A Toolkit for Change

This book is about how we as human beings make decisions —and how anyone involved in the field of social change can help individuals or groups to make positive choices using decision science. It draws on the latest thinking in behavioural economics, neuroscience and evolutional psychology to provide a powerful practical toolkit for fundraisers, campaigners, advocacy specialists, policy makers, health professionals, educationalists and activists.

At the heart of the book are the fascinating and powerful insights that we have gained in the last 10 years about how our brains work when making decisions—often summarised as behavioural economics. It also shows how techniques in common use in commercial settings can be applied to the social sector.

"Mahmoud and Ross deliver a well written and insightful read on a complex topic for the social and humanitarian sector."

—Andrew Rizk
Director, Finance & Administration
International Federation of Red Cross and Red Crescent

change for Good

Good for

USING BEHAVIOURAL ECONOMICS FOR A BETTER WORLD

Bernard Ross & Omar Mahmoud

Cover and interior design: Susana Cabrera/semioSCreation
Typesetting: Rosa Trujano
Proofreading: Martha Hurley

Published by The Management Centre, London, UK
and semioSCreation simultaneously in NYC

The Management Centre
2 Old Malling Farmhouse
Lewes
BN7 2BY

Ordering Information:
Quantity sales. Special discounts are available on quantity purchases by corporations, associations, and others. For details, contact the The Management Centre.
Orders by U.S. trade bookstores and wholesalers. Please contact semioSCreation:
Tel: +1(718) 715-2433; subeca4@gmail.com or visit www.semioscreation.com.

ISBN 978-0-692-06436-8 (Paperback)
Printed in the United States of America

the management centre

Contents

Introduction
Another Book on
Behavioural Economics?

This book is about how we as human beings make decisions —and how anyone involved in the field of social change can help individuals or groups to choose to make a positive change.

At the heart of the book are the fascinating and powerful insights that we have gained in the last 10 years about how the brain works when making decisions. Many of these have come from the field of behavioural economics, and in particular the work of leading thinkers such as Kahneman, Thaler, Barden and Ariely. But the insights come from broader fields such as psychology, economics, neuroscience, and evolutionary psychology.

Those of us involved in social change probably need to recognise that the advertising and marketing industry generally is far ahead of us in all this. For at least a decade these commercial marketers have had access to some leading edge scientific insights into how people make decisions. By implication they know how experiences or activities can be designed to encourage people to make those decisions in a particular way—whether it's to buy a specific candy bar, to take advantage of a promoted hotel offer, or to regard a particular behaviour as normal. We see the evidence for this in the way goods are displayed at a certain height on the supermarket shelves, in the way clothes in fashion stores are lit, in the pop-ups which say 'book now only three left at this price,' or in the financial products we select online which are not obviously in our best long-term interest.

However, the fact that businesses are more advanced allows us to use their applied learning for social good. There are obvious links between fundraising and this commercial use for example. And the same techniques which allow us to understand how to get people to eat more of a sugary product may also help us to understand how to encourage the same people to stop.

Governments are also increasingly using behavioural economics to change citizen behaviour in the areas of environmental protection, tax compliance, energy consumption, and many other domains. But we have also worked hard to find examples of progressive not-for-profits and non-governmental organisations (NGOs) who are making use of these approaches.

Structure

The book is divided into three main parts:

- The first part explores the key principles underpinning what we know about the brain and about how we make decisions. This folds in what we know about Behavioural Economics—but goes further. This is a fast moving field, but we try to incorporate the latest thinking.
- The second part takes some very specific techniques technically called heuristics, and some wider frameworks, and shows how they can be applied to fundraising and more general social change issues.
- The third part explores how to apply practical principles of how we decide, and we also raise some concerns about ethics and the challenge of applying theoretical concepts to real-world, mission critical issues.

Dedication

To every human being who wants to create a better world in small ways. Thank you for investing in this toolkit for change. In your honour we will gift the profits from this book to Médecins Sans Frontières and other humanitarian agencies dealing with so many of the world's crises.

With Grateful Thanks

We have used a large and varied set of references. However, a few works have been particularly foundational and helpful. These four key texts are:

- Daniel Kahneman's *Thinking, Fast and Slow*.
- Dan Ariely's *Predictably Irrational: The Hidden Forces that Shape Our Decisions*
- Richard Thaler and Cass Sunstein's *Nudge: Improving Decisions About Health, Wealth and Happiness*
- Phil Barden's *Decoded: the Science Behind Why We Buy*

We are indebted to a number of people who have generously given their time, talent, ideas and case studies.

From Bernard:
Among those I want to offer special mention to are:

Meredith Niles, the dynamic Executive Director of Fundraising and Engagement at a wonderful UK charity, Marie Curie. She offered invaluable insight, opinion and examples.

Mike Colling, CEO of MC&Co, one of the outstanding direct marketeers of his generation, who offered encouragement and constructive comment.

Clare Segal, my brilliant co-director at =mc, who offered challenge, support, and wine, depending on the need.

From Omar:
This book has also benefitted from discussions with many colleagues over the last few years during our day to day interactions, conferences, and workshops.

Their opinions, challenges, and suggestions have been instrumental in writing this book. To name a few: Vinay Ahuja, Bo Beiskjaer, Francois Berge, Jill Van den Brule, David Cravinho, Francesco De Flaviis, Eric Dekoninck, Dorian Druelle, Martin Gimenez-Rebora, Christina Gkouvali, Bernadette Gutmann, Tatjana Ivanova, Jan Kamphuis, Mary Lynn Lalonde, Ben Lones, Daniel McDonnell, Arpad Michaux, Vicky Nef, Emer O'Doherty, Ben Riondel, and Angela Travis.

Finally, thanks to our ultra-hardworking, talented production team led by the outstanding designer Susana Cabrera. Great work too by Rosa Trujano and Martha Hurley.

Omar Mahmoud
Bernard Ross
Geneva and London
February 2018

Prologue:
An Ethical Note
on Behavioural Economics

Throughout the book we are almost unrelentingly positive about the potential applications of decision science, and specifically behavioural economics. We know from the number of speaking engagements and consultancy assignments we have been asked to undertake in the last couple of years that there is real excitement in the not-for-profit world about the potential of these approaches. And in the commercial world still, where every visit to the supermarket or online visit provides evidence of the use of these techniques. But there are some legitimate ethical concerns that we need to address, especially on the bold claim of 'changing behaviour without changing minds.'

The anxieties about uses and abuses by the commercial sector are perhaps obvious. Techniques from decision science are used by marketers to encourage acquisition or consumption for its own sake, with the one goal of driving profits. When these techniques are used without an ethical framework, that can lead to targeted consumers buying inappropriate financial products, eating foods that are bad for them, or even entering into commercial relationships that will prove exploitative or parasitic.

This specific challenge is raised and explored by Richard Thaler, 2017 Nobel Laureate for Economics, and Cass Sunstein in their outstanding book *Nudge: Improving Decisions about Health, Wealth and Happiness*. They talk about a World divided between *Econs* and *Humans*, a typology that complements System 1 and System 2. But their typology goes further and suggests that individuals have a dominant preference for one or more of the thinking or deciding modes.[1] The *Humans*, they suggest, are these targets for many manipulative System 1 techniques used with little reference to their well-being. A troubling dystopian possibility in our view.

But the commercial world does not have the monopoly on malpractice. There should properly be concerns from those of us working within a social change agenda about using techniques to 'persuade' individuals to increase their gifts, to sign up to a petition, or to change their behaviour. There are some techniques we might consciously avoid for ethical reasons. We need to ensure we don't inappropriately target vulnerable individuals. We also need to recognise that if we're battling a major corporate entity they may well have more ammunition and capital at their disposal than we do. Nudging eaters towards healthier options involves a battle against major corporations spending many millions trying to persuade us to eat supersized, addictive and unhealthy options.

Those challenges grow in scale when governments or large public agencies try to get people to take part in, or stop, activities which fit with social policy objectives. For example, taking exercise, eating healthily, smoking less, safeguarding sexual health, agreeing to sign up to organ donor schemes, supporting policies like taxes on alcohol, etc.[2]

---

[1] In Sunstein and Thaler's topology Humans struggle to make informed and positive decisions for themselves, buffeted as they are by behavioural 'do this' messages. Econs make more balanced and objective judgments. But there are few of them.

[2] Sunstein caused controversy in 2012 when he tried to explain that Mayor Michael Bloomberg's attempt to ban 'big gulp' fizzy drinks/sodas in New York was what he called 'non-libertarian paternalism'. (Bloomberg had proposed a ban on the sale of sugary beverages in cartons over 16 ounces in any of the city's restaurants, delis, cinemas, or even from the ubiquitous street carts. Bloomberg's entirely laudable goal was to reduce the ill health impacts of these high sugar drinks—including tooth decay, diabetes, and obesity.) The problem, Sunstein pointed out, was that logically two

In the UK David Cameron, former Prime Minister, very consciously promoted this approach and with Thaler's help established a specific team—nicknamed Nudge Unit—to use Behavioural Economics techniques to provide what he called 'an option between nanny-style state intervention and the unrestrained market maximizing its own benefit.' Their job was to advise UK Government departments on how to collect taxes faster, persuade people to become organs donors, opt for more energy efficient approaches, etc. (For more on this, see **Chapter 3**.)

Some people have claimed a nudge unit could very easily turn into a *Ministry of the Mind*. This would be a move way beyond what Thaler and Sunstein call *libertarian paternalism*, where there is general agreement on what is 'good' for an individual or society. The worry often expressed is that we will end up in an Orwellian, *1984*-type dystopia. You may remember in the novel, O'Brien, one of Big Brother's thought police, points out to anti-hero Winston Smith, that he cannot have original thought: 'We create human nature. Men are infinitely malleable.' This chilling aphorism might seem a distant nightmare, but there is no doubt that governments do try and make their populations conform to various ideological positions. And behavioural economics offer some ideas on how to do that without people necessarily being aware.

The UK Nudge Unit experiment has gained traction. It has had some UK successes, and now has contracts all over the world to advise governments on how to help change their citizens' behaviour. *Nudging* has become a global industry. And it is being replicated in Singapore, in Germany and in the US. For more on this see David Halpern's excellent book *Inside the Nudge Unit*.[3]

16-ounce Coke-style drinks are the same as one 32-ounce 'supersized' coke look-a-like. What was to stop companies pricing two cups to make it sound attractive and customers ordering two drinks instead of one? Sunstein maintained that ordering two would be a nudge that would have an impact.

[3] Halpern was the CEO of the UK's Behavioural Insights Team. Prior to that he was Chief Analyst at the Prime Minister's Strategy Unit from 2001–2007.

Increasingly, democratic governments have come to favour cognitive approaches that seek to shape people's lifestyle choices through positive reinforcement, indirect suggestion and incentives, alongside more legislative approaches. This new *educative state* is growing rapidly and its techniques becoming more prominent. What it means we will need to see. Whatever happens we cannot ignore it. And as practitioners in social change we need to embrace it.

How do You Make Decisions? And are They Good Ones?
A Quiz

Before you read this book, or even if you are just reading in a bookshop, try this quiz. It is based loosely on work by Daniel Kahneman, the Nobel Prize winning economist, and his talented colleague Amos Tversky. Their work is the inspiration for much of what follows. (The quiz itself is adapted from a 2011 *Vanity Fair* article.) You can see the scoring and rationale at the end of this section. Let's see how good you are at making decisions:

1. A town has two hospitals: one is large and one is small. Assuming there is an equal number of boys and girls born every year in the UK, which hospital is more likely to have close to 50% girls and 50% boys born on any given day?

A. The larger one

B. The smaller one

C. About the same (say, within 5% of each other)

2. A team of psychologists performed personality tests on 100 professionals, of which 30 were engineers and 70 were lawyers. Afterward, brief descriptions were written for each subject. The following is a sample of one of the resulting descriptions:

Jack is a 45-year-old man. He is married and has four children. He is generally conservative, careful, and ambitious. He shows no interest in political and social issues and spends most of his free time on his many hobbies, which include home carpentry, sailing, and mathematics.

What is the probability that Jack is one of the 30 engineers?

A. 10-40%

B. 40-60%

C. 60-80%

D. 80-100%

3a. How many dates did you have last month? / How many dinner parties did you attend? (Please choose whichever relates to your life style!)

A. 1–3

B. 3–5

C. 0

3b. On a scale of 1 to 5, how happy are you these days (5 being the happiest)?

A. 1

B. 2

C. 3

D. 4

E. 5

4. Imagine that you decided to see a play and you paid €10 for the admission price of a ticket. As you enter the theatre, you discover that you have lost the ticket. The theatre keeps no record of ticket purchasers, so the ticket cannot be recovered. Would you pay €10 for another ticket to the play?

A. Yes

B. No

5a. Choose between getting €900 for sure or a 90% chance of getting €1,000.

A. Getting €900

B. 90% chance of getting €1,000

5b. Choose between losing €900 for sure or a 90% chance of losing €1,000.

A. Losing €900

B. 90% chance of losing €1,000

Solutions and explanations

Question 1: The most common answer is C. We normally expect things to follow a proven pattern regardless of size. But size matters. A small sample size (i.e. the small hospital) will often contain extreme proportions, while a large sample size (i.e. the large hospital) will more likely reflect real-world distributions. The heuristic shown here can be used to understand some forms of prejudice—if you haven't been exposed to a large number of people from a certain group, you are more likely to have incorrect assumptions about them. When you do not account for the size of a sample, Kahneman and his colleague Amos Tversky say, you have used the *representativeness* heuristic.

Question 2: If you answered anything but A (the correct response being precisely 30%), you have fallen victim to the representativeness heuristic *again*, despite having just read about it. When Kahneman and Tversky performed this experiment, they found that a large percentage of participants overestimated the likelihood that Jack was an engineer, even though mathematically, there was only a 30-in-100 chance of that being true. We have an irrational affection for rich details. We especially like ones that we believe are typical of a certain kind of person (e.g. all engineers must spend every weekend doing maths puzzles), is yet another shortcoming of our decision-making processes.

Questions 3a and 3b: Regardless of how you answered, it is likely that your answer to question 3a) is positively correlated to your answer to question 3b)—that is, you rated your happiness higher if you had more dates or more dinner parties and lower if you had fewer dates or dinner parties. However, when the order of these questions was reversed, as was done by two German researchers, people's happiness became untethered from their dating-dining life.

This experiment demonstrates the brain's deferral to System 1, the faster and easier of the two thinking processes we have. When faced with an *objective question* (in this case, *How many dates or dinner parties did you have or attend last month?*), followed by a *subjective one* (*How happy are you these days?*), people often simply carry over their answer for the first to the second. This heuristic is called *substitution*.

Question 4: If you answered 'no', as most people do, consider the following question:

Imagine that you decide to see a play. The tickets are €10, which you will pay at the door. As you prepare to enter the theatre, you discover you've lost a €10 note. Would you still pay €10 for a ticket to the play?

Both scenarios result in the net loss of €10. If you answered 'yes' to this, you seem to have fallen victim to what Kahneman and Tversky call the 'framing effect': being swayed by the way in which questions are worded, rather than responding just to their substance. When Kahneman and Tversky performed this experiment in 1981, they found that 46% of participants would pay for another ticket, while 88% of participants would purchase the ticket after they had lost €10. The framing effect is also used to explain the influence of positive and negative information on our decisions—for example, why consumers prefer to buy minced beef labelled 80% lean rather than 20% fat.

Question 5: The results of this simple problem set, for which most participants answer A and then B, were used to develop their *prospect theory* thesis that would make Kahneman and Tversky famous. In a 1979 paper, they documented a peculiar behavioural tendency. When people faced a loss, they became risk averse, when they caught sight of a possible gain, they became risk seeking. As a result of their discovery, Kahneman and Tversky debunked Bernoulli's *utility theory*, a cornerstone of economic thought since the 18th Century. (Bernoulli first proposed that a person's willingness to gamble a certain amount of money was a product of how that amount related to his overall wealth—that is, €1 million means more to a millionaire than it does to a billionaire.)

If you're surprised by your answers, or by the explanations, then this book may offer you the insights you need to improve your decision making and that of the individuals or groups you aim to engage.

Part 1

Decision Science:
10 Things We Know About How We Make Decisions

Decision Science:
10 Things We Know About How We Make Decisions

These are exciting times in the field of social change and social justice—whether you are working in an international non-governmental organisation (INGO), for a public agency, with a United Nations (UN) body, or even volunteering with a community group. It is true that the challenges we face are growing: climate change impacts, health issues like obesity, increasing social exclusion, and growing wealth inequalities. Despite these challenges, the good news is we now understand more about how to make a difference and how to encourage others to make a difference.

Specifically, we understand more about how people come to make decisions about what to do in a given situation—from how much to donate, to identifying which policy to support, to adopting more energy efficient approaches, and even how to change their diet for the better.

Much of that knowledge comes from developments in three linked areas of science which we can now bring into our work.

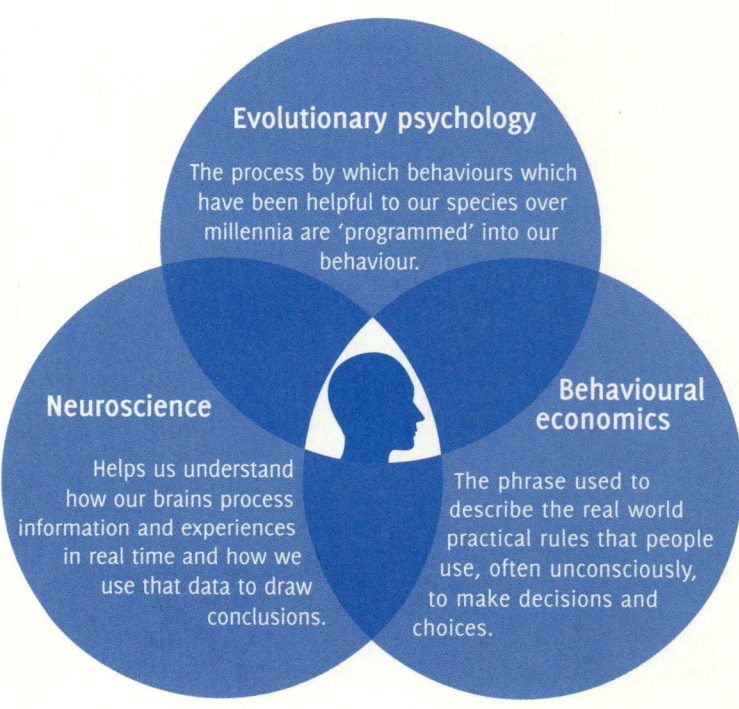

The combination of these three powerful scientific perspectives offers us insights into key principles that determine how we think and act in specific situations. Together these form a body of practice called *decision science*. Throughout the book we'll use examples from our experience and the experience of others involved in campaigning, fundraising, advocacy, or practical action, that show how these principles work in practice.

We'll share proven social approaches with leading edge thinking from academics, and learning from those working in the commercial field. Our perception is that the social sector is maybe 10 years behind the commercial sector in using much of this thinking, so some of the 'best' examples come from business.

If you're involved in social change this book is designed to help you with ideas and approaches on how to be more effective—whether the focus is encouraging supporters to become more engaged, securing greater commitment to tackle an issue, promoting better health outcomes, or challenging attitudes and prejudices between groups.

You will also find out, and learn from:

- Why Nigerian scammers deliberately misspell their emails and offer such improbable deals.
- Why neighbours in NYC ignored the cries of a person being murdered.
- How poor Mexicans and Americans are being helped to avoid punitive payday loans.
- Why 'old-fashioned' direct mail packs perform better than online video for fundraising.

And even:

- How to stop paying for that 'bargain' magazine subscription you don't need.

Let's begin with a quick introduction to each of the scientific perspectives, outlining the different contribution each brings to our understanding of how people make decisions.

A VERY SHORT INTRODUCTION TO EVOLUTIONARY PSYCHOLOGY

We have essentially the same brain in the industrial, internet-connected, city-dwelling, virtual media world, that our ancestors had in the pre-agricultural, isolated, savannah-dwelling-among-the-wild-beasts, small tribe era.

In that primitive environment, our behaviour was driven by fundamental instincts such as survival, territorial protection, and sex. These basic drives, evolutionary psychologists argue, imbued us with certain attitudes—for example, preferring prevention and safety to risk and chance-taking. Put simply, our ancestors thought it was more prudent, by and large, to suppose a dark thin shape on the ground and not quite in view, was a dangerous snake and not a potentially useful tree branch that had fallen. So, the internal advice was 'when in doubt walk past,' and seek a safer 'stick' opportunity. Thousands of years later, this 'risk-aversion bias' still influences our decisions at home and work.

Our brains—only 2% of body weight—use 20% of the body's energy. This ratio means we are predisposed to be energy efficient or, in layman's terms, lazy. The basic desire for low energy consumption means we are programmed to look for shortcuts in our thinking, in order to reduce the processing time and energy used. These shortcuts also mean that we prefer to make decisions fast, rather than waste energy fully working through the rational implications. It is largely our fast-moving *emotions* that have most impact on our decisions. The implication is that appealing to reason can influence *opinions*. Contrary to popular belief, it's not that emotions simply drive direct behaviour. As Phil Barden pointed out to us in correspondence, it's rather that emotions are a response to a stimulus. What drives behaviour is motivation. This connection between stimulus—response—emotion-behaviour is especially strong when we need to decide something quickly.[1]

---

[1] Barden shared this useful explanation of his thinking. 'There are some exceptions (e.g. anger makes us hit the car horn) but, as Baumeister et al found in a meta study of <3,000 papers, such examples are primitive and immediate (e.g. fear can lead to fight or flight) and don't explain why we buy brands or services. There are cases of us seeking to regulate an emotion which link to your sector specifically (e.g. I see a charity ad which makes me feel sad/anxious and I act, via donation, to bridge the gap between my current state and my desired state). However, in studies on "mood freezing", where respondents were told that their emotions would not change (because they'd been given a placebo "drug" to freeze their moods) irrespective of their actions, then their behaviour did not change when faced with situations where they would normally have acted differently—this shows that it's not the emotion itself that motivates us.'

A VERY SHORT INTRODUCTION TO NEUROSCIENCE

Neuroscience is generally defined as the study of the nervous system including the brain, and the brain-mind connection. Originally neuroscience was classed as simply a branch of biology. But our ability to study in detail how the nervous system works means that it is now a discipline in its own right despite the fact it overlaps with a range of other fields such as chemistry, psychology, genetics, computer science, linguistics, mathematics, and even artificial intelligence.

In part, these developments in our understanding have been fueled by improvements in technology. Thanks to imaging techniques such as fMRI[2] scanning, we can now study interactions at a molecular level while people are actually thinking about issues. We can also study how movement and different kinds of sensory stimulus such as smell or touch, impact on the brain and its processes. This means we can, for example, plot the way in which habits, such as drinking under stress, are formed neurologically. Put simply, the way in which 'neurons that fire together wire together.'

This has led to some challenging findings such as:

- The same neurons fire when we *observe* someone eating a banana as when we eat a banana—evidence for the importance of body language 'mirroring.'[3]
- Strong brands do not cause greater excitement in a brain but rather less. Rather than stimulating us more, strong brands work in the background.

---

[2] Functional Magnetic Resonance Imaging (fMRI) is a procedure that uses MRI technology to indirectly measure brain activity by detecting changes associated with blood flow. Because we can now study neurological activity in real time we can gain profound insights into the areas of the brain involved in different kinds of thinking and decision-making.

[3] For more on this and the science behind it see Chapter 10.

• There is some evidence we can encode information genetically, for example, our tendency to *avoid* rather than *take* risks. See the stick/snake choice on the previous page.[4]

Neuroscientific insights mean we can study the actual processes that take place in our brains, and from that we can understand how to replicate the processes in our attempts to communicate or influence.

A VERY SHORT INTRODUCTION TO BEHAVIOURAL ECONOMICS

The term behavioural economics describes a school of thought that combines economics with psychology. The beginnings of behavioural economics go back to the second half of the twentieth century when economists *and* psychologists began to realize that traditional economic theory could not explain much of human behaviour.

Traditional economics is based on the assumption humans are rational beings who make choices based on a logical cost/benefit-type analysis. So we will act consistently in our own best interests.

Behavioural economics says we all work within a *bounded rationality*. That human rationality is limited by a number of factors: our mental abilities, the level of information we have to deal with, our cognitive and emotional biases, peer pressure, and time pressure. With such factors at work, behavioural economists say, we resort to heuristics, or mental shortcuts, to make fast and frugal decisions. These can be useful and save us time and energy, but they can lead us astray. They may not be in our own best interests. And they are definitely not rational.

For example, you go to a supermarket to buy a bar of soap and see two brands on the shelf. *Brand A* is a bit better quality—let's say 10% better—but it is also 30% more expensive than *Brand B*. Deci-

---

[4] See Phil Barden's book, *Decoded: The Science Behind Why We Buy*, Wiley 2013.

sion? Logically you might say, 'Buy B.' Many economists and most people *believe* that this is how they actually behave. It is also how we like to think we make choices about a whole range of issues: where to live, our career options, our 'healthy selection' at restaurants. In reality, we often buy Brand A, because its green packaging suggests it is natural, or because the price per bar, not gram, is lower, or even because we saw someone else buying it.

> *If you look at economics textbooks you will learn that the economic man can think like Albert Einstein, store as much memory as IBM's Big Blue, and exercise the willpower of Mahatma Gandhi.*
>
> Richard Thaler, author, with Cass Sunstein, of *Nudge*, 2008, Winner Nobel Prize for Economics 2017

Behavioural economics is not based on ideology, assumptions or beliefs. Rather, it says, 'When in doubt, find out what actually happens.' The research in this field shows there are a number of specific systematic and common mistakes—shortcuts—that people make when they are trying to make decisions. These shortcuts are technically called *heuristics* and **Section Two** explores the implications of ten of these.[5] Once mistakes are identified and codified they can be used by third parties, including us, to help shape the way people make decisions. We can use this insight for good or evil, ethically or unethically.

This book explores what these shortcuts are and how you can use them to promote positive social change.

---

[5] A number of researchers have claimed there may be as many as 150 heuristics, though not all are equally powerful.

IMPLICATIONS

The terms System 1 and System 2 were first developed and brought to worldwide public attention by Daniel Kahneman, who won the Noble Prize in economics in 2002 for his work helping us to understand how people really think. (It was Kahneman who popularized the phrase 'behavioural economics' with his book *Thinking, Fast and Slow.*) We are indebted to him, and to Thaler, who won the Nobel for Economics in 2017 plus others like Dan Ariely, Rory Sutherland, and Phil Barden. Much of what we have covered here owes its origin and insight to them.

To summarise, these three disciplines provide us with a well-rounded if challenging perspective on human behaviour and decision-making. *Behavioural economics* observes and tests actual behaviour. *Evolutionary psychology* helps explain the origin of our behaviour. *Neuroscience* shows us the biological processes that govern our thinking and behaviour. Throughout the book we will refer to decision science, but will be combining all three under that one heading.

For the sake of simplicity, we have organised some of the key ideas into a list of '10 Things We Now Know About Us, and How We Make Decisions'—and explain their importance and relevance.

TEN THINGS WE NOW KNOW ABOUT US, AND HOW WE MAKE DECISIONS

1. We Have Some Basic Psychological Drives and These Shape Lots of What We Do

If you've seen or heard of the Disney cartoon *Inside Out*, you will be aware of the idea that there are some very basic drivers that guide our behaviour. In the movie a young girl's social development is shown through the metaphor of five emotions living in her head that discuss what appropriate action to take in the face of different challenges. *Inside Out* is only a children's animation, but many neuroscientists sign up to the concept of key emotional drivers underpinning our behaviour.

A number of these experts agree that there are five basic drivers for behaviour, mostly at a subconscious level.[6] The most commonly identified ones are:

- Survival
- Power
- Territoriality
- Nurturance
- Sex

For our ancestors on the African plains millennia ago these five served very practical uses. Living in pre-historic times we needed to be sure that we were safe (survival), that we understood where we were in the tribe hierarchy (power), that we knew our domain (territoriality), that we felt part of a community (nurturance), and that we could find a mate to feel loved, and to keep the tribe growing (sex).

These same drivers still shape our behaviour today, under modern cultural veneers. *Survival* in a twenty-first century context is having a source of income such as a regular job or enough money in the bank. *Power* is having a clear position in a company, organisation or even family. *Territoriality* is our own house or apartment, or an office space ideally on a corner, or responsibility for a geographic area in a business. *Nurturance* covers connections with people in power positions or a large network of friends and acquaintances. *Sex* is being attractive to someone and having access to desired partners.

While all are important, our brains respond to one overarching driver—*survival*. This is often referred to simply as the 'fight or flight' response, which kicks in automatically whether we are lost in

---

[6] David L. Weiner, *Battling the Inner Dummy: The Craziness of Apparently Normal People.*

the mountains, or we're worried about how the presentation to the Board might help or hinder our careers.

Survival itself may be split into *Promotion* (seeking opportunities for food, looking for a mate, etc.) and *Prevention* (fearing risks, avoiding becoming dinner). Evolutionary biologists, interestingly, often suggest this driver is what helped us evolve to be *mostly* risk averse. Throughout our history, avoiding risk has been much more important to survival than benefitting from opportunities. Running away at any sign of perceived danger, such as not stopping as we walked across the savannah to find out whether that mystery object was a stick or a snake, was crucial for survival. The key issue was the high impact of getting it wrong.

We still carry this coded message in our heads. So today, any offer made to persuade us to buy a product, use a service, or support a cause must carry a perceived disproportionally higher potential benefit than cost.

Remember, our basic *emotional* brain doesn't know that the world around it has changed compared to 200,000 years ago. Our rational *cortical* brain has to keep reminding it, and sometimes there is no time for the consultation to take place. On those occasions, the emotional brain acts on its own. It asks for forgiveness, not permission. (See page 31 for an explanation of our brain structure and why this is important.)

Similarly, territoriality and nurturance have contemporary importance. For most of human history, people lived in small bands and tribes, with very limited mobility. They cohabited with family and friends they knew very well. Coming across people from outside their circle was often met with suspicion. They lived in an *Us vs. Them*[7] world. In short, their survival depended on belonging to a group and distinguishing their group from others.

Today, unless we clearly have something in common with other people, our first reaction is often one of indifference, suspicion, or even dislike. Sadly, we see this reaction to otherness in the response

---

[7] For more on the important idea of *Us vs. Them* see **Chapter 8.**

to the many contemporary refugee crises in the world. Seen *en masse* refugees have been called a 'swarm' or a 'flood'—suggesting something subhuman or inhuman. But we may change our view when we hear an individual telling their story, or see a dead child swept up on the beach, or when the 'faceless' refugees turn out to be mothers, teachers, daughters, music lovers, etc. That is, we can change our minds more easily when these people turn out to be like us.

One Brain, or Three?

We talk a lot about *the* brain in this book. But over time our brain has actually evolved into three parts. This model is often called the Triune brain.

- **Reptilian:** This is the oldest part, shared, as the name suggests, with reptiles. It controls basic survival functions such as blood circulation and maintaining body temperature. It functions unconsciously almost all the time.
- **Mammalian:** We share this brain with other mammals and it is responsible for essential emotions and drives such as power, territoriality, nurturance, love, etc. It determines much of our behaviour with other people.
- **Cortical:** Is the most recent in terms of development. It is the smallest of the three, and unique to a small number of primates, though clearly most developed in humans. It controls higher order operations such as language, mathematics, logic, etc.

The reptilian and mammalian parts occupy most of the brain, and conduct most of its work, mainly at a subconscious level, so we're not aware of what's going on. This means most of our information processing and decision-making also happens at subconscious level, only *sometimes* in consultation with the conscious brain.

As influencers we need to craft our messages for action to reach the subconscious as well as the conscious brain, with an emphasis on the former. The language of the *subconscious brain* is emotions, images, visuals, metaphors, stories, and music. The language of the *conscious brain* is text, logic, facts, and numbers.

2. We Respond to Subconscious Context

Fundamental to decision-making science is the premise that much of our data processing and decision-making is subconscious and fast.[8] Deciding is so fast, even changing our minds can be difficult. According to some recent research at Johns Hopkins University if we change our minds within roughly 100 milliseconds of making a decision, we can successfully revise our plans. If we wait more than 200 milliseconds, however, we may be unable to make the desired change.[9] But it's not just our thinking process that's important. Some senses, for example, are important, especially smell. In a test between two Nike stores, one with a very faint 'consciously undetectable' scent and one without, customers were 80% more likely to purchase in the scented store. In another experiment at a petrol station with a mini-mart attached to it, pumping the smell of coffee into the store saw purchases of the drink grow 300%. And if you take the time to wander into the M&M World store in Leicester Square London, you might now notice the smell of chocolate. When it first opened in 2011 it didn't have the smell and sales were disappointing. They hired a company called ScentAir who specialize in adding signature scents to stores. The managing director of the company, Christopher Pratt, said in an article describing the effect: "It looked like the place should smell of chocolate, it didn't. It does now." And sales have moved in response.[10]

When you visit a charity website, the *conscious* brain analyses the message content. (What is the cause I am being asked to support? What do they want me to do—donate, sign a petition or join up?) At the same time the *subconscious* brain continuously interprets the

---

[8] Not only is the decision process subconscious the decisions are made in a fraction of a second. For more on the implications of this see this *Harvard Business Review* article by Gerald Zaltman, Emeritus Professor at Harvard Business School *https://hbswk. hbs.edu/item/the-subconscious-mind-of-the-consumer-and-how-to-reach-it.*

[9] For more on the speed of decisions see this interesting article *https://www.scientificamerican.com/article/the-neuroscience-of-changing-your-mind/*

[10] *http://www.independent.co.uk/news/media/advertising/the-smell-of-commerce-how-companies-use-scents-to-sell-their-products-2338142.html* August 15, 2011 *The Independent.*

subtle background and peripheral cues. (How you feel about the colours, images, celebrities involved, etc.)

> *I always thought the brain was the most wonderful organ in my body. And then one day it occurred to me, 'Wait a minute, who's telling me that?'*
>
> Emo Philips

Your subconscious brain has a mind of its own. And some subtle cues can have unexpected influences. For example, in an experiment people exposed to a smell of baking cookies were more likely to help strangers than those who did not smell the cookies. The participants didn't recognise any connection; the data, their behaviour, simply said there was. In the same way when a brand is associated with a celebrity, many of the celebrity's qualities are assumed to 'rub off' on the product: elegant, sophisticated, sexy, etc. Even though people may deny the impact.

Some signals also come from inside us, and we look unconsciously for opportunities to confirm our inner state. When we are in a good mood, we are more likely to tolerate our colleagues and partners, and are more likely to donate to charities. These activities become a way to validate or confirm our inner feelings.

Are You Looking At Me?

In some companies, employees can serve themselves coffee or tea, after putting the relevant amount in an 'honesty box,' next to the drinks in a kitchen. In an experiment run over ten weeks, researchers at Newcastle University in the UK found that employees were open to subconscious influence based on the picture that they saw. People put more money in the honesty box in the weeks when there was a small, 13cm x 3cm, picture of *eyes* on the wall of the kitchen, than when it was a similar-sized picture of *flowers*.[11] Researcher

---

[11] Reported in New Scientist June 28, 2006. Original article in *Biology Letters* (DOI:10.1098/rsbl.2006.0509).

Melissa Bateson reported staff paid 2.73 times more, on average, when the eyes rather than the flower picture was present.

(Over three days at the International Fundraising Congress in Holland we repeated this experiment using soft drinks. Delegates did indeed put more money in the tin provided when overlooked by a picture of eyes than they did with a picture of tulips.)

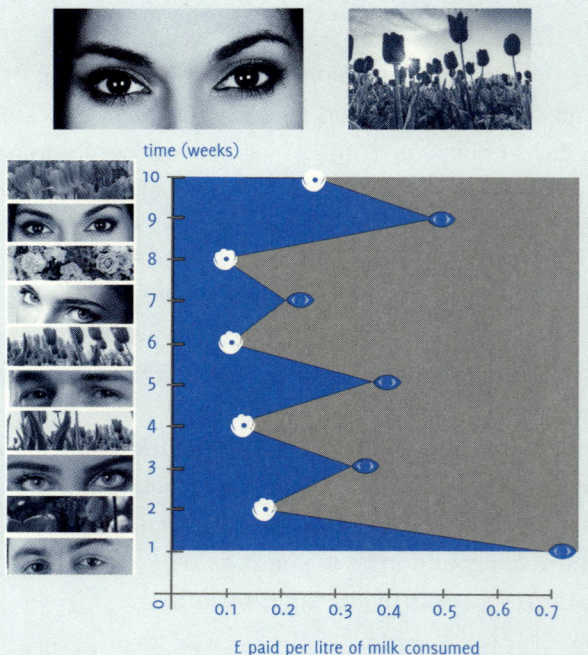

None of the respondents in either experiment *consciously* noticed the difference between the two images when they were subsequently questioned. But at some subconscious level the impact of eyes was important.

The original research concluded that eyes[12] act as a symbol of social supervision, suggesting someone is observing you. Without reference to the

_____

[12] Meredith Niles, one of the UK's leading fundraisers and thinkers about behavioural economics, points out that" the 'eye of providence' or 'all seeing eye' (visible on every US dollar bill) representing an omniscient god has been used across cultures for many centuries to encourage 'correct' behaviour. We may not have always had the science to demonstrate the impact of the eye, but we have had strong intuitions about

conscious brain, they activated employees' social consciousness urging them to do what is socially correct. An excellent illustration of the power of the subconscious brain to process information and take decisions all by itself.

In these, and in many other related experiments, subjects are not only unaware of the cues that drive their behaviour, they refuse to believe that such cues had any influence on their decisions, when told about the experiment.

In fact there is real evidence that our *expressed attitudes* are not a great guide to our behaviour. We don't always do what we say we would do, but will come up with a rationale for why not. Colin Camerer, respected behavioural scientist, has a blunt explanation. 'The human brain is like a monkey brain with a cortical "press secretary," who is glib at concocting explanations of behaviour and who privileges deliberative explanations over cruder ones.'[13]

What is the implication of this subconscious processing for individuals involved in social change? Websites, mailings, video clips, and other communications media can deliver subtle cues in the background to drive subconscious behaviour while the conscious brain believes it is assessing 'the cause' in a rational way. The same 'eyes' experiment could encourage employees involved in food preparation to wash their hands after visiting the toilet. Or, as suggested above, you could try putting eyes on or near a static charity collection box in a shop, hotel reception or pub counter to see if that increases your donations. We have seen it a number of times near cycle racks, discouraging thieves from stealing bikes.

---

the power of being watched. She also offers some great additional examples of the impct of eyes on charitable behaviour.

* https://www.danielnettle.org.uk/download/097.pdf: Eyes placed over a charitable donation box increased donations 48% vs. control with no eyes.

* https://www.ncbi.nlm.nih.gov/pubmed/26181843: A robot "watching" subjects undergoing an experiment on a computer led subjects to donate 29% more.

* http://www.sscnet.ucla.edu/anthro/faculty/fessler/pubs/HaleyFesslerEyespots.pdf: Eye cues on a computer screen increased altruism in a dictator game, and when the salience of the eye cue was increased, the altruism increase.

[13] Camerer, C. F., Loewenstein, G., & Prelec, D. (2004). *Neuroeconomics: Why Economics Needs Brains.* The Scandinavian Journal of Economics, *106*(3), 555-579.

Macmillan Cancer Support, a major UK charity, has taken this idea of personal 'eyes' interaction to a whole new level. They tested the advert below in a London shopping mall. It uses face recognition technology to change the message displayed according to whether it is mostly men or mostly women walking past. Women get, 'No Mum Should Face Cancer Alone' and men, 'No Dad Should Face Cancer Alone.' Both versions then prompt a £5 text donation. When the immediate audience is less than 60/40 in one gender, a generic ad is shown, 'No One Should Face Cancer Alone.'

Easy to Read = Easy to Do?

The same subconscious processing applies to text. What is seen as *easy to read* is also seen as *easy to do*.

Tuck your chin into your chest and then lift your chin upwards as far as possible for 6-10 repetitions. Lower your left ear towards your left shoulder and then your right ear towards your right shoulder. Do 6-10

Tuck your chin into your chest and then lift your chin upwards as far as possible for 6-10 repetitions.
Lower your left ear towards your left shoulder and then your right ear towards your right shoulder.
Do 6-10

In an experiment these two pieces of text, describing the same fitness exercise, participants were asked to say how difficult it was to complete the physical activity described.

They scored the *exercise* described in the cursive, harder-to-read-script on the right as more difficult than the same *exercise* in the easier-to-read, plain typeface on the left.

The *content* is no different, but participants conflated the difficulty of reading the typeface with the difficulty of the exercise itself. This is a process may be called physical/psychological transfer, and what it tells us is *how* we present ideas makes a significant difference.

Conversely, you have probably noticed that in 'fancy' restaurants the management will often present the menu in a more elaborate script, signaling the sophistication of the cuisine. See **Chapter 4** on *Framing* for more on how restaurants manipulate our decisions with menus. And **Section Three** on the design of menus.

3. We Think Fast and Slow

One implication of the first two 'what we know' points is that our brains have two ways of making decisions. Daniel Kahneman calls these two ways *System 1* and *System 2*, which, he says, 'respectively produce fast and slow thinking'. (Hence the title of his most famous book.) For our purposes these two systems can also be thought of as the contrasting processes of intuitive and deliberate thought.

System 1 System 2 Experiment

Kahneman uses a simple experiment to illustrate the difference between the two systems.

A bat and a ball cost $1.10 bought together. The bat costs $1 more than the ball. How much does each cost? Answer the question quickly in your head.

If you're like most people you divide up $1.10 neatly into $1 and 10 cents, rather than correctly into $1.05 and 5 cents. (Think about it for a moment. If the ball costs 10¢ more than the bat, then the total cost will be $1.20—10¢ for the ball and $1.10 for the bat, so the total can't be $1.10.)

The distinctive feature of this seemingly easy puzzle is that it evokes an answer that is intuitive, appealing—and wrong. Kahneman suggests that this demonstrates the relative power of System 1 over System 2.

By the way, don't feel bad, many thousands of university students have answered the bat-and-ball puzzle, and the results are shocking. More than 50% of students at Harvard, MIT, and Princeton gave the intuitive, incorrect, answer. At some less grand universities, the rate of failure to check with System 2, and come up with the wrong answer, was more than 80%.

The systems have different characteristics:

- **System 1:** Operates automatically and quickly, with little or no effort and no sense of voluntary control. It kicks in most of the time, especially when dealing with a familiar issue such as driving your car home by a familiar route. You rely on your intuitive and emotional system to do this.
- **System 2:** Allocates attention to the effortful mental activities that demand it, such as complex spreadsheets, calculations, and tackling issues that need rational, logical consideration such as learning to play a new instrument or sorting complex data into a coherent report. This is our slow, rational, tiring, deliberate system.

The automatic operations of System 1 can generate surprisingly complex patterns of ideas, but only the slower System 2 organises thoughts in a logical series of steps. When all goes smoothly, which is most of the time, System 2 generally adopts the suggestions of System 1 with little or no modification. (In other words, you believe your first impressions and act on your desires.)

If asked to pick which kind of thinker they are, most people say System 2. But in reality System 1 is how we *actually* make decisions. In fact, having made very fast System 1 choices, it is only when asked to *explain* the reasons for their choices, that people switch to System 2 to rationalise their decision.

However, when System 1 runs into difficulty, it calls on System 2 to deliver more detailed and specific processing to solve the problem. This is what happens when you have to multiply 17 × 24—somewhat harder for most of us than multiplying 2 × 2.

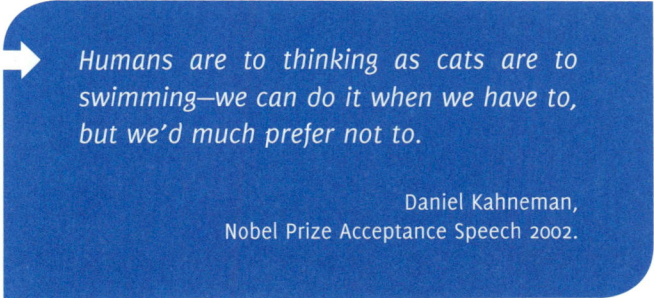

Humans are to thinking as cats are to swimming—we can do it when we have to, but we'd much prefer not to.

Daniel Kahneman,
Nobel Prize Acceptance Speech 2002.

Autopilot and Pilot

Most of the time we are on System 1, the *autopilot*, because most of what we do is repetitive. We wake up and go through the same motions—visit the bathroom, eat breakfast, brush teeth, take shower, get dressed, walk out of the house, take the bus, or drive the same route to work, smile at the boss, frown at colleagues, drink coffee, complain, take lunch break, etc. This explains why it is so easy to forget whether we've locked the door or switched the lights off. We perform these operations on autopilot.

It is only when something unusual happens that our *pilot* gets activated—we have to go to the doctor before work, we need to follow a diversion while driving, our boss is unusually pleasant in the morning, our normal coffee isn't available and we have to make another choice, etc. When this happens surprise activates and orientates our attention. Often you will stare, and search your memory for a rationale that makes sense of the event.

System 1 and 2 summary

System	System 1	System 2
Characteristics	• Fast, effortless, unconscious • Looks for patterns • Creates stories to explain events	• Slow, effortful, conscious • Looks for logic • Uses analysis to explain events
Advantages	• Responds quickly in a crisis • Comfortable with the familiar • Makes associations	• Demands consideration • Weighs up pros and cons • Establishes consequences
Disadvantages	• Jumps to conclusions • Unhelpful emotional responses • Makes 'mistakes' unconsciously	• Slow to decide • Requires energy and effort • Becomes tired thinking

The table above shouldn't suggest that there is a crude 'flick' between the systems. They're not binary. Kahneman describes them as working seamlessly together in an intertwined way. System 2 is, after all, involved in every decision even simply as a 'lazy controller.' (Thanks to Phil Barden for this insight.)

4. Our Brains Are Lazy; So We Invented Some Quick Fixes

System 2 uses lots of energy. And switching between System 1 and System 2 is a challenge. Our brains are fundamentally lazy, and look for the simplest, fastest, easiest answer or quick fixes. To put it more politely the unwritten but powerful *Law of Least Effort* means we are predisposed to like mental shortcuts.[14] So we use these quick fixes —heuristics—to help us save energy and get to an answer quickly.

---

[14] The reason behind this laziness is that though it is only 2% of the total body weight, the brain uses 20% of total energy consumption measured in blood circulation. There is a good physiological reason that our ancestors learned this 'minimum effort' approach.

When faced with a choice between two tasks, the brain opts for the easier one. Remember, this usually happens on the subconscious level.

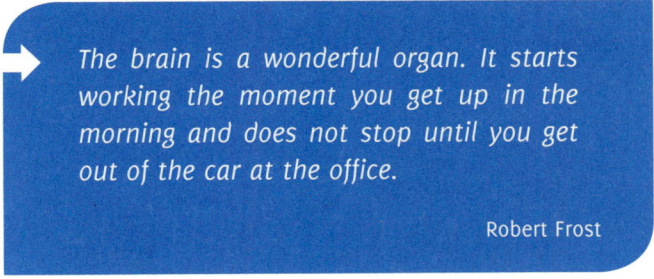

> The brain is a wonderful organ. It starts working the moment you get up in the morning and does not stop until you get out of the car at the office.
>
> Robert Frost

A linked implication of *The Law of Least Effort* is a need for completion or closure. This becomes very important when we listen to a story. We are keen to know the end. Our brain concentrates on following the story as it unfolds and will only rest when it finishes. That is when you 'cannot put a book down'—one more chapter, and another, just one more. It is also why we hate movies with ambiguous or unresolved endings. Stories without an end tax our brain, making it wander and wonder. For more on this see **Chapter 7** on stories.

5. We Wire What Fires Together

The brain stores information in networks, not individual bits. When stimuli appear at the same time the brain automatically makes an association between them. When the brain experiences the same signals together several times, a strong 'associative memory' is formed by connections being established between our neural circuits. This is reinforced with every new exposure.

Pavlov's Dog Experiment is a classic example of associative memory. He and his team first locked up a group of dogs in cages and starved them. They then brought in plates of freshly cooked meat. They placed the plates near the ravenous dogs. Aroused by the inviting smell, the dogs salivated. At the same time the scientists rang a bell.

The process was repeated a number of times. Then the experiment was changed. The bell was rung *without* the presence of the meat, and the dogs started salivating as soon as they heard it. They had established an associative memory—an *anchor*—connecting the sound of the bell with the arrival of food. For more on this see **Chapters 1** and **8.**

Many of us have similar associative memories we have unconsciously developed. They may be connected with our childhood, such as a smell or a sound that evokes a powerful memory of parents or past home life.

Sometimes companies deliberately create an association between unrelated senses and objects. For example, in an experiment reported by Charles Spence, Professor of Experimental Psychology at the University of Oxford, food eaten with heavier cutlery in a restaurant was rated as tastier, and people were prepared to pay more for it.[15] Much advertising also relies on the power of subtle, and sometimes not so subtle, association. This is technically known as the *halo effect*.[16] Nespresso, for example, has consciously built an association with 'smooth and classy' and George Clooney. More generally, the halo effect occurs when one aspect of a product influences our perception of the performance of the product in other areas: a white laundry detergent with blue speckles can make consumers think it removes dirt better; a soap with a stronger perfume is believed to clean better; coffee made with granules rather than powder is perceived as tasting better. In the same way, association with a celebrity can make us feel more positive about a brand.

---

[15] http://www.futureoffood.ox.ac.uk/sites/futureoffood.ox.ac.uk/files/impact%20of%20tableware.pdf. In another example a cosmetics company identified that a different, more luxurious-looking, jar improved consumers' perception of the quality of the skin cream they produced. They tested exactly the same cream in different jars in different cities. The results were conclusive. Consumers thought that the skin cream *itself* was better when placed in a more luxurious-looking jar. When the consumers who had taken part had the experiment explained to them, many refused to believe they had been influenced by the jars. The cream 'quality' assessment happened on a subconscious level, influenced by the packaging.

[16] Halo effects can be triggered by all kinds of sensory signals: product packaging, colours, perfumes, music, and celebrities. There is more on this interesting phenomenon in the discussion of cultural differences and consumer responses in **Section 3.**

This is why brand consistency is important, if it is to leave strong memory traces in the brain.

6. We Only Can Deal With WYSIATI

In *Thinking, Fast and Slow*, Kahneman, refers to What You See Is All There Is (WYSIATI) as the most common factor limiting our rational thinking.

Our lazy brain is impatient. It tries to reach a conclusion fast. But to reach a conclusion, it must assume that it has all the information it needs to answer a question or make a decision. But how can the brain assume that what it sees is all there is? Well, in the absence of adequate external stimuli, it uses what's already there to 'bulk out' the available data.

For instance, we form impressions about people within a few seconds of meeting them. In recruitment, this may translate to an interviewer coming to a conclusion about the candidate within about 30 seconds of beginning the interview. When tested these initial notions about the applicant and their abilities are often wrong. Interviewers who are trained to not form instant judgments about someone do a better job at screening and selecting candidates who succeed in job roles.

There are other ways the brain completes the missing parts of any picture. Here's an example from Kahneman. Read the description below, then answer the question.

Description: *Steve lives in the US and is very shy and withdrawn. He's invariably helpful but with little interest in people or in the world of reality. A meek and tidy soul, he has a need for order and structure and a passion for detail.*

Question to answer quickly: *Is Steve more likely to be a librarian or a farmer?*

Where we have introduced this question in workshops, two-thirds of participants guess that Steve is a librarian. As it happens, male farmers in the United States outnumber male librarians by a ratio of about 20 to 1. So statistically he is more likely to be a farmer. Had we included this framing or information, participants might have concluded that Steve is probably a farmer. But because most people focus only on the information in the description, they come to a wrong conclusion.

This example demonstrates two problems in the heuristics associated with System 1 thinking. The first is straightforward stereotyping. The description *fits* that of the librarian stereotype. Steve fits the stereotype, therefore he must be a librarian.

The second challenge relates directly to WYSIATI. What evidence do people need to draw a conclusion? Our experience is no one asks for extra information in the Steve exercise. This is often ascribed to the availability bias: people make a decision based on the information that is easily and readily available rather than searching for more. To discover more on this, see **Chapter 9.**

7. We Think Perception is (Almost) Reality

When people were given a vanilla pudding to eat that had been coloured brown using a tasteless food colouring, they described the delicious taste of ... chocolate. Why?

First, perceptions—visual, auditory, touching, smell, or taste—do not just provoke a straightforward stimulus-response reaction. The brain is not a blank slate. The eye is not a camera. The brain's perception *combines* the incoming signals with existing expectations. So the lack of a flavour is compensated for by the strong chocolate colour. We can re-imagine the chocolate flavour from the colour stimulus.

In fact, some perceptions are so strong and emotional that they can prevent you from giving up bad habits or adopting good habits. Some research suggests the less a product is presented as healthy, the better its perceived taste. Some readers may know the classic 'naughty but nice' advertising slogan for cream. As a complement, a mouthwash that tastes slightly unpleasant, like medicine, is more easily perceived as more effective than one that's sweet.

We also try to make sense of perceptions according to some basic but unreliable rules. Have a look, for example at the following two tables. Which is bigger? Some people choose A and some choose B.

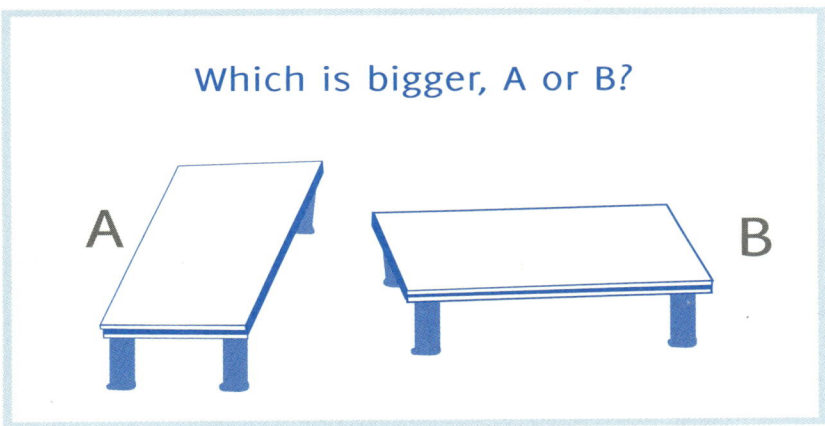

The truth is both are exactly the same. If you're not convinced, photocopy the page and cut out the tables. Check them. Now do you see?

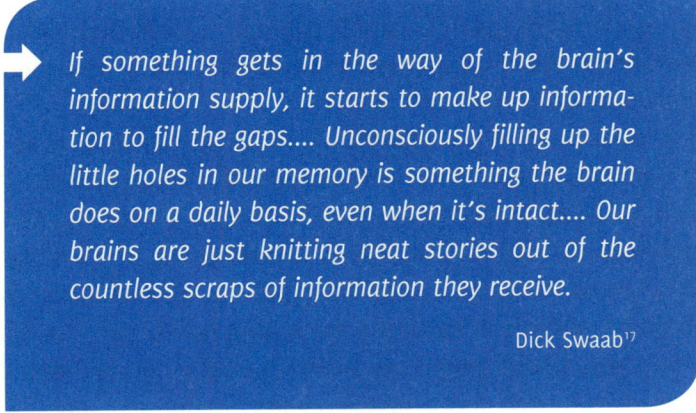

If something gets in the way of the brain's information supply, it starts to make up information to fill the gaps.... Unconsciously filling up the little holes in our memory is something the brain does on a daily basis, even when it's intact.... Our brains are just knitting neat stories out of the countless scraps of information they receive.

Dick Swaab[17]

[17] *We Are Our Brains*, Penguin 2015, p. 152.

We are also deluded in terms of how our behaviour compares to that of others. Below is a piece of US research comparing actual giving behaviour to the average. (See the discussion in **Chapter 10** on how we make a mental distinction between average, ideal, and normal behaviour.) Essentially most donors to charitable causes think they are more generous than the average, when the truth is almost three quarters are less generous. Helping to readjust this inaccurate perception is important for long term fundraising success.

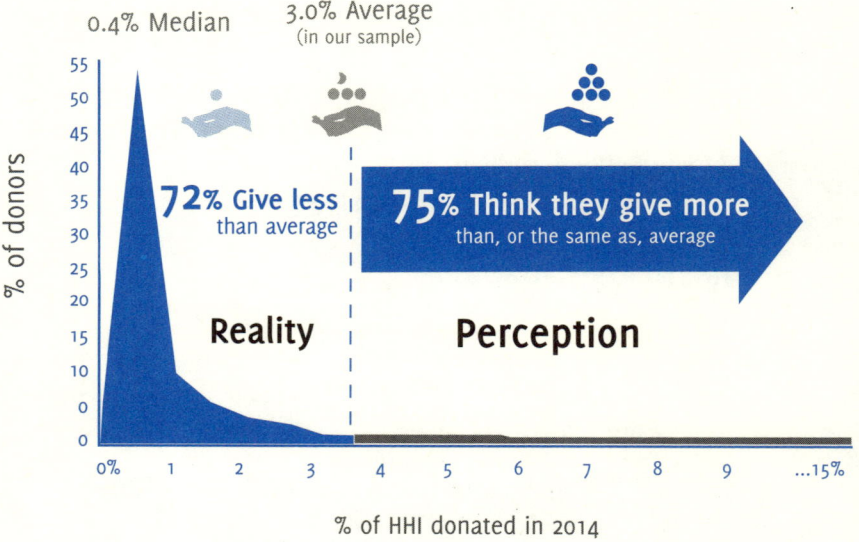

8. We Recognise, and Like, Patterns

We store information in our brains as patterns and frameworks, technically called schemas. For example, it is much easier for us to count multiples of 3 in an ascending order: 3, 6, 9, 12, 15, 18, 21, 24, 27, etc., than to recite them backward, even though the chunks of information remain the same. Simply, we prefer certain pattern sequences more than others.

Even if some information is missing, we often identify the pattern by filling in missing information. If, for example, we are reading from left to right and have already seen and recognised the letters, A, P, P, and L, the 'APPLE' recogniser will predict that it is likely to see an E in the next position. It will send a signal down to the E recogniser saying, in effect, 'Please be aware that there is a high likelihood that you will see your E pattern very soon, so be on the lookout for it.' The E recogniser then adjusts its threshold such that it is more likely to recognise an E. If an image appears next that is vaguely like an E, but is perhaps smudged such that it would not have been recognised as an E under 'normal' circumstances, the E recogniser is likely to still indicate that it has indeed seen an E, since that is what was expected.

Our brains can do amazing things with patterns, and become better at them as we practice. Look at the message below. Try reading it out loud—you find you get better as you progress.

But the brain is adaptive ...

7H15 M3554G3
53RV35 7O PR0V3
HOW 7H3 8R41N C4N
D0 4M4Z1NG 7H1NG5!
1MPR3551V3 7H1NG5!
1N 7H3 B3G1NN1NG
17 W45 H4RD BU7
N0W, 0N 7H15 LIN3
7H3 8R41N 15
R34D1NG 17
4U70M471C4LLY
W17H 0U7 3V3N
7H1NK1NG 4B0U7 17,
B3 PROUD!
0NLY C3R741N P30PL3 C4N
R34D 7H15

Nimble decision scientists can exploit this desire for patterns. On the next page is a banner Bernard spotted in Glasgow. He stopped, as did a number of other people, to complete the pattern. Can you work it out? Our desire for a pattern is a way to attract attention.

How we interpret facts, data, information, etc., is influenced by the way the data is framed. *Framing* (about which more in **Chapter 4**) is an important notion in this information processing and patterning. Essentially, the way we perceive a painting, picture, or information is influenced by the frame we put it in.

For example, the annual membership of a fitness centre can be framed as:

- Fitness Centre annual membership fee £350 *or*
- Only £1 a day for your fitness and wellbeing *or*
- Your health for a year for less than the price of a daily cup of coffee

An even more effective kind of framing is *emotional framing*. The rational message is the picture, and the emotions—the context, story, packaging, images, colours, logo, and celebrities we put around it—are the frame. What we say about the functionality of a product, or service, is the painting.

Brand acts as a powerful frame for our experience of the product. The famous Coca-Cola vs. Pepsi 'taste test' was first run out in the 1980s, but is still used today. When consumers sip both products in a 'blind' test, the majority prefer Pepsi. (Apparently, because it is sweeter.) But when consumers drink the products identified by their brand names, the majority prefer Coca-Cola. Neurological tests based on this experiment traced brain activation while people drank the identified and unidentified products. What they discovered was that different parts of the brain were activated with Coca-Cola, than with Pepsi. With Pepsi, the reward parts of the brain were activated, in recognition of its taste and sweetness. With Coca-Cola, the memory and happiness parts of the brain were activated. This was, and is, largely due to successful and consistent branding.

The conclusion is that Coca-Cola's global market leadership is not driven by its product, but rather by its brand—or frame.

We can conceive a similar exercise in charity fundraising. Send the same fundraising appeal to two comparable samples of potential donors, but with different organisation names at the top. Any difference in response will be due to the brand power (frame) of the charity, and not to the product, or the appeal itself (painting).

This exercise shows how our brain organises any incoming information into schemas, or categories. These are meant to make the process of retrieving known information, and assessing new information, easier. We have a schema for a hospital (building, operations, doctors, nurses, machines, analyses, medicines, etc.), a school (class, desk, teacher, blackboard, desk, homework, etc.), a company, a city, home, etc.

Imagine your brain is a library. There is a librarian inside your head who receives information—'books.' The librarian looks at the book title, identifies the category to which it belongs, and shelves it accordingly. If the book does not belong to a category inside your existing library, the librarian will often ignore it. This is especially true in the way we respond to information about people. Take politicians. If we have a specific opinion about a politician we interpret or select incoming information that supports our point of view about them. In the 2016 US presidential election, supporters of Donald Trump heard his more outrageous comments as evidence of his plain speaking and common sense. Opponents heard them as evidence of his racism, misogyny and bigotry.

9. We Have Goals and Try Really Hard to Meet Them

None of the principles we've articulated so far take place in the abstract or simply for a whim. Underlying all our behaviour is the idea of *goals* —outcomes or results that we aspire to and direct our action towards.

These goals may be very concrete and *physical*—to reduce hunger, to make sure we don't feel cold, to have a safe place to stay. Or they may be *psychological*—to feel wanted, to feel affinity, to feel security. You can clearly see how well-established pieces of psychological theory fit in here. (It even fits with some old school thinking like Maslow's Hierarchy of Needs.)

A great deal of contemporary decision science is designed to convince us that by acquiring a specific product or service we will satisfy one or more of our goals.[18] We have goals, but there remain a number of challenges to getting what, as the Spice Girls put it, we "really, really want."

We may *not be able to fully articulate or understand what our goals are or how we might achieve them*. We believe, or are *led* to believe, that if we owned *that* car or wore *that* garment we would feel young and sexy. Or if we purchased *that* burger and fries we would feel contented and replete. The sad reality is that acquiring the product or service often doesn't actually satisfy the goal.

We may be *encouraged to prioritise one goal over another, more socially useful, one*. While our System 2 brains might think it's useful to spend time reading a novel or studying Spanish on a commuter trip, Our System 1 brain is stimulated to believe it's more relaxing to play mindless games of Candy Crush because we 'deserve' the relaxation. (It's also less effortful—hence the expression 'mindless activity.')

---

[18] If you are keen to know more about this then Phil Barden's chapter on goals in *Decoded* is an interesting and enlightening read. He sees marketers as trying to influence behaviour in favour of their brands/products/services. Goals help them to understand why people buy categories and brands. As Barden points out, there are numerous instances now of 'purpose'—a kind of goal—being what drives companies, and consumer choice, (Unilever's *Sustainable Living Plan* is a good example.)

If you are involved in the social change agenda the good news is that people do very often have positive or altruistic goals. It is then your job to explain to these individuals that taking this specific responsible action, or making a donation to this charity, or reducing their consumption in this area, will help achieve an important societal or personal goal—despite the fact many other commercial stimuli are suggesting the reverse. Within the basic drives discussed earlier we can distinguish many goals, some positive and some negative. A brief list of the reasons why people give money to charity, for example would include to feel good, to help others like them, to help others less fortunate, to be like other generous people, to gain social status, to follow a religious belief, to assuage guilt, to impress an important individual etc.

Commercial agencies are well ahead of not-for-profits when it comes to identifying and using goals—implicit or explicit—in marketing. A famous example is discussed in the *Harvard Business Review* article, *Marketing Malpractice: The Cause and The Cure*.[19] Here Clayton M Christiansen, Marketing Professor at Harvard, talks about the 'job' for which a product is hired by consumers. His core idea is that the key function of a marketer is to create an experience that matches a specific consumer goal. (See below for *The Milkshake Mystery* case study.)

The Milkshake Mystery

Christiansen relates the case study of a fast-food restaurant keen to increase sales of milkshakes. The initial approach followed classic marketing techniques: interviewing current and potential consumers, establishing their demographic and personality traits, exploring with the segments what their interests were and how the current product met them, and establishing what new features or benefits would be worth paying for.

Sadly, after all this work and a significantly improved product, in line with the research, there was no significant impact on sales.

---

[19] 1 December 2005.

A new team of behaviourally-focused marketers was brought in. They began, not with the milkshake, but with the *goal* which a milkshake might satisfy. From observations with consumers in different real-life settings, they identified two key goals which a milkshake could satisfy that the current product didn't quite do:

- **Goal 1: To postpone hunger and boredom:** the research observed that a surprising number of *adults* bought milkshakes in the morning on the way to work. The rationale for this was not clear until the marketers spoke to those adults about why they'd made a purchase. The answer was simple—many of them had left for work early and without breakfast to get to the office, so they were hungry. They knew that they couldn't stop to eat and they'd have to spend a long time in slow moving traffic. Buying a milkshake gave them something that would help fill them up and avoid hunger pangs while driving. *And* since the milkshake is thick, it would take a while to consume, giving them something physical and tactile to do—so reducing the boredom of the commute. Further, their perception was that they could gain some *nutritional value* through the milk. Finally, there was even some evidence that sucking through the straw added a significant amount of value to the experience, satisfying some basic childlike desire, as well as being convenient for driving, and making the search for 'last drops' a fun activity.

- **Goal 2: To reward children:** the second cluster of consumers looking to meet a goal were parents buying milk shakes for their children later in the day, maybe after school or as part of an evening meal. The parent could use the milkshake as a reward for good behaviour earlier in the day, or even as a payoff for simply eating the 'nutritious' burger that had been offered. ('If you eat up all your burger then you get your milkshake. You don't eat the burger, you don't get the milkshake.') On further exploration, the behavioural economists noticed that a milkshake, again connected to the straw and the thickness, could take quite a long time for a child to consume. An adult would often be able to talk to another adult, make a call on their mobile, or finish reading a newspaper while waiting for the child to finish. Result? All round winners, if you ignore the nutritional implications.

These two pieces of goal analysis allowed the marketers to work with food scientists to identify the 'jobs' that the milkshake was meant to do for the people who wanted to 'hire' it. From this the key improvements became fairly obvious:

Make the shake thicker so it takes longer to consume, and formulate it so it retains its consistency while it's being consumed.

Engineer the straw to be thinner so the consumer has to suck hard to get at the product, and make sure that a secure plastic lid on the cup reduces spills

Include some unusual elements, e.g. 'chunky' ingredients, that create an element of surprise, so the whole experience changes and becomes more fun.

The key message for the social sector is that if we are trying to orientate people towards specific social outcomes or behaviour, we need to analyse carefully which of our supporters' personal goals we are meeting. What goal-delivering job are you being 'hired' to do—is it emotional, physical, psychological or social?

Activate the Posterior Superior Temporal Sulcus, Not the Nucleus Accumbens. Clear?

Thanks to technological advances, we know there are specific areas in the brain activated for reward, pleasure, memory, fear, etc. The latest fMRI scanners allow us to see in extraordinary detail, and in real time, what's happening while a person is exposed to a certain stimulus; reading a message, watching a video clip, eating chocolate, engaging in exercise, etc. For example, we often see heightened activity in the reward area triggered by eating chocolate. This is not as precise as spotting a broken bone in an X-ray, because even with sophisticated neuro-technologies like fMRI we can only see which parts of the brain are activated. We don't see specific ideas, thoughts, or dreams floating around—perhaps fortunately. We also know that ideas, thoughts, or dreams often create responses in different parts of the brain at the same time—across a neural network, not a single neuron.

The same kind of stimulus can produce different responses. For example, experiments show that when people play a video game which earns or loses them money as they play, the *nucleus accum-*

bens is activated. This is a primitive part of the brain associated with the pleasure of sex, drugs, and gambling. However, when people play a video game in which winning results in making donations to charity, a different part of the brain is activated, the *posterior superior temporal sulcus*. This is responsible for social interaction, and how we perceive others, relate to them, and bond with them.

10. We Can Be Easily Confused

Our brains are in one sense wonderful—they can create fantasies, make intuitive connections between events, and help us make altruistic rather than selfish choices. But they have relatively poor raw computational power and the environment in which they have to operate is complicated with too many choices, inadequate information, and relatively little time. Technically, this operating context is what makes our rationality bounded.

These constraints mean that people in general, and especially consumers keen to get on with things, need fast strategies to make choices. Hence the need for the ten major heuristics we discuss in the next section.

Common sense, and some research, suggests that more information leads to better decisions. But this is true only up to a point. Beyond the optimum input, more information can cause confusion and may actually lead to poorer and slower decisions, albeit ones made with greater confidence.

We have already discussed how Kahneman and his colleague Tversky provided a psychological underpinning to the challenge of how people deal with all this complexity. They were not, however, the first to have made this connection. In the 1950s Herbert Simon came up with the concept of *bounded rationality*.[20] In this concept,

---

[20] Others built on Simon's work. Gerd Gigerenzer, author of *Simple Heuristics That Make Us Smart*, among other books, came up with the idea of 'fast and frugal' thinking. He suggested that the rationality of a decision depends on the frameworks available for consideration—which might vary by culture, by age, by social setting, etc. So

our decision processes, and maybe even our minds, can only really be understood relative to the environment in which they evolved and are working. The decisions made are not always the best, because there are restrictions in our ability to take in or process information. And, of course, our computational capacities may depend on time of day, mood, sobriety etc.

So Kahneman's 'heuristics and biases' insight was not entirely revolutionary. Though the fact he and Tversky developed and implemented a rigorous experimental approach meant that the field moved on massively. In the years since Kahneman's Nobel Prize, more evidence has confirmed that bounded rationality informs much of business and social psychology. It helps explain how our decision confusion is not some unfathomable mystery, but simply us bumping up against the limits of our processing power.

Glass Half-full or Half-empty: The implication of this limited processing power is, for example, that how something is framed—positively or negatively—has an enormous impact on how information is processed, even if the outcome is identical.

Let's say you've been diagnosed with a very serious illness, and two different doctors come to tell you what happens next:

- **Doctor A:** 'With proper treatment, you have an 80% chance of a full recovery.'
- **Doctor B:** 'There's a 20% chance that you'll die after being treated for this illness.'

Which doctor would you want to work with? Even though the prognoses are exactly the same, most people will pick Doctor A, because an *80% chance of recovery* sounds way better than a *20% chance of*

---

people are 'ecologically rational' when they make the best possible use of their limited information-processing abilities. They do this by applying simple and intelligent algorithms. In this way they'll *normally* make a good choice—what's called in the jargon a 'near-optimal inference.' An example might be 'If it smells bad it's probably not good to eat,' or 'If it's a popular choice of hotel then it's probably good,' or 'If it's expensive then it's probably high quality.' These heuristics are, in general, useful.

death. (This could have a significant impact on how you frame a charity appeal or call to action.)

Don't Think of an Elephant: The preference for positive framing, in certain contexts, may be related to the notion that we cannot 'unthink' of something. This is illustrated by George Lakoff in his book *Don't Think of an Elephant.* If you ask a person not to think of a pink elephant, they will only be able to think of a pink elephant. If you want someone to bring you a glass of water safely, it is better to say 'Hold the glass carefully,' rather than 'Don't drop the glass,' which will cause the brain to think 'drop, drop ...'

In the context of fundraising, pay attention to how much you talk about the *problem*, and how much about the *solution.*

The power of expectations is one main reason why placebo medicines, and other types of placebo offerings—expensive wine or branded coffee—work so well. We look for data to support our *confirmation bias.* This occurs when we warp or select data to fit or support our existing beliefs or expectations. The effects are often found in religion, politics, and even sometimes in science. (For example, in 1986 NASA scientists ignored the data that suggested the O-rings on the Challenger craft might fail in cold weather, as the launch was always assumed to take place in warm weather. The world later watched as the shuttle broke apart just 73 seconds into the flight, killing all on board. It was a cold day.) As Abraham Maslow said on another occasion, 'If the only tool you have is a hammer you tend to treat everything as a nail.'

KISS: Keep It Simple for Supporters: When a supporter looks at campaign or fundraising material on a website, email, or direct mail envelope, she scans it quickly to see what it is about. If she finds lots of text, many numbers, several boxes with different insights, she may well automatically switch off promising herself to get back to it later (a.k.a procrastinating). If you're looking to persuade someone to signup to an online campaign or to commit to a programme of personal action you should, where possible, encourage immediate action or commitment. There are some straightforward ways do that:

- Shape the process to make engaging easy
- Make the process of engaging easy
- Frame the choices appropriately
- Reduce the barriers to action

Our bounded rationality means we can be confused about a number of things.

Our feelings: We are often not clear about our *feelings*. There is significant evidence that what people see and feel about various stimuli (their *remembered utility*) doesn't always match up to what they actually experience (their *experienced utility*.) While people often believe they remember their entire experience, people are much more likely to remember the peaks and troughs—and the end of the experience—most strongly. Morris Altman, Professor of Behavioural and Institutional Economics at Victoria University in Wellington Australia shares a real-world example.

'If you had a painful operation that lasted four hours with limited anesthesia but the pain diminished markedly in the last half hour or so, you would remember the experience as not being all that bad. On the other hand, if the four-hour operation was largely painless but the last half-hour was excruciatingly painful, you would remember the operation has been very painful—despite the fact that the total pain in the first scenario was much greater than the total pain of the second scenario.'[21]

We can see the same effect in terms of customer or supporter care. If you deliver a poor experience to a customer, but then apologise and recover, the customer will often form a much more positive view of the overall experience.

Ourselves: We can also be confused about *ourselves*. The Dunning-Kruger effect is a cognitive bias which encourages people to have a false sense of their own ability. It was first detailed in 1999 by David Dunning and Justin Kruger of Cornell University. The effect works in two ways. First, people mistakenly assess their ability as much

---

[21] *Behavioural Economics for Dummies*, Morris Altman, Wiley, 2014.

higher than it really is—literally they think they are capable of things they are not. (If you have ever watched the auditions for the British TV show *X Factor* or the US show *American Idol* you can see plenty of evidence for this.) Conversely their research also suggests that highly skilled or competent individuals may *underestimate* their relative competence, with the negative consequence that they assume that tasks that are easy for them will also be easy for others.

Why does that matter? Because an inability to look outside of your existing belief systems will vastly limit your ability to grow and improve, both in business and in your personal life. And you may find it hard as a manager or coach to understand why someone can't do something that to you seems easy.

Consumers today have access to a wide range of products and services. And many people claim to value this level of choice or personalisation. However, the job of choosing between hundreds of products or offers can be daunting especially when money is involved. For example, you are probably aware of how hard it is to choose the 'best' mobile phone package when there are so many providers and so many options.

And an Eleventh Thing We Know

We organised the material in this first section around a list of 10 easy-to-follow-ideas, even though the actual content is 'messier' and more complex than that. There's a good reason for this.

People like reading lists—especially prioritised lists. They like them in magazines, in books, and on the web. The lists they like cover a spectrum of topics: 10 Steps to Guaranteed Weight Loss, the 10 Cutest Cats, 20 celebrity photos you'll never forget, the 50 Wealthiest People in the World, or the 15 Best Country Walks. Indeed, numbered lists go much further back than the internet, maybe beginning with the 10 Commandments or the 7 Deadly Sins. Whatever the reason, we love lists.

Lists, of course, fit in with a number of our key principles—especially those to do with being easy for our brains to use, offering us a pattern, and fitting into our sense of social conformity. Lists provide us with data which is already pre-filtered, so they are easy to consume. And if they are based on a survey, or are compiled by expert authors, they have some social proof.

Part 2

Key Decision Frameworks

Chapter 1

Prime and Anchor Ideas

Summary

The choice we make in a given situation can be significantly influenced by our unconscious response to a previous experience or to previous information we've received. This can happen through two linked heuristics called *priming* or *anchoring*.

Priming can take place when we are exposed to one or more stimuli—sounds, pictures, touch, words—that trigger a physical, cultural or social 'memory.' This memory then unconsciously influences our subsequent response. For example, simply getting people to read a list of words to do with tiredness will encourage them to slow down when asked to complete a subsequent physical task. Showing them a picture of an inspirational figure can help with confidence[1].

Anchoring is a more targeted or specific version of priming. Here the very specific first stimulus we're exposed to may well function as an *anchor*. For example, in a shop, showing a label with a previous higher price, and then highlighting a current reduced price produces

_____

[1] A study has shown that women who are exposed to images of other powerful women can be primed to feel more confident and assured when public speaking. In the experiment women were asked to speak in a room where they could see at the back of the room a large photo of a powerful and admirable female political figure. (Angela Merkel and Hillary Clinton performed strongly as primes.) Iona Latu *et al.*, 'Successful Female Leaders Empower Women's Behaviour In Leadership Tasks,' *Journal of Experimental Psychology*, Vol. 39, Issue 3, May 2013.

a sense of a 'bargain,' even if the actual price paid by the customer in the end isn't, objectively, a good deal. We judge the discount price using the 'original' price as the anchor.

Both priming and anchoring are key mechanisms through which System 1 exercises control over System 2 without us being aware of it. Cialdini, the legendary social psychologist, says these elements are part of what he calls pre-suasion—unconscious convincing.

As a fundraiser approaching prospects to consider making a gift, you might let them know that other donors have already contributed at a significant level. Within certain constraints, if you do this you're more likely to secure a larger gift. The introduction of the higher value gift 'anchor' creates a reference point for any subsequent discussion or decision.

We also need to be aware of the dangers implicit in priming, either conscious or unconscious. These can underpin prejudices and unfairness that we need to address and avoid. Individuals, whether they are judges reviewing sentences, poor people trying to borrow money, or recruiters selecting candidates, can pick up an unhelpful bias from a specific context or communication. We can help them develop a useful balance if the data is presented in a different way, or they are made aware of how their assessments can be distorted.

Decisions, Decisions

People find it hard to make decisions in a vacuum. They like something—a benchmark or a reference point—against which to compare their decision. This is especially true when they make a decision that involves numbers, such as buying something or making a donation. Often the reference point comes from past experience, 'I usually buy X for Y amount.' Or 'We normally donate Z every month.' But when a person is in unfamiliar territory, it is a good idea to provide them with a starting point that makes the decision easier, as it gives them a mental shortcut *and* appeals to their lazy, System 1 brain.

Consider this example, originally from Kahneman, which we've adapted. A roomful of people is divided into two. Half the participants are asked to close their eyes and cover their ears.

The others are shown a slide with the following questions on it.

- Was Gandhi 144 years old when he died?
- How old was Gandhi when he died?

They are asked to write down individually:

1. Answer 'yes' or 'no' to the first question.
2. Make an estimate of Gandhi's age when he died.

This first group is then told to close their eyes and cover their ears.

The other half of the room is asked to open their eyes and unblock their ears. They are shown a second slide, with slightly altered questions:

- Was Gandhi 35 years old when he died?
- How old was Gandhi when he died?

Both ages given for Ghandi's death, 144 and 35, are clearly ridiculous for anyone with the slightest grasp of history, or biology in the case of the first figure. This data, therefore, should *rationally* be dismissed and not taken into consideration when considering the second question—as would happen if System 2 was in charge.

What is interesting, is that in this experiment, and we've now done it a number of times in different countries and with different demographics, the two groups come up with very different answers. Those shown the larger initial 'age at death' stimulus tend to estimate a significantly higher number than the group shown the lower number, usually the difference is as much as 15 or 20 years. (This is a powerful and safe-to-try-at-home-or-work experiment. Give it a go. And if you must know Gandhi was 78 when he was assassinated.)

The stimulus of the first number, although it's clearly wrong and should be ignored, impacts on the 'age at death' guess. In feedback, both groups recognise the first age suggestion is ludicrous, and usually claim they dismissed it from consideration. But the evidence is they are *subconsciously* influenced. That's an anchor at work.

For a charity fundraiser, this has some important implications. Think about the stimulus you might introduce to a major donor or a prospect when meeting them. For example, even asking, 'How much do you think it costs to run a school for 500 students in India for a year? £100,000, or more?' before soliciting a £50,000 gift, might deliver a higher gift result because the potential supporter anchored round the higher number.

Do You Want to Give Me $30,000?

In the US Girl Scouts go door-to-door selling cookies to raise money. The cookies are popular and tasty. But, normally speaking, raising a lot of money is not easy on such low value items. Markita Andrews is famous as the Girl Scout with the largest ever cookie sales record.

There's a minimum price for the cookies, but the Girl Scouts were aiming to raise as much as possible. To help achieve this goal, Markita Andrews would knock on a door and begin by asking for a donation of $30,000.

If the homeowner said 'No,' as they always did, then she would say 'Then please buy a box of cookies and pay what you can.'

The proof of the anchoring pudding? In 12 years she sold $80,000 worth of cookies. And in 1985 she sold a remarkable 11,000 boxes of cookies in one year.

She was so successful Disney made a sales training film about her which was shown worldwide to multi-national companies, and she wrote a bestselling book. All at the age of 13.

Business uses the anchoring heuristic, but with less ethical intent, and sometimes more subtlety in what is called stealth marketing. Robert Levine, in his book *The Power of Persuasion: How We're Bought and Sold,* shares a great case study. A US cable TV company was keen to raise its subscription rates, but wanted to use the anchoring effect to make it appear that they were actually saving people money. In a careful PR stunt they announced to the press that the 'rumours' they were planning to increase their subscriptions by \$10 a month were completely false. 'You can relax. It's not going to happen. And the great news is, the rate for basic cable is only increasing by \$2 a month.'[2] As a result, many customers had a more positive view of what was still in fact a price rise and fewer than expected cancelled their contracts.

Surely Smart and Savvy Marketers Wouldn't Fall For a Technique Like This?

You might imagine this heuristic is so obvious it wouldn't work on a sophisticated fundraising or marketing audience. Happily, for those of us using decision science, that's not true. Here's an example of an experiment showing *anchoring* in action. It has the added twist that people feel they have made some kind of free choice about the original stimulus. (Note that in the Gandhi example the anchoring 'value' was pre-chosen by us.)

In October 2015, we were speaking at the world's most prestigious fundraising event—the International Fundraising Congress in Holland. As part of our research we decided to conduct a number of experiments onsite.

We prepared two bags. One bag contained 100 pieces of paper with the figure 10 written on them. A second bag contained 100 pieces of paper with the figure 65 written on them. The only other prop we had was a bottle of not very prestigious champagne.

We approached 30 delegates at the conference, all of whom were experienced figures in the European and global fundraising market. You might imagine they had a sound grasp of sales psychology. Certainly they thought so. Their inner System 2 dialogue and perhaps their inner Dunning-Kruger bias[3] reinforced this view.

---

[2] Robert Levine, *The Power of Persuasion: How We're Bought and Sold.* 2003, pp. 100–101).

[3] This bias suggests people tend to have a significant overestimation of their own ability. For more on this see Dunning-Kruger effect in **Section One**.

We stopped each person individually and showed them only one of the two bags. We told them that in the bag were 100 pieces of paper with *different* numbers, 1 to 100, written on them. (Though this was not true, of course.) We explained we were asking them to take part in an experiment, and that for the purposes of the experiment they first had to draw a 'random' number from the bag. The number was simply to allocate them an anonymous record in our survey data.

Once they had selected the number—always a 10 or a 65—we wrote it down on a test sheet, repeating that it was their 'random' number. We also gave them some small meaningless praise such as, 'Goodness, that's unusual to pull such a low number.' Or 'Goodness, 65—what a high number.'

We then produced the bottle of champagne. We explained it was not a *grande marque* but was a perfectly sound brand. (None of the respondents had heard of it, so they didn't have a price association.)

In the low value number variant, participants were first asked if they would pay €10 for the champagne, and to answer 'yes' or 'no.' Then we asked them to state what *maximum* price they would pay for the champagne as a gift for a not-very-special occasion, and a not-very-special friend. The €65 example followed the same process.

The results are shown below. As you can see what's really interesting is that these experienced, sophisticated individuals who received the initial stimulus of *choosing* the apparently random '10' produced a much lower average price in terms of maximum they would pay. And those equally experienced, sophisticated individuals who were given the original random stimulus of 65 produced a much higher average price, by a factor of almost €30. There are a few outliers in the results, as you would expect, but the average is solid.

What is also worth highlighting is that most of those who started with the high figure (65) gave lower estimates than that number, while most of those who started with the lower figure (10) gave a higher estimate than that number. However, they were still influenced, or anchored, by the original figure.

Respondents Shown €65 Anchor	Respondents Shown €10 Anchor
65	15
10	25
5	25
65	25
40	20
40	15
23	15
15	25
80	15
25	23
100	15
65	10
45	20
60	15
50	18
Average	**45.9**	**18.5**

We have since repeated this experiment in the USA, China, UK, Slovenia, Germany, Egypt, France, Chile, Argentina and Switzerland. In each case the participants were sophisticated fundraisers and marketing savvy. And many were quite suspicious. Despite this the results remain consistent in all locations.

In our view, this experiment demonstrates that even the cleverest individuals can be led to think they are making a *free, informed choice*, when in fact they are being encouraged in a very specific direction[4]. Anchors are powerful drivers of behaviour without conscious choice. Anchors complement *Nudges*, a different kind of deliberately influenced choice. See **Chapter 3** for more on this.

---

[4] Helping someone believe that they were in some way responsible for *choosing* the original number stimulus gives higher ownership of the result and seems to give higher results. (This links to the IKEA effect, see **Chapter 5**, and to the limited ability to assess information discussed in **Chapter 9**.)

Rough Justice: Anchoring and Unconscious Bias

Anchors can have some troubling impacts, and you need to take care to avoid bias especially in situations where fairness and equity are key.

One experiment demonstrating this involves German judges, each with an average of 15+ years experience of courtroom decisions, so you would presume scrupulously fair. Each judge first read the same case about a woman who had been caught shoplifting. They were then asked to roll a pair of dice. What the judges didn't know was that the dice were loaded. Every roll resulted in either a 3 or a 9.

As soon as the dice came to a stop, the judges were asked two questions:
- Would you sentence the woman to a prison term more, or less, in months, than the number on the dice?
- Please state the exact prison sentence in months you think would be fair for the shoplifter.

The results are a tribute to the power of random anchors. On average, those who had rolled a 9 said they would sentence her to 8 months. Whereas those who rolled a 3 offered the lower sentence of 5 months. The anchoring effect impact was 50%.[5]

The implication is that we need to watch carefully for biases that can creep into our judgments, no matter how experienced or objective we believe we are. (There is an complementary explanation here. You could also argue that this shows how the brain, depleted of energy (low blood sugar), defaults (System 1) to the norm of no parole.)

Of course, you might argue, the judges' decisions in the 'Rough Justice' case were not affecting any real people. But if the judges could be affected by a random number on a dice, how might watching a TV news report with some similarities, or reading an advert about shopping with a prominent random number affect them? How might a similar stimulus affect a salary negotiation, or a vote in an election? Many UK electors report being strongly influenced, perhaps deceived, by the much-quoted figure of £350M coming back to the UK every week from Europe if people voted for Brexit. The figure, of course, had no real empirical base.

---

[5] Daniel Kahneman, *Thinking, Fast and Slow*, 2011 pp. 125-126.

There is further disturbing evidence about how something as simple as the time of day or the state of the judges' stomachs might affect their sentencing decisions. From another experiment, we know that whether a judge is hungry or tired can affect decisions-making. This example is drawn from the *US Proceedings of the National Academy of Sciences*.

The study was based on eight parole judges in Israel. They normally spend their whole day reviewing parole applications from prisoners. The cases are normally reviewed in random order, to avoid bias.

The judges devote an average of only 6 minutes to each case. The default option is denial of parole; 65% of requests are refused. In a study over several weeks, the exact time of each judge's parole decision was recorded, as was the timing of the judges' three food breaks—morning, lunch, and afternoon. When the scientists mapped the proportion of approved requests against the time since the last food break there was a strong and unhappy correlation. The proportion of 'yes's to parole requests spiked after each meal. At this point, almost two thirds were granted. But during the next two hours or so until the judges' next meal break, the approval rate dropped steadily, to about zero just before the next meal. Implication? A full or empty stomach acts as an anchor—and against the interests of justice.

By identifying and tackling these often unexpected relationships, we can help remove the potential for unconscious injustice or inequity. You might not be deciding about a person's freedom, but watch out for an element of unconscious bias in the way you select candidates for jobs, or assess project proposals for support.

Priming Primer

Let's explore priming a bit more.[6] For example, how someone fills in the missing letter in this word:

SO_P

---

[6] Much of this section owes a great deal to some terrific insights from Behavioural Architects www.thebearchitects.com, published in *Marketing Week* https://www.marketingsociety.com/tags/behavioural-architects.

Depends on whether they were thinking about cleansing and hygiene or eating and hunger. (Soap or Soup.)

Priming can make a difference in our attitudes to people. Solomon Asch ran an experiment in which he wrote a series of adjectives to describe an anonymous individual, then sequenced them differently to share with two different groups. **Group 1** read a description of someone who was 'intelligent, industrious, impulsive, critical, stubborn and envious' **Group 2** read a description of someone who was 'envious, stubborn, critical, impulsive, industrious, intelligent'.

In **Group 1** 32% subsequently rated the person described as happy, 74% as good-looking, and 64% as restrained. In **Group 2**, 5% rated the person as happy, 35% as good-looking, and 9% as restrained. The order in which even subjective information is received can make a massive difference to perception. (And notice too that people have opinions about qualities not even described— 'good-looking' was not a quality in the original description.[7])

According to those clever people at The Behavioural Architects,[8] a leading insight consultancy, there are four main ways that priming can impact on us and our subconscious:

- **Enable us or identify something faster:** One very simple example is when a person is exposed to the word 'yellow,' they seem to be slightly faster in recognising the word 'banana' in a later context. This seems to happen because the words 'yellow' and 'banana' are linked in our memories. (This is technically known as *semantic or conceptual priming.*)

  In a charity setting we might want to associate our logo with a key idea, as does the Red Cross with their universal symbol.

- **Affect our perception or judgment:** People tend to evaluate their own personalities and abilities more positively in comparison to

---

[7] Quoted in *#Hooked,* Patrick Fagan, Pearson 2017. Asch, S. E. (1946). Forming impressions of personality. *The Journal of Abnormal and Social Psychology, 41*(3), 258-290.

[8] http://www.thebearchitects.com.

other people. For example, Europeans, when they work or meet others in an Asian context seem to rate themselves and their culture more highly.[9] (This is technically known known as *construal priming*.)

Those of us involved in social change might seek to ensure that we challenge racist perceptions of, say, Africans as unable to manage their economies.

- **Impact on subsequent actions**: We gave the example earlier of the effect that words about tiredness can have on subsequent performance. The behaviour architects share a similar example, where people primed by reading lists of words associated with impolite behaviour are subsequently more likely to behave rudely—such as talking over others. This is technically known as *behavioural priming.*

  We might consider how using action-orientated words and images might affect our perception of, say, the Médicins Sans Frontières (MSF) brand in handling emergencies.

- **Align our goals and motivations**: Finally, we might want to prime someone with an attitude or approach that aligns their goals with what we want to achieve. In the social sector, we are obviously keen to prime people with the concepts of altruism and philanthropy. This means that in a wide range of situations the person in question will think and act in the interest of others. This is technically known as *goal priming.*

  An agency like Greenpeace might be keen to encourage ideas around environmental awareness by showing celebrities recycling or avoiding waste

---

[9] For some interesting Chinese research on this: *https://www.frontiersin.org/articles/10.3389/fpsyg.2017.01759/full.*

Priming Through Sequence

Simply changing the *order* in which questions are asked or information is shared can dramatically change how audiences or individuals respond to propositions or questions. In his book on influence,[10] Cialdini talks about a mental health charity that stopped people in a public park and asked them to consider volunteering against two contrasting offers asked in sequence:

Offer A

1. 'Would you be prepared to volunteer to spend a day at the zoo as a companion for individuals with a mental health challenge?' To this 17% of respondents said 'Yes.'

2. This was followed by, 'Would you consider committing to being a two-year counsellor for the same group of individuals [with a mental health challenge]?' To this 100% of respondents said 'No.'

The sequence was then reversed.

Offer B

1. 'Would you consider committing to being a counsellor for individuals with mental health challenges for two years?' Again 100% said 'No.'

2. Followed by, 'Would you consider spending a day at the zoo with the same group of individuals [with a mental health challenge?' In response to this proposition 37% said 'Yes.'

The *sequencing* of the ask produced a different priming effect. In Offer B, it obliged respondents to assess the relative reasonableness of the second proposition.

You can even deliver an impact by linking unconnected issues. A team of three researchers, Schwartz, Strack, and Mai, asked Group A respondents:

Q1. 'How happy are you with life in general?'

Q2. 'How often do you normally go out on a date?'

---

[10] *Influence: The Psychology of Persuasion*, Harper Collins, 1984.

In this sequence, the question and the answer were closely correlated. By and large, people decided they were broadly happy, and then replied to the dating question as an afterthought. However, when the questions were reversed, for a Group B, responses were very differently correlated. They answered in a way that suggested they were overall less happy than the first group.

The sequencing of questions influences responses. More specifically, people's response to the first question influences their response to the second. In Schwartz, Strack and Mal's experiment,[11] the change produced a less happy response. (By the way this result is not just to do with dating and young people. We have carried out similar experiments at a number of events, and produced a similar reversal of correlation.) On issues such as salary and making love:

Q1. 'How happy are you with your salary?'

Q2. 'How often do you make love with your partner?'

In each case the conflict between our automatic System 1 process and our more rational System 2 process are highlighted.

Similar effects might be useful when asking questions asked about sexual health or drinking habits, and trying to encourage people to be completely candid. If you ask, 'How many sexual partners have you had?' And give a range of '0, 1–5, 6–10, 11–15, or more?' you'll get a different answer than if you anchor the numbers as 'Less than 10, 10–15, 15–25, or more than 25?' (Or a similar question about alcohol or food.) Choosing the range—and anchoring it sensitively—can help people to be more candid.

As you can see from the examples above, priming is important if you're designing any kind of survey to measure satisfaction or the attractiveness of different action options. The learning for anyone trying to persuade people to save more for retirement, to adopt a better diet, or to make a donation, is to consider carefully the anchoring information, and the sequence in which it is given, against any choice.

---

[11] https://core.ac.uk/download/pdf/42101251.pdf

Helping Poor People Make Good Credit Choices

People living on the financial margins—poor people—might be expected to always make careful, rational judgments about spending and borrowing, because they have to be very careful with money. In fact, research carried out by Anandi Mani and others has shown a strong correlation between lacking money (or time) and making poorer decisions 'possibly because poverty imposes a cognitive load that saps attention and reduces effort.'[12]

The reality is those most at risk financially make some of the least appropriate choices. In the UK, this is most evident through what are commonly called payday loan services, such as Wonga, which may charge up to 2,000% a year in compound interest for loans. But borrowers, many of whom are already in financial trouble, seem unaware of the true cost of a loan from these companies and its very serious financial implications. In their adverts the companies, you might notice, emphasise the *ease* of the borrowing process, 'just one call and in 5 minutes the money is in your account,' and neglect to stress the very serious, and unfair, long-term cost implications.

The World Bank has been exploring innovative ways to help poor people make good financial choices. Specifically, they have been looking at how to ensure people in developing nations improve their use, and understanding of, credit options. Previously the Bank's focus was on proposing regulation of credit suppliers, and attempting to ensure the terms of any credit option are transparent. They have had some success with this approach, but these initiatives still

---

[12] Taken from an article in *Science,* 'Poverty Impedes Cognitive Function', 30 August 2013, by Anandi Mani et al. The team gathered evidence from shoppers at a US shopping mall in New Jersey, and also from farmers in Tamil Nadu, India. They found that when people were considering a possible important financial decision, such as how to pay for a car repair, there was an impact on performance in unrelated complex or reasoning tasks e.g. working out the cost of a shopping trip, calculating how big a floor or field area was etc. Lower-income individuals performed poorly in these extra tasks if the repairs were expensive, but did well if the cost was low. In contrast, higher-income individuals performed well in both conditions. So, the assumption is the projected financial burden of the bigger bill imposed no cognitive pressure. Similarly, the sugarcane farmers from Tamil Nadu performed a range of cognitive tasks better after harvest than before.

assume that people make sensible and considered choices[13] using System 2. Unfortunately, they don't.

In recognition of this, the World Bank has increasingly worked to use behavioural economics to help shape real world choices by vulnerable consumers. In a 2016 report, they discussed the impact of various approaches in practical field trials among poor and low-income groups in the US and Mexico—two very different countries. (See footnote 8 for the outcome in Mexico.)

In the US, individuals seeking payday-type loans were divided into two groups. The control group was sent the paperwork and a proposition that a 'normal' payday loan-type company would issue. This consisted of an envelope with an explanation of the borrower's cash amounts to pay back and the due dates. Like this:

a. The standard envelope
A payday borrower receives his cash in an envelope. The standard envelope shows only a calendar and the due date of the loan.

The second group was offered the same proposition, but with a different explanation. The envelope they received showed how the cost in dollars grows very fast when a loan is outstanding for three months. Moreover, it compared the cost of the payday loan to the fees for

---

[13] Often the very poorest people adopt inappropriate credit methods with extraordinary high interest largely because they are unable to secure any other form of finance —from the bank, from relatives, or from a credit union. This leads people to borrow money, perhaps for basics to buy food or to pay rent, in a context where they have no choice. And, of course, they may not feel able to consider the longer-term consequences.

borrowing a similar amount on a credit card. (Clearly a credit card is a *bad* way to borrow, but it is still better than the payday lender.)

b. The envelope comparing the costs of the payday loan and credit card borrowing
In a field experiment, randomly chosen borrowers received envelopes that showed how the dollar fees accumulate when a payday loan is outstanding for three months, compared to the fees to borrow the same amount with a credit card.

How much it will cost in fees or interest if you borrow $300			
PAYDAY LENDER (assuming two-wee fee is $15 per $100 loan) If you repay in:		**CREDIT CARD** (assuming a 20% APR) If you repay in:	
2 weeks	$45	2 weeks	$2.50
1 month	$90	1 month	$5
2 months	$180	2 months	$10
3 months	$270	3 months	$15

The idea was that the prospective borrowers could anchor their perception of the relative cost of the two options through the comparison, and hopefully see the disadvantages of the payday lender.

The good news is the results confirmed that the borrowers *were* influenced in a positive way. What is also interesting is that this counteracted the way the payday loan companies themselves were priming the 'small dollar' cost of the transaction in a quite misleading way, for example: 'Only $15 to pay for a two-week loan of $100!' Complementary research confirmed that individuals under financial pressure were often misled by these apparently low costs, and found it difficult to work out the real cost over time, or recognise the enormously high interest rate.

The specific outcome of this simple 'back of an envelope' initiative, according to the World Bank, was that 'Compared to the control group, individuals who received the envelope with the "dollar anchor" were 11 percent less likely to borrow from the payday lenders in the four months that followed the intervention.'[14]

---

[14] A parallel experiment was conducted with low-income residents in Mexico City. In this case participants were invited to a classroom-style setting to choose the best, cheapest, loan from a set of five options typical of actual credit options offered by local

This experiment also indicates that providing reference points makes decision making easier, because our brain evaluates options in relative rather than absolute terms. We intuitively, and often subconsciously, ask 'Compared to what?'

Using Priming and Anchoring in Fundraising

The priming and anchoring technique is clearly important. In a charity fundraising department it can make a significant difference in a range of ways by:

- Engaging potential supporters in feeling they are choosing the way[15] they engage with your cause—even if that choice is artificial. This also gives supporters a feeling of being in control, a strong behavioural motivator.
- Clearly signalling a stretch gift or level of engagement already given by others creates an aspirational anchor—making that goal, or total sum—seem worth considering or even possible.

Here is a specific example of anchoring at work in fundraising. At a North American museum, three separate but similar clusters of environmentally concerned visitors were asked to make a donation to address the ecological damage caused by oil tankers in the Pacific. The visitors were asked for help as they entered the museum. Each cluster was exposed to one of three ways to help:

---

banks. The task was to identify the cheapest way to take out a one-year, $800 loan. Attendees were offered rewards to get the 'right' answer, ensuring there was motivation. The researchers reported a significant difference in outcomes. 'When using the banks' descriptions of their products, only 39 percent of the people could identify the cheapest credit product. When using the more straightforward summary sheet, [produced by the researchers] 68 percent could identify the cheapest credit.'

[15] Note, though, the importance of limiting choice as a way of encouraging engagement; too much choice seems to confuse us. See **Chapter 9**.

- *Version 1* 'Would you be willing to donate to save 50,000 offshore Pacific Coast seabirds from small offshore oil spills?' *[No specific gift requested]*
- *Version 2* 'Would you be willing to pay $5 to save 50,000 offshore Pacific Coast seabirds from small offshore oil spills?'
- *Version 3* 'Would you be willing to pay $400 to save 50,000 offshore Pacific Coast seabirds from small offshore oil spills?'

The average donation offered by those asked *Version 1* of the question, where no specific amount was specified, was $64. For those given a relatively low anchor of $5 the result was a relatively low average of $20. Finally, participants given the high anchor of $400 came up with an impressive average donation of $143. You can see the impact of the anchor, high and low, at work. You can also see how donors respond to the scale of the challenge indicated by 50,000 birds when asked to judge their own gift level. (Version 1).

These results confirm an important underlying implication—there's no generally accepted answer to the question of how much anyone should give in a specific circumstance. Moreover, there's no realistic answer to how much to give when a prospect recognises that there is clearly a huge problem, and one that needs investment way beyond the ability of an ordinary donor. As Kahneman reflects: '[in such circumstances] it is not surprising that people who are asked difficult questions clutch at straws, and the anchor is a plausible straw.'

It is also worth noting that people do not opt for the exact amount of the anchor. The anchor *influences* their choice but doesn't dictate it. It is hard to tell in advance what the exact effect of the anchoring will be. That's why it is important to test different approaches against different outcomes.[16]

---

[16] You might be interested to note the effect of what is called a 'mid-term anchor' For more on this see **Chapter 2**. A mid-term anchor occurs when donors can see the pattern of previous gifts, and then an individual, or the agency raising funds, makes a contribution that is much higher than all previous gifts in a range to try and anchor a number of higher subsequent gifts. The intention is when supporters see the number stimulus they respond with an upgrade. But if the stimulus is too high they can perceive it completely 'out of their league' and it has no effect.

Priming and Anchoring a New Category

Priming and anchoring don't just apply to something as simple as price or gift amount. You can also anchor a *category*. When Steve Jobs introduced the first iPad he was concerned to reframe potential customers' attitudes to what it *was* as well as how much it should *cost*.

He began his introductory presentation at that landmark Apple conference in 2010 by showing off the iPad and its various features. He then rhetorically asked, 'What should we price it at?' (There had been much discussion on this question before the launch, the product itself had been well trailed.)

He went on to say, 'If you listen to the pundits, it's hard to see how we could price it under $1,000.' (A figure more closely associated with laptop-style devices.)

At this point the figure $999 came up on a gigantic screen behind him. He paused and then in a wonderful piece of theatre and psychology he said, 'I am thrilled to announce to you that the iPad pricing starts not at $999 but at .... just $499.' The spoken impact was reinforced by a visual effect. Behind him on the giant screen, the $999 image was crushed by the figure $499 dropping down on top of it.

The effect was to make $499—still a lot of money—appear a great deal less.

He was doing something very clever by creating a perception of what the iPad was and was not. His point was it should be compared to a laptop *in price terms*. By this comparison at $499 it looked like a bargain.

Make it Physical—Priming and Anchoring Through The Senses

Look at the image on the next page. Which of these price tags will drive the greater sales: the one on the left or the one on the right? (Note that they both offer exactly the same deal in the same way. All that has been changed is the font size and sequence of the relative offers.)

According to Phil Barden, in his book *Decoded*, the one on the right has been shown to deliver higher sales—in one case 28% more —than the one on the left. This says something significant about anchoring through our senses: the *semiotics* of anchoring are crucial too. What seems to be important here is the relative font size of the two numbers. The label on the right makes more impact on us because it crosses out the bigger number. And, the smaller font suggests a smaller price. The anchoring here is *visual*. Other senses can be used. See our earlier example where the weight of the cutlery used impacted on perceptions of quality of the food; different senses can reinforce a key impression.

A good friend and colleague, Christoph Müller-Gattol, Director of DIRECTmind Social Marketing Agency in Austria, explored the same idea using an envelope. He sent a fundraising direct mail (DM) appeal to potential supporters of a medical research charity with a picture of a magnifying glass on a regular-sized envelope, asking essentially 'how long will they have to wait for a cure?' He then sent a similar group of potential supporters exactly the same DM appeal with the same envelope image. But this time he used a much longer envelope, which meant the message, 'How long will they have to wait for a cure?' had a physical anchor in the envelope size. The income from the second version of the appeal was 40% higher.

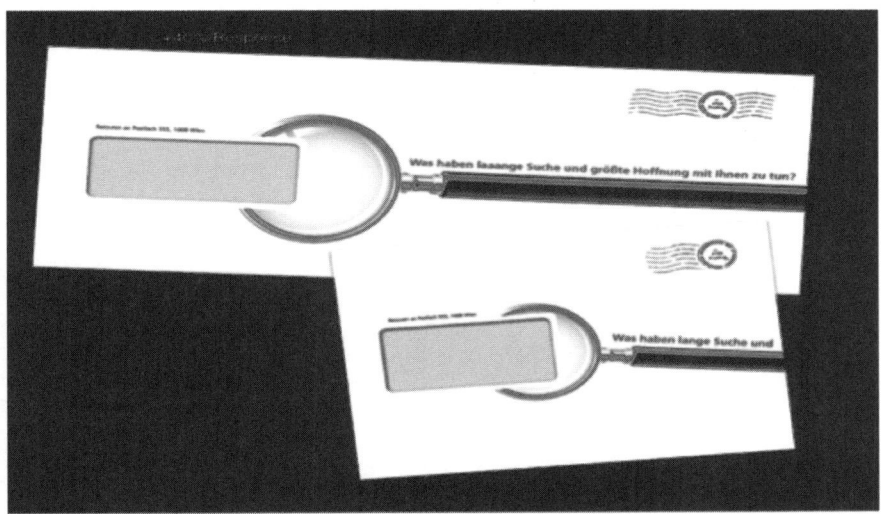

Priming With Words

There are many other examples of priming outside the world of numbers. We've already mentioned the impact of the Thaler experiment on groups asked to read different stories with frequent references to words connected with age and degrees of tiredness. Here's a fuller explanation:

One group had more words in their story to do with youth and energy, the other had more words to do with age and strain. Halfway through the exercise, participants were sent off on a supposed errand, which involved walking some distance. The individuals who had been exposed to the tiredness and age words took longer to complete the trip than the others primed with youth and energy words. They had been primed to an attitude of tiredness. And that attitude had a measurable physical impact.

In a social change setting this choice of language could be important—such as when encouraging healthy life choices, explaining the profile of a campaign, or seeking specific action.

Size is Important

Even the smallest word can make a massive difference. Dr. Robert Cialdini, Psychology Professor at Arizona State University, studied the donation mechanic for the American Cancer Society, one of the world's largest Not for Profits (NfP). His research contrasted the phrases used by door to door solicitors.

Word Formula 1: One group of prospective donors were asked:
'Would you be willing to help by giving a donation?'

Word Formula 2: A second group were asked:
'Would you be willing to help by giving a donation? Every penny will help.'

The impact was significant. 28% of prospects approached using Formula 1 gave, but those approached using Formula 2 were almost twice as likely to donate

There were two further interesting insights from this study: the amount donors gave didn't change with the addition of the 'every penny' qualifier. And follow up interviews suggested making people aware that even a penny could help encouraged those who might not otherwise have given.

In a complementary piece of consumer-based research Carnegie Mellon University researchers changed the description of an overnight shipping charge on a free DVD trial offer from 'a $5 fee' to 'a small $5 fee.' Simply adding the word 'small' increased conversion by 20%.

Priming with Smells

In another great example mentioned by the behavioural architects, a study by Dutch psychologists investigated the impact the smell of cleaning fluid might have on how clean and neat we are. In the experiment students were asked to complete a questionnaire while sitting in a room. In the same room for some of the subjects was a bucket of water scented with lemon cleaning fluid. A control group completed the questionnaire without exposure to the scented water. Once both groups had completed the questionnaire they were asked to go to another room. This one had no lemon scent.

Both groups were then given an exceptionally crumbly biscuit to eat and were videotaped eating it. In comparison to the control group, the group exposed to the lemon scented cleaner tidied up the crumbs more thoroughly. Clearly, a smell associated with cleanliness had primed them to behave in a clean and tidy way.[17]

Priming Ethics

In his book *The Life You Can Save*,[18] Peter Singer explores the issue of philosophical anchoring. He explains that he teaches a practical ethics course in which he asks his students to think of the following hypothetical scenario:

'On your way to work, you pass a small pond. On hot days, children sometimes play in the pond, which is only knee-deep. The weather is cool today, though, and the hour is early, so you are surprised to see a child splashing about in the pond. As you get closer, you see that it is a very young child, just a toddler, who is flailing about, unable to stay upright or walk out of the pond. You look for the parents or babysitter, but there is no one else around. The child is unable to keep his head above the water for more than a few seconds at a time. If you don't wade in and pull him out, he seems

---

[17] In a follow up study researchers tested the impact of three different smells in the same way: an orange smell (pleasant, but with no common association to cleanliness); a grass smell (pleasant too, but with no association to cleanliness); and a sulphur odour (unpleasant, and definitely not related to cleanliness). The participants exposed to the sulphur smell did much less cleaning than those exposed to the more pleasant smells.

[18] Singer, Peter. *The Life You Can Save: Acting Now to End World Poverty*. Picador, Great Britain, 2009.

likely to drown. Wading in is easy and safe, but you will ruin the shoes you bought only a few days ago, and get your suit wet and muddy. By the time you hand the child over to someone responsible for him, and change your clothes, you'll be late for work. What should you do?'

Singers reports that students respond almost 100% of them say they would save the child. When he reminds them that their shoes will be ruined, they brush that aside. He suggests that most readers will respond in the same way. He moves on from this hypothetical scenario to another that may hit closer to home. He points out that if readers are drinking a bottle of water or a soda while reading his book when safe tap water is available, they are spending money on things they don't need. And they could use that money to save children's lives. In his view that's an ethical choice. And his purpose is to anchor every occasion readers drink a soda or bottled water.

▰▸▰▸▰▸▰▸▰▸▰▸▰▸▰▸▰▸▰▸

What are the Lessons From Priming and Anchoring?

- In traditional economics, the belief is it is the facts that matter. People will make rational judgements if given quantifiable data. In behavioural economics, *how* the facts are presented and sequenced matters a great deal and significantly impacts on the choices that people make. Priming and anchoring appropriately by audience significantly impacts on the choices they make.
- Priming is an important tool for social change practitioners. It teaches us that our System 1 brain can be guided towards making a choice without being aware it is. The first piece of information given, or choice made, can make a difference to subsequent decisions. Our brain can *believe* it is making a sensible and logical System 2 choice when it is not. These two simple implications are important for anyone trying to influence behaviour.

- Number anchoring—is especially useful for those working for charities in fundraising and development. Asking for a gift and positioning that gift alongside another higher stimulus—someone else's gift, the 'normal' gift, or even an associated number—can make a significant difference in the size of the outcome level of support.
- Priming can be used outside the world of numbers, with which it is most often associated. The words, images, sounds, textures and even smells we use can make a huge difference in how people perceive a situation, or the way in which they respond to a request. When you share a message consider the way in which different senses can be used to impact the decision or choice you want people to make.

Chapter 2

Make Progress, but Choose Your Time!

Summary

Goals are important to people. Our behaviour orientates us towards them. And when individuals feel they have made progress towards a goal, they become more committed to it. They feel good about what's been done so far and the closer they get to the goal, the harder they work to achieve the desired result.

We especially like to see progress at particular stages in a process. Emphasising progress at these times will encourage further commitment. (At its simplest, a progress bar for a software download showing only 10% left can encourage people to wait for the download to complete—even when they have no idea how long the 10% will actually take.) When we're trying to encourage a particular behaviour we should pay attention to this progress preference.

In the behavioural economics framework this is called the *endowed progress* heuristic.

Progress is hard at the start. You need to reduce what's called friction, barriers to starting, at the beginning of any process. Barriers might include complicated forms to fill in, elaborate registration processes, too much text to read, or even just a slow loading web-page. An additional barrier occurs when progress is not recognised when it has actually taken place. This can cause people to lose motivation. If someone *feels* they are making little or no progress, even if they objectively are, they are more likely to give up. This has important implications for educationalists and health professionals.

Two critical progress points are: a) at the beginning of a project, indicating success in overcoming inertia, and b) towards the end of a project, promising completion. Both progress points reflect qualitative change and can deliver a strong emotional impact. The first signals a change from nothing to something, the second a move from something to everything. All other change in between is seen as quantitative, or incremental.

Progress Not Results

The *endowed progress* heuristic is often illustrated by a compelling case study which demonstrates the power of the *idea* of progress rather than *objective* progress. This case study is based on an experiment originally conducted by two behavioural scientists, Nunes and Dreze, in a carwash in a US city. The basic experiment has been repeated a number of times since, in different locations and in different settings.

Two rival carwash companies offer a similar service in terms of price and quality, but a different loyalty scheme.

- **Company A** gives you a loyalty card which allows a free car wash after 8 visits. The loyalty stamps on the card begin at 1 and go up to 8. You get a stamp for each visit.
- **Company B** gives a loyalty card which also allows you a free car wash after 8 visits, but the presentation is different. On Company B's card there's a 10-visit cluster. But you start with two free 'starter' contributions.

Your logical System 2 tells you in both cases you need eight stamps from paid-for visits to receive the free car wash. The only difference is that the card on the right gives a 'start' of two free stamps. Yet the card on the right drives very different customer behaviour.

- Those customers who began with two 'free' stamps reclaimed the free car wash more quickly
- *And* the time between their visits got shorter the closer they got achieving the 10
- *Plus* their redemption rate was 34% against those who started from scratch, which was only 19%
- The *uplift in sales* for Company B was 79%

We have repeated this experiment in an independent local UK cafe. We adjusted the offer to encourage coffee-drinkers to revisit the same cafe more regularly. While the increase in take-up was a more modest 21%, the increase in visits was still noticeable.

The simple technique of offering customers a 'head start' seemed to drive three positive pieces of behaviour from a marketing point of view. There are two linked factors at play here: *endowment* and *progress*.

Endowment: When we own something—like the two stamps in the carwash card—we value it highly and do not like to lose it. (This also links closely to the idea of *loss aversion*. See **Chapter 5**.)

Progress: The closer we are to completing a goal, the more effort and money we are willing to put in to complete it. This is related to the *sunk cost effect* where, having committed so much money and effort, we feel it would be a pity not to bring it to completion. If we did not carry on, we would feel the investment to date was wasted.

The car wash study provides practical evidence for the power of the endowed progress heuristic. Making progress towards a goal, even if it is clearly a construct, encourages people to work towards that goal. It's interesting to note some follow up research on this specific type of experiment from the company Posterboy Printing.[1]

There are four additional lessons here:

- When you hand out a new loyalty card for maximum impact the retailer should stamp it there and then in front of the customer or supporter. This gives that customer a real time, visceral experience of progress. So in the car-wash example you would begin with the card needing 10 stamps. But you mark the two free ones at the point of purchase. This feels much more personal as well as immediate.
- Offer a reason for the bonus. For example 'because you are a new customer', 'because it's St. Patrick's Day'. The 'reason' seems to make the offer more attractive. Interestingly slightly spurious reasons seem to be regarded more positively by customers than the obvious real one—to promote customer loyalty. And customers seem to recognise this is a one-off rather than *expecting* a bonus the next time.
- Avoid valuing any reward in cash terms. Make the collection mechanic in points, coffees, car washes, etc. The direct cash calculation can make the offer seem less significant, or even a bad deal. (Customers do the calculation about your direct item cost versus competitors.)
- Make sure that the number of points or purchases to be collected before fulfillment is small—say 6–8 additional purchase commitments. Even when the same *percentage* is available, say 5 free stamps on a 15-stamp card, or 2 on a 6-stamp card, there is much greater take-up on the lower number. People don't want to defer the gratification too long.

As a charity you could use these lessons to encourage people to take part in a behaviour change programme—for example, losing weight

---

[1] For a longer discussion on this see: www.posterboyprinting.com.au/content/loyalty-cards-trick/

or reducing alcohol or drug use. Or you might use it in fundraising to reward special supporters. Why not have rewards cards for these people?

The progress principle also explains why people also like the Amazon and Dell websites, which show them the progress of a purchase from the warehouse to their home. And this progress mechanic *is* used by charities. For example, Oxfam UK have a great interactive graphic on their website showing how goods for humanitarian relief are being moved from a central store to the setting where they are needed—a village or refugee camp. You can see it here at http://www.oxfam.org.uk/what-we-do/help-oxfam-deliver.

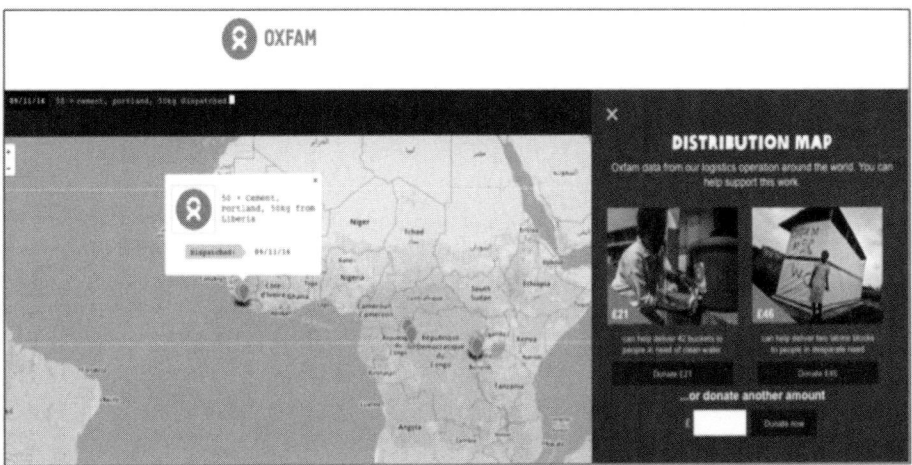

Another interesting example of the use of the *idea* of progress comes from Doctors Without Borders in the US. They achieved a 16% hike in response rate by changing their message to regular donors from 'we need your gift to respond to this crisis' to 'thanks to your regular gift our team has already left for the crisis zone.'

Endowed Progress in Fundraising

The carwash case study focuses on progress at the *start* of a process but there is evidence of a similar impact blip at the end.

Some of this evidence comes from a study linked to the micro-finance platform Kiva.org. Kiva has been enormously successful, raising over $4 billion in project funds in 10 years. This US-based agency offers 'social investors' the chance to support micro-entrepreneurs in developing nations. The micro-entrepreneurs, normally helped by a development agency, put up a project idea—to set up a bakery in Malawi, to run a hairdressing salon in Peru, to build a small fish farm in Vietnam, etc.—on the Kiva website. The entrepreneurs set a start up target to raise, usually between US$350–$750 and then the investors, generally individuals in a developed nation, can contribute a percentage of that initial cost.

The research team studying how people invested in Kiva measured the rate of investment at various stages of an individual project's funding journey. What they found was that, as a specific entrepreneur's project got closer to its target, the *rate* at which investors contributed increased. Follow up research suggested that the motivation for these later social investors was that they wanted to be part of the clearly-likely-to-happen-success—to be part of the *result*.

We have seen a similar result in a major global campaign we have advised on for the Global Polio Eradication Initiative. Their core proposition is illustrated in the two maps below. In the one on the left you can see in how many countries polio existed in 1988. Compare that to 2014 on the right. (And since then Nigeria has been declared virus free, leaving only two countries in the world where the polio virus is in the wild.) In various forms this graphic has made a transformational difference to the fundraising campaign. Who would not want to 'Help eliminate polio from the Earth' when success is this close? Notice, too, the power of the *visual* representation.

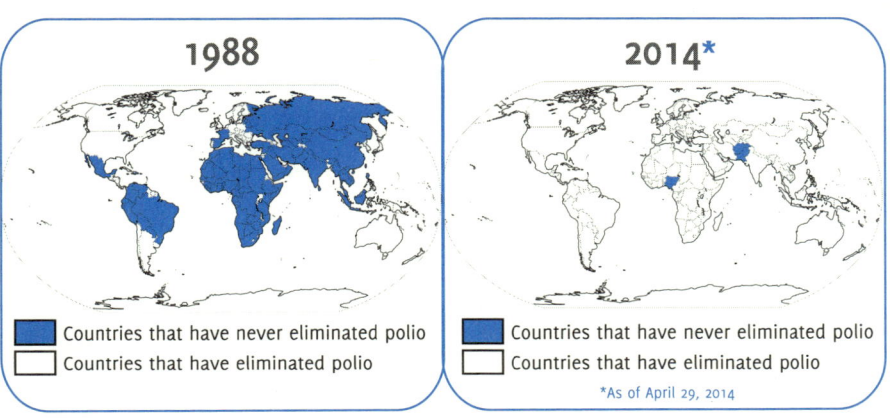

This graphic is designed to appeal to donors who are High-Net-Worth Individual (HNWI). In fact, the financial 'heavy lifting' to eliminate the disease has already mostly been undertaken by governments over the last three decades. These governments have a much more System 2 approach to social investment. But individuals, especially HNWI, are keen to 'share the podium' now that the goal is close. (By the way, when the World Polio Eradication Initiative succeeds, polio will be only the second disease to be declared eliminated globally since smallpox in 1979.)

Kiva adds to the more modest motivating narrative it shares on its website by actively promoting details about projects and loans which are close to meeting their target. For example, Josefina Del Carmen has already raised 75% of the money she needs to buy what she needs to set up her farm:

Josefina Del Carmen

El Salvador | Agriculture | Agriculture

A loan of $300 helps Josefina Del Carmen to buy seeds, fertilisers, herbicides and pay the workers to cultivate corn, beans and sorghum.
Read their story >

Funding via Fundacion Campo

75% raised

———————

$300.00

Lend $25

People's keenness to be part of the result, or to complete the process is also proactively used by JustGiving (www.justgiving.com) the UK peer-to-peer charitable giving site. They take the 'progress' illustration even further by:

- Showing potential donors who visit the site the *total cash* raised to date.
- Demonstrating how this relates to the *desired goal* in percentage terms.
- Reinforcing this data as a form of *graph*, which has a particular impact.

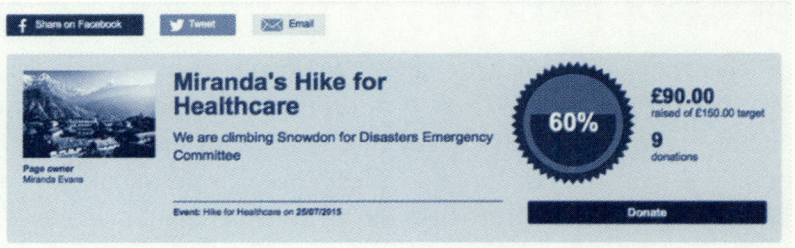

This visual illustration of progress means donors can see themselves in a powerful position—able to tip the balance towards helping to make the target achievable, and edging closer to the 100%.

Through JustGiving, donors can also influence others to join in by posting to social media their satisfaction at having brought the result even closer. Importantly, the update takes place in real time—the progress graph goes up as you hit the 'donate' button. Social media, especially in real time, can act as a strong communicator of progress and a driver of this peer-to-peer effect. (This links strongly to the *normalising* heuristic discussed in **Chapter 10.**) And real time updating gives us a strong sense of 'agency'—the ability to take action and see we are making an impact.

By combining progress with the *anchoring* heuristic discussed in **Chapter 1,** you can track the progress effect in a very direct way on websites where supporters are making contributions and can see the contributions of others. Here again the impact is not uniform, it is strong at the beginning and the end of a process. But there is an interesting, and perhaps unexpected, impact in the middle. The graphs below show how different levels of gift made in the middle of a fundraising campaign can strongly influence subsequent gifts. If someone makes a rather larger gift in the middle of a sequence, there is a lift in subsequent gifts. Conversely, if a low gift is made then it reduces the subsequent level. This is a kind of moving anchor.

Visible effect of previous donations on Justgiving / Virgin Money Giving website

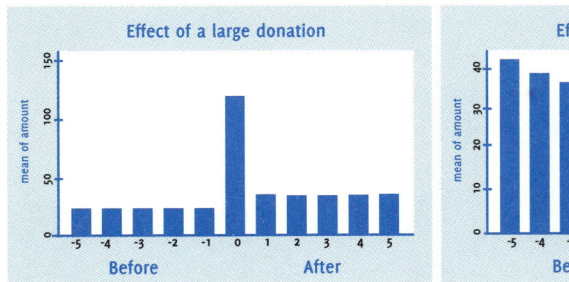
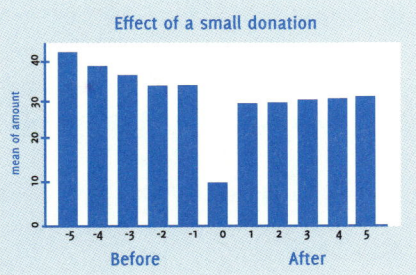

We tested this phenomenon while raising money for Syrian refugees in Tunbridge Wells, a small, quite conservative town in the UK. Using the JustGiving platform over a six-week period we made donations in varying amounts under different identities to an online campaign we set up. Higher contributions we made drove up donations made by later supporters. We were looking for an average of £35 per gift. If we had a run of £20 donations, by making a small series of £33–40 donations ourselves, we could 'push' the average back up.

However, when we made a gift significantly out of the norm e.g. £250 when the gifts had been coming in at around the £40 mark ... it had no effect. Our hypothesis is that would-be supporters then see the high contribution as being out of their frame of reference. This links to the idea that behaviour needs to be normative, see **Chapters 6 and 10**. It's important to judge accurately the *potential* for your audience to contribute and to encourage progress from there. A challenge for supporters and donors is that they don't necessarily know what the right amount to donate is. So you have to provide guidance on that and keep reinforcing it.

The Power of a Graph

Graphs and other forms of visual information are enormously powerful as a convincer whether you are putting together a business case for senior managers, designing a website for shoppers or donors, or assembling a presentation to convince sceptical colleagues at a meeting. We have already seen how the graphic representation of progress on peer-to-peer sites has an impact, but it goes further than this.

A recent experiment[2] shared at a medical conference showed two variations of an advert. In both cases the advert used copy which suggested a specific medicine was effective in treating a particular illness.

- In advert **Version 1**, the drug was promoted using clear copy, including data supporting the claim the drug was effective.
- For advert **Version 2**, the experimenters used a chart instead that showed exactly the same data as the copy-only version.

Despite the clear, strong copy in version 1 only just over two thirds of those who read the advert believed, in follow up research, that the medicine was as effective as claimed. But for those who saw the data as a *graph* the percentage of readers who *believed* the drug to be effective increased. The difference?—from 67.7% in the text-only version, to an astonishing 96.6% with the chart. There is great power in a visual representation of data, especially when it shows progress.

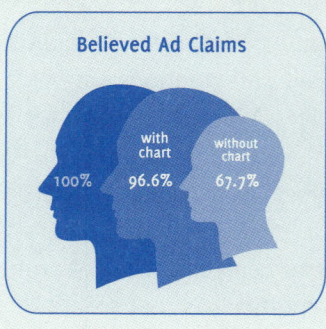

Believed Ad Claims

100% with chart 96.6% without chart 67.7%

[2] Researchers from Cornell University published this in the journal *Public Understanding of Science*. In one experiment, 61 participants were presented with written information about a new medication explaining how it had been found in trials to reduce colds by 40 percentage points, from 87% to 47%. This result was compared to a control drug, and it was made clear that FDA approval was pending. Half the participants were also shown a simple bar graph, which visually depicted this 40% difference in effectiveness. Of those who saw the graph, 97% believed the drug was effective, compared to 68% of those who had only read the text.

Focus on the Number

In his book *Misbehaving*, Richard Thaler cites an example he thought intriguing in terms of perception of progress. At the end of an academic term, he shared his class's average score in essay work: 72%. Most of the students were upset, and felt it was a low score.

At the end of the next term, rather than give an average percentage, Thaler gave his class the raw average score of 96/137. (137 was the total number of marks available.) The students were much more satisfied with this description of their results, even though such a score actually equates to a *lower* result of 70%. Thaler suggests the students were better pleased because 96 *feels* high—possibly they were subconsciously comparing it to 100, which is close. (In the previous case 72 seems far away from 100. It seems that we are more familiar with the base of 100, relating it to percentages, than with other systems or raw numbers.)

The technique of focusing on numbers and reinforcing them in different ways is useful when presenting ideas to supporters or even to sceptical audiences. Further evidence for its effectiveness can be found in a piece of research conducted by two researchers, Karlan and List. This builds on the JustGiving example earlier.

The researchers studied a campaign at the University of Central Florida. There, with the institution's agreement, they were allowed to alter the way a specific fundraising campaign was presented online. The researchers were keen to track the impact of various changes in showing progress. Specifically, they wanted to establish the impact on supporters' gift levels by how the percentage of the target raised was displayed at various points.

Their results confirm the importance of the progress heuristic, and Thaler's observation on the power of percentages:

- Artificially displaying the percentage already raised of the goal for a specific project from 10% to 67% significantly improved response rates.

- Almost 1 in 10 prospects contributed at the higher level when solicited. But under 1 in 20 of those approached contributed at the 10% point.

The impact goes further than this. Showing progress didn't just bring in more prospects, it also increased the *size* of donations:

- On seeing the campaign was at 10% of goal, the average gift was US$15.
- At 33% of goal, the average gift went up to US$26.[3]
- And at 67% of goal, the average gift went up to US$40.

In summary, donors gave larger—more than US$20—gifts more frequently, and fewer small donations when they believed a significant percentage of the target had been achieved. This was entirely unconnected to the proposition.

So we know this progress technique works. But why is posting the percentage of the goal achieved effective in reaching a result? Karlan and List came up with a number of possible explanations based on behavioural science:

1. The simplest explanation is that donating to a campaign close to its target is simply more appealing. (Clearly the podium effect seen on the Polio Campaign.) A supporter seeing a target close to the last $100 can appreciate how their $10 is directly driving concrete progress, or helping achieve completion.
2. Another was that growth was used by supporters as an indicator that the cause in question was worthy or deserving. Contributing then became an aspect of the 'social norm' we know from **Chapter 6**.[4] We seem to be reassured: we won't be challenged for our behaviour, since others are doing the same.

---

[3] Note though that this result—a growth in the middle range—is not duplicated elsewhere.

[4] Interestingly, JustGiving further prompts the social norm effect by including details of the most generous donor to date in their breakdown of individual sponsorship progress. This can be a compelling message.

3. Finally, we have a preference for payoffs today rather than future gains—the *present bias* we explore below. Decision scientists call this *time inconsistency*—knowing a gift today helps meet the target soon is more motivating than a distant ambition.

What this suggests is, if you plan to raise money for a cause, then launch your campaign while emphasising:

- How much has already been raised.
- How close you are to the desired target.
- That the campaign will close soon.

The same principle could also apply to, for example, a membership drive in a campaign or a petition that needs a million signatures.

If you're encouraging peer-to-peer fundraisers make sure they know about the power of endowed progress. Suggest to them that they first contact their warmest, closest friends—the ones they know will definitely donate—and ask them to donate early in the campaign (hopefully a good number to set a nice anchor) to their page. Only after securing a number of donations at the right value should they go out to their wider networks.

Choose Your Timing

This general principle can be demonstrated more precisely. In a further study based on Kiva.org, researchers measured the precise giving rate at various stages of a project's funding. They confirmed the previous finding that as the project got closer to its goal the contribution rate increased. (But they also found that the initial rate of contribution was significantly lower. See the graph below.[5])

---

[5] Source Nuns, Joseph C. and Xavier Druze, 2006, 'The Endowed Progress Effect: How Artificial Advancement Increases Effort'. *Journal of Consumer Research.* 32 (March), 504-512. Cryder, Cynthia E., George Loewenstein, and Howard Seltman

And finally, they found a significant drop-off in donations in the middle.

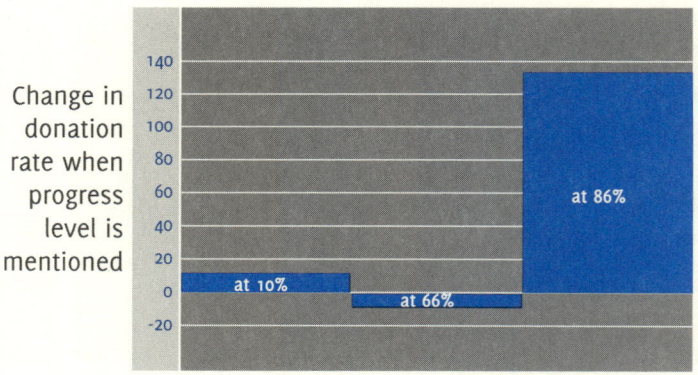

To our suggested tactics above, then, we can add a fourth:

- Don't show the campaign as being in the middle.

This may mean that you have to split any campaign into different chunks rather than lay out the whole effort. Phase 1 becomes the first 20% of your overall goal. You're more likely to succeed faster if you can show you are 75% of the way through the that phase, rather than at 15% of the overall goal.

Using Imagery to Suggest Progress

There are many different kinds of visual information that can drive engagement besides graphs. The advert below is by the charity Cancer Research UK. It shows the endowed progress effect using the idea of bottles of chemicals or drugs as a metaphor for successful progress. What is more, the bottles themselves have a liquid that is coded for the Cancer Research brand Pantone® colour. (There are several semiotic elements going on in this image.)

(2013), 'Goal Gradient in Helping Behavior,' *Journal of Experimental Social Psychology*, 49 (6), 1078-1083.

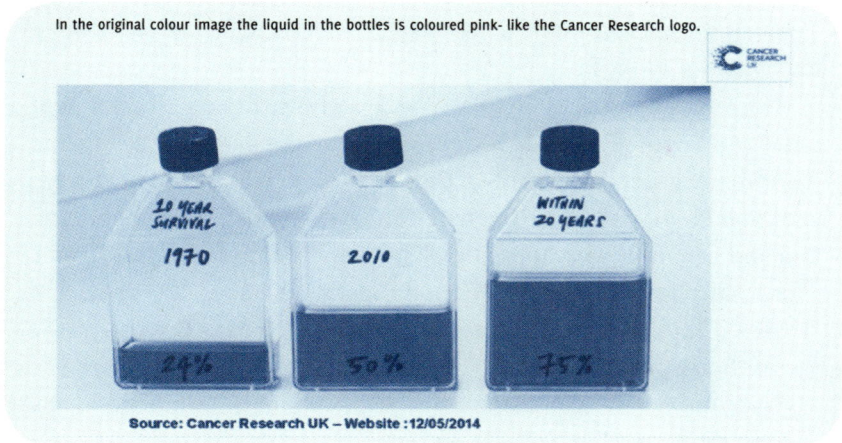

In the original colour image the liquid in the bottles is coloured pink- like the Cancer Research logo.

Source: Cancer Research UK – Website :12/05/2014

Winners and Losers in Time

Progress is also defined by our *perception* of time. Imagine that you're watching a vital world cup football game between **Team A** and **Team B**. After extra time both teams are level, so there is going to be the dreaded penalty shoot-out. Both sides choose their five players to each take their single penalty shot. As is normal, the teams take turns to shoot. The one with the most goals at the end of the five attempts wins.

Here is how the scoring unfolds.

Player	Team A	Team B
Player 1	Scores	Scores
Player 2	Scores	Misses
Player 3	Misses	Scores
Player 4	Scores	Scores
Player 5	Misses	Scores
Goals	3	4

Team B are the winners. This is all pretty straightforward from a logical point of view.

Now imagine you are in the crowd watching the sequence of penalties. As **Team A's** player 5 steps up to the penalty spot each team has already missed one shot so the score is even at 3-3. He takes his shot and balloons it over the bar. **Team A** supporters are heartbroken and can only now hope the player from **Team B** does the same. The final player for **Team B** coolly steps up, takes the shot, and strokes it into the left-hand corner of the net. **Team B** wins, to the joy of their supporters.

Now answer these questions quickly, without thinking too much. In your opinion, who, would you say:

- Is the *most responsible* for **Team B's** success? The first penalty taker or its last one?
- Is the *most responsible* for **Team A's** loss? The third penalty taker or the last one?

Most people pick the last penalty taker as the hero in **Team B** because his goal ensured the victory. People tend to give more credit to the last player's goal even though, as a matter of pure logic, the goal scored by the first penalty-taker *had an identical impact on the outcome*. In other words, people tend to favour the later event in the time sequence. And conversely, the last miss may stain the reputation of player 5 on **Team A** forever. (Anyone who is a supporter of England's national football squad knows this feeling.)

It is this insight that led the researchers to set up the Kiva study referred to earlier. They wanted to check out a hypothesis—that *potential* donors would imagine receiving more 'social credit' for donations made to campaigns that were close to reaching their targets. This effect works in the same way that the last goal scorer gets more credit for the result than the first goal scorer did in our example. This effect, they continued to theorise, would lead more people to give as a campaign progressed and drew closer to its overall fundraising goal. Their research, reinforced through interviews with donors and from data about gift-timings, suggests they were right. This phenomenon might also be related to the *need for completion effect* discussed in **Chapter 7**.

Supporter Onboarding

Onboarding is the technical term for bringing a staff member into your organisation and up to speed with its processes and approaches. But it can also be used to describe how a customer or charity supporter registers interest in your work and moves though a number of stages to full engagement. It is a process that needs to progress as fast as possible and reduce what we've earlier called friction. If there is too much friction, the process takes too long, or it's too complex, or you need to look up things that are not easily available online, potential supporters can very easily time-out and not complete the process. They may even become disenchanted with your bureaucracy.

Onboarding often starts with some kind of registration.

- For a *business*, this might involve a customer opening an account, having decided to make a purchase. They can have no idea how long this process takes, since many different forms of registration exist. And they may be suspicious if the company asks for more than address and credit card details. Sometimes you are taken off the main site to go through a third party agency that processes your payment.
- For a *charity*, it could include a supporter trying to register their commitment to a campaign. The supporter might want simply to register an opinion. But you want to find out about them, in the hope you can convert them to a donor further down the line. Like the business customer, the supporter may also be anxious since they don't know why you're asking if they want to be contacted by phone, text, etc.

Many people, whether commercial customers or would-be charity supporters, give up on even these first processes without completing the task. Common reasons include, not being clear how long it will take, wondering why a certain bit of information is needed, or even what the payoffs are for them to share this level of information. There are a number of ways to reduce the friction here and make the core process more effective:

- Reducing the number of fields in your online registration process. Beate Sorum, Norwegian charity web consultant, has some interesting examples of how simplifying helps in onboarding. In one case, she shows that reducing the number of fields a donor had to fill in as part of registration from 11 to 4 led to completed donations increasing 140%.
- Using a variation of the progress chart. Displaying a progress bar —similar to those used when downloading software—throughout onboarding can be a great motivator to completion. For example, look at how LinkedIn encourages onboarding within their site. People like to feel they have reached 100%.[6]

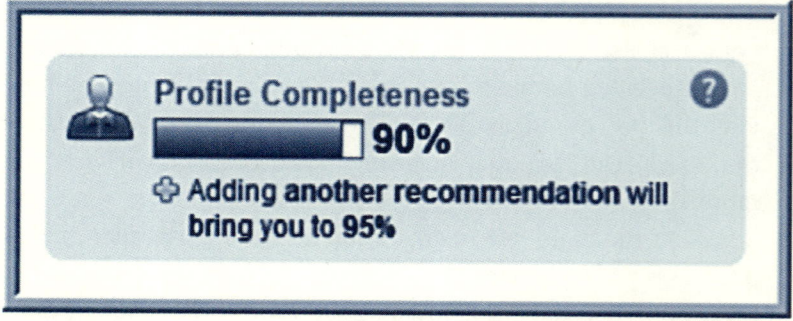

Once you have passed someone through the initial stages of onboarding you need to think about how to keep supporters engaged.

---

[6] At a conference session run by LinkedIn's Marketing Director it was made clear that they rarely if ever let you get to 100% on your profile completeness, because they want to keep you coming back. They will keep adding new features for you to adopt, or suggest that you add more abilities, or another of something you already have, or that you endorse a friend or colleague.

The travel site, TripAdvisor, tells users how respected and admired their reviews are. And it rewards them with badges and levels to show their progress as a respected commentator. And users do all this for free—just for the chance to share their opinion, and in exchange for a series of meaningless accolades. Here is Bernard's score as a level 11 restaurant reviewer on TripAdvisor. He has done a lot of work providing reviews to secure that meaningless 'expert level badge.' He's even collecting 'points' that have no seeming purpose. But it all *feels* like progress.

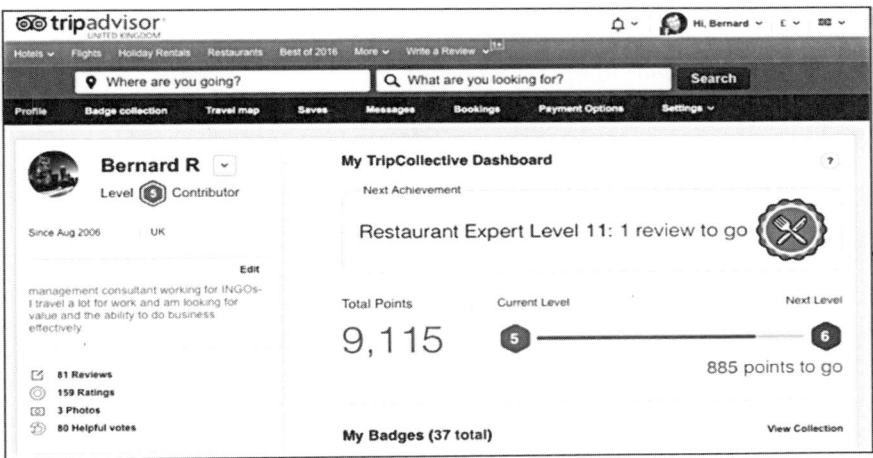

'Save More Tomorrow' Gives Pensions a Boost

There is a well-known early test of delayed gratification, an important element in emotional intelligence in children. It involves asking a child as young as three if they would like one marshmallow now, or two marshmallows later. The potentially conflicted child is then left in a room with the first marshmallow in front of them. They are told they have to wait five minutes alone without eating the marshmallow to secure the second one.

This test, when given to four-year-olds, is surprisingly accurate at predicting their ability to control their impulses—one aspect of emotional intelligence—in later life. If they succeed in resisting the marshmallow they seem more likely to develop the patience for deferred gratification, than if they do not. Too simplistic for adults? Consider that in the UK online sales of lottery tickets for the weekly draw are falling. This is having a significant effect on the charitable funds made available through a share of the lottery spend. But more people are opting to buy scratch cards looking for the instant gratification even with a lower value win. Marshmallows come in many forms.

Many adults have not had the benefit of this insight growing up. And indeed, they struggle with the basic idea of giving something up now in exchange for 'more' or 'a payoff' later. This gives us a clue to the *present bias* heuristic. You can see a version of this in the way some products are priced. Many consumers buy a really cheap inkjet printer and then pay a fortune for ink cartridges—failing to work out the overall cost of printing copies over the 2-3-year life of the printer. Some companies take advantage of this bias, tying consumers in with an attractive cheap 'now' offer, and not disclosing what the long-term cost will be.

As an instructive example, Sony actually loses money on every XBox it sells. But then makes money back on the games which can only be played on its own system. This basic business model was devised by King Gillette, who invented the disposable razor blade in the early twentieth century. He sold the razor handle and first blade cheaply, and then increased prices for the blades once the consumer was tied into the system. A brilliant model that builds on our biases, and that still works today.

This bias is especially important in the area of retirement savings, the ultimate long-term investment. There is always a good reason to spend income now, and put off long-term financial planning. Most people in UK, for example, accept *intellectually* they will have to take responsibility for their own long-term financial needs as the overall economics of state pensions, social care, etc., don't make great financial sense. The problem is many people seem reluctant to take positive action to safeguard their personal financial status until it is too late.

The UK Government is trying to change this, so it set up the National Employment Savings Trust (NEST). In this scheme, all employees are automatically enrolled in workplace pensions. The scheme draws on lessons from the Save More Tomorrow (SMT) scheme in the US, set up by Professor Shlomo Benartzi, co-chair with Thaler of the behavioural decision-making group in the Anderson School at UCLA.

The SMT scheme auto-enrolled employees in workplace pensions. It was designed to address a conflict: retirement was a far distant prospect for many people; and there is always something that is wanted or needed now. The programme was cleverly constructed to actually play to people's *current time* focus rather than challenge it. Participants only had to commit to make small contributions to the scheme at first. Then, as their salaries increased, as is normal over time, the savings were automatically increased.

SMT has seen savings rates at participating US companies grow by 400%. It is so successful it is now used by more than 60% of US companies offering defined contribution pensions.

Auto enrollment is also central to the UK's NEST scheme. This means participants have to opt *out,* playing to the lazy brain's desire for an easy life. To make life and onboarding easier still, the software fills in much of the data when you enroll. This works to counter our natural inertia when it comes to form-filling and seemingly complicated decisions. There's a huge body of evidence that both auto-fill in and auto-enrollment improve participation and retention rates. (There is some important learning here for charities and public bodies. Even something as simple as a look-up that allows people to type their postcode and then the address is filled in will reduce initial friction.)

Critics of this model in the US and the UK say it can appear patronising. They argue people should be able to make sensible, System 2-type decisions about their own future in their own time. But in a 2015 *Financial Times* interview Professor Benartzi dismisses this. 'The thing a lot of [critics] miss when they say, "it feels paternalistic," is if you don't have it, you have also decided what the default is—that is, without auto enrollment, most people will do nothing. I like to talk about the choices as 'auto takeoff' and 'auto grounded.' As evidence of how benign auto enrollment is, he points to his own further research, which shows if the initial level of contributions is set too high, 'everyone opts out.' So the scheme to some extent self regulates.

'Are we tricking them? Maybe a little bit,' Professor Benartzi admits. Is it socially justified? We think that's your call.

What Are the Lessons From Progress and Timing?

There is a whole series of implications arising from the way in which we perceive and make sense of time. Our sense of time and progress is neither linear, nor logical. We prefer to contribute to progress at specific points, and we prefer current gains and future payments to current payments and future gains. We like to see, and be part of, what we perceive as progress. Indeed we prefer to contribute to progress at specific points, and are more inclined to do so when information on the progress is presented in specific ways and at specific times. Among the most powerful communications are illustrative representations of progress, like graphs.

Some key ideas to consider when using this heuristic:

- **Work to help overcome initial inertia:** You need to reduce barriers —or friction—for example, by reducing the information that people have to take in, or data that they have to input to make progress. Be aware of the importance of time perception. Don't set a long timeline, focus on action *now*, even if the impact is later.
- **Cluster progress into chunks:** Break down a big goal into a number of smaller goals. Reinforce progress regularly and in real time, ideally. It helps reinforce impact and encourage engagement.

- **Present different kinds of progress:** Money, time, results. And do it in a number of ways. Visual representations, especially graphs, are important.
- **Choose how you share numbers:** Percentages or raw numbers. This choice makes a big difference to how people see a result.
- **Organise your proposition and campaign:** In a way which makes people consider they are making a distinct difference at that point. Presenting potential supporters with a key tipping point is essential—where they think they can make a step-change or worthwhile difference.
- **Be aware of how people think about time:** It's not logical. People will be much more aware of time at the beginning and near the end of a process. They will give greater weight to contributions then. And are more likely to contribute themselves.

Chapter 3

Nudge Gently and Ethically

Summary

Nudge is a word popularised through a particular approach to decision science developed by two US academics Thaler and Sunstein.[1] (Thaler won the Nobel Prize for Economics in 2017.) It is also the title of their 2008 book, which looks at 'Improving decisions about health, wealth, and happiness.' The book complements Kahneman's work, and looks at the small communications changes we can make which will influence decision-making. Importantly, Thaler and Sunstein acknowledge that most nudges operate at a *subconscious* level, but are keen that people should have a choice.

Specifically, the two main aims of *nudges* are to drive people towards a particular outcome by helping them to:

- Consider issues in an appropriate framework.
- Make better decisions for themselves and others.

In this chapter we'll look at health, fundraising, and a range of other areas where nudge theory helps leverage significant behaviour changes. These small changes often achieve much better results

---

[1] It is interesting to note that the idea of a 'nudge' has become popular almost as a brand itself. And where Kahneman has largely remained in the academic world, Thaler has gone on to write a number of other popular books, most recently *Misbehaving*, 2015.

than more conventional thinking. Conventionally, if you are the parent or guardian of a young person due to take an exam, you might:

- Offer a *reward* for desired behaviour: 'You'll get an iPod if you work hard and get an A grade in your exams.' *Or*
- Impose a *sanction* for unacceptable behaviour: 'You won't be allowed out for two weeks if you get a C grade.'

Nudging avoids what it sees as these simplistic and maybe dramatic carrot-and-stick approaches. It reinforces the idea of 'choice'—but subtly steers people towards a specific action. Indeed, some changes are so subtle they may seem almost insignificant. For example, the UK National Health Service (NHS) managed to reduce the number of 'no shows' for appointments by 11% when receptionists asked patients to verbally repeat the date and time of their appointment. Thaler describes such nudges as SIFs: *Seemingly Irrelevant Factors*.

What is a Nudge?

Thaler and Sunstein do not offer a definitive definition of *Nudge theory* in their book, although they do suggest a useful 'what it is and what it is not' outline near the start:

> ... *A nudge, as we will use the term, is any aspect of the choice architecture that alters people's behaviour in a predictable way without forbidding any options or significantly changing their economic incentives. To count as a mere nudge, the intervention must be easy and cheap to avoid. Nudges are not mandates. Putting fruit at eye level counts as a nudge. Banning junk food does not....*

Note that this 'sort-of' definition refers to an early case study about shaping choices to alter behaviour in a cafeteria queue—hence the 'fruit at eye level' reference. People may well recognise they are being nudged, whereas with some other principles, such as *priming* and *reciprocity*, they may not.

The Oxford English Dictionary definition of the word *nudge* may also help in appreciating Thaler and Sunstein's approach to the idea:

Nudge [verb]

- *'Prod (someone) gently with one's elbow in order to attract attention.'*
- *'Touch or push (something) gently or gradually.'*
- *'Coax or gently encourage (someone) to do something.'*

Nudge [noun]

- *'A light touch or push.'*

If you are a social activist the good news is that there are lots of great not-for-profit examples of nudges. In this chapter we'll look at some of these—and also consider some of the ethical challenges they create.

Encouraging Healthy Eating in America

Nudging is concerned with encouraging 'desirable' behaviour. Let's look at a key challenge for desirable behaviour—tackling obesity, a major health issue in the developed world. The starting place for good eating habits is in childhood. Schools and education authorities have for years been looking for ways to get children and young people to eat more fruit and vegetables—not an easy task. The debate about how to change eating habits has focused largely on what is provided in schools. Public health advocates argue that chips (french fries), biscuits (cookies), and fizzy drinks should be banned. And some schools have done that. (In the UK, chef Jamie Oliver[2] famously campaigned to get un-healthy 'turkey twizzlers' banned and to introduce healthier food.)

In response, food manufacturers who supply schools say that such 'denial' approaches only encourage students to get their 'fat fix' elsewhere. And indeed in the UK we saw mothers turning up to schools with burgers at lunchtime and pushing them through the fence in response to their children being 'forced' to eat salads and other healthy food. There is a similar challenge with cafeterias in workplaces.

In New York, the Department of Health decided to research a different approach in schools. They asked Brian Wansink, Director of the Food and Brand Lab at Cornell University, to find out how much a school would need to cut its prices for apples, oranges and bananas to increase sales, and consumption. After an initial review, he soon fed back that this was the wrong question. 'Price,' he said, 'wasn't the problem. It was the presentation.'

According to a report in the *Washington Post*,[3] in the school caf-eterias Wansink reviewed, fruits were displayed in unattractive steel bins in poorly lighted areas of the lunch queue. As a result, no-one chose them. His solution was to go to a discount store and buy a cheap wire fruit rack. And then he found a desk lamp, which he used to illuminate the fruit. 'Sales of fruit in one school went up 54 percent. Not in a semester: by the end of the second week,' Wansink said. 'It would have gone up faster, but they kept running out of fruit.'

This, and similar experiences with adults at companies like Google and Apple, means people with responsibility for nutrition in workplaces and education settings are now paying much more attention to how food is presented. What we're learning is that deci-sion science—often with very limited financial investment—can help fight obesity. And the answer is not to ban, but to nudge.

---

[2] http://www.theguardian.com/society/2005/mar/06/schoolmeals.
[3] www.washingtonpost.com piece by Jane Black, *Washington Post* Staff Writer, 9.6.10.

Don't Let Anyone Deny it, Size Matters. And Brains Don't.

Nutritional challenges are not simply the preserve of people who don't know about calories and saturated fats. In 2002 Wansink organised an ice cream party to celebrate a promotional success of a colleague who worked in his nutrition unit. Unable to resist the temptation, Wansink turned the opportunity into an experiment.[4]

When they arrived party-goers were randomly given a smaller (17oz) or a larger (34oz) bowl and a smaller (2oz) or larger (3oz) ice cream scoop. After they had helped themselves, each nutritionist had their bowl weighed and was asked to complete a short survey. Those with a smaller bowl and a smaller ice cream scoop provided the benchmark level of ice cream consumption. The result:

- Those provided with a larger bowl ate 31% more than the benchmark
- Those with a larger scoop ate 14% more than the benchmark

Even *experts* can fall for a nudge.

David Just, a professor at Cornell's Department of Applied Economics and Management, describes the *nudge nutrition* educational approach in a blog: 'Rather than implementing outright bans on certain foods, its goal is to design sustainable lunchrooms that guide smarter choices.'[5] Professor Just's key word is 'guide.' 'Simply replacing pizza with whole wheat flatbreads, and fries with roasted sweet potatoes doesn't allow kids to learn how to make real-world choices.'[6] Importantly, he went on 'We set [the cafeteria] up so that everything is available and the kids are enabled to see how to make a decision, or how to make decisions.' Making those decisions proactively, he says, leads to 'good' long-term habits.

The attraction of nudge approaches here is obvious. They are not just low-cost, they are also flexible and scalable. And they do not

---

[4] https://www.ncbi.nlm.nih.gov/pubmed/16905035.

[5] Blog: *The Nudge, Cafeteria Part III*, March 9, 2009.

[6] There is some interesting data that suggests we are more attracted to fatty high calorie food—presumably in response to our ancestral need to stock up on energy until the next uncertain meal. https://www.nationalgeographic.com/foodfeatures/evolution-of-diet/.

impose a lack of choice, which might well fuel rebellion—especially among young people.

Nutritionists have often led the way for nudging. Here's a list of eat-well nudges culled from various sources. You might like to look at your own organisation's approach if you have a café or canteen. Anyway here are our 7 Top Tips:

- Invest in smaller plates to make food portions look larger, and therefore better value.
- Put salads and vegetables near the front of any queue so that people can fill their plates with them first.
- Design the layout of the salads so you don't have to reach far for broccoli, but you do for grated cheese.
- Put ice cream in a 'frosted' or opaque chest freezers—ideally with a lid you have to roll back—so there is just a bit more effort to reach it.
- Create separate cash-only lanes for unhealthy foods such as calorific desserts and fizzy soft drinks.
- Describe healthy foods in richer detail e.g. 'rich vegetable medley soup' instead of 'vegetable soup.'
- Bury items like fish and chips in the middle of the menu while the grilled fish is at the top and wilted greens at the bottom.

If you're *really* interested in nutrition Cornell has launched a great web site, www.smarterlunchrooms.org, for work and school lunch managers, that helps coordinate ideas on 'nudge cafeterias'.[7] There are also some excellent ideas here: www.nudges.org/tag/cafeteria/ #sthash.dGKPkNkl.dpuf.

Colour-coding food choices in a cafeteria is a semiotic nudge,[8] which can make a significant difference to eating habits. People

---

[7] http://www.sas.upenn.edu/~baron/journal/11/11213/jdm11213.pdf.

[8] Semiotics is the study of communication codes, made famous by Roland Barthes the French philosopher. From a semiotics perspective, everything in or around a message is a communication code: images, graphs, data, colours, music, fonts, design, shapes, etc. Think of a direct mail package. The fact that you are using a direct mail

associate green with 'go', amber with 'think about it', and red with 'stop right there'. So colour coding foods like that can guide choices, when coupled with simple advice. ('Have at least two green food portions and no more than one amber or red one.') Or see the advice from the Google canteen below. A similar system has now been adopted in UK on a range of food packaging in supermarkets.

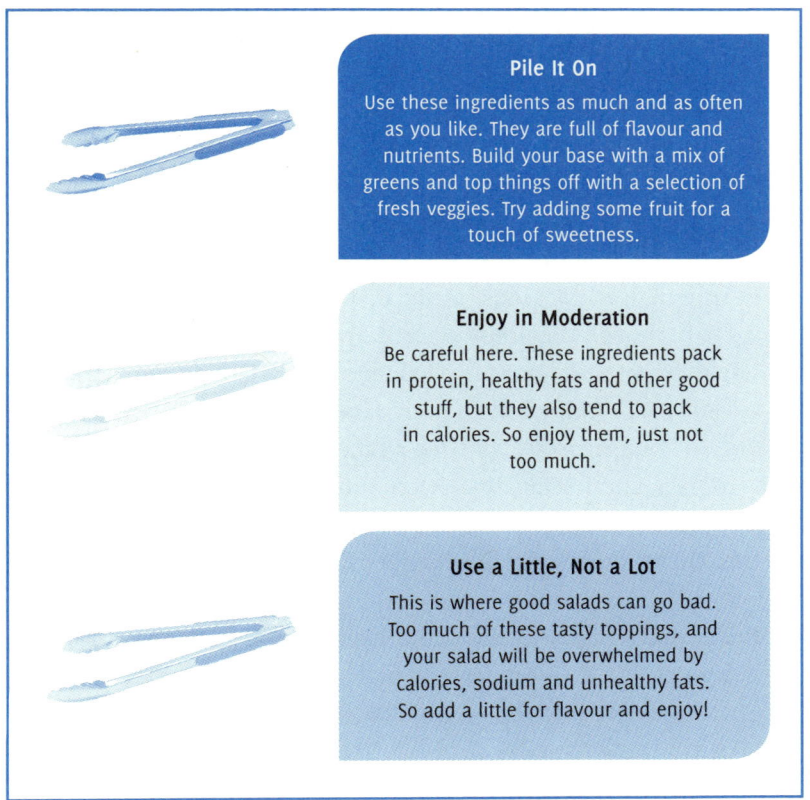

Pile It On
Use these ingredients as much and as often as you like. They are full of flavour and nutrients. Build your base with a mix of greens and top things off with a selection of fresh veggies. Try adding some fruit for a touch of sweetness.

Enjoy in Moderation
Be careful here. These ingredients pack in protein, healthy fats and other good stuff, but they also tend to pack in calories. So enjoy them, just not too much.

Use a Little, Not a Lot
This is where good salads can go bad. Too much of these tasty toppings, and your salad will be overwhelmed by calories, sodium and unhealthy fats. So add a little for flavour and enjoy!

---

instead of email or a phone call is an aspect of semiotics. The size, colour, and shape of the envelope are communication codes, and so is the paper type, font, images, etc. Some codes are pretty much universal (e.g. traffic lights in different colours) while others are local (e.g. the meaning of a horseshoe, the impact of colour red, or the number 8.)

The UK Nudge Unit

Thaler and Sunstein's nudge work has been put into practice very specifically and systematically across a range of social issues, especially in the UK. The former British Prime Minister, David Cameron, was an early convert to nudging. He set up the world's first government run Behavioural Insights Team (BIT), popularly called 'The Nudge Unit', in 2010 just after he won a general election. His aim was to find a way of improving public services *and* saving money. Over the next five years the team undertook a number of assignments covering a wide range of social issues—from improving diversity in the police service, to reducing smoking, improving tax revenues, and even reducing theft of mobile phones. In a series of fascinating experiments, explored below and elsewhere in the book, they also looked at how to improve charitable giving.[9]

In true nudge style, most of the changes applied by the Unit were very small, though the ambition was always to have a significant impact. In their work the team applied three important principles of decision science: accepting not all their experiments would work, at least on first roll out; rigorously testing a range of options to see which has most impact; and imaginatively combining a range of techniques and frameworks to develop in the end an effective decision architecture.

Despite some failures, BIT has an impressive list of achievements:

• **Reducing fraud and debt**: the team introduced a new form of reminder letter to anyone who had been slow to pay their income tax. The letter told recipients that most of their neighbours had

---

[9] In 2015 the BIT team were spun off as an independent social enterprise. Halpern, the CEO of the unit was clear about its role: 'The key point [of any assignment] is that it has to have a social purpose.' As an example of their social purpose he explained the team would *refuse* to help an alcohol company improve sales—but they would *consider* a project helping a company to reduce sugar. In this sense they are significantly different from many of the commercial agencies using decision science simply to sell more product. The privatised unit still gets significant assignments from UK Government ministries and it has also undertaken work for a range of public agencies worldwide including the UN, the World Bank, and other governments.

already paid the amount due. The simple peer comparison 'nudged' forward the payment of £30 millon a year.

However, this approach had limited impact on the 5% of people who seemed to be the worst offenders. After significant testing the team identified a distinct message that *did* impact on this group: 'Not paying tax means we all lose out on vital public services like the NHS, roads and schools.'[10]

- **Reducing dropout rate in adult literacy classes:** The UK Government subsidises adult literacy classes, but these historically have had a high dropout rate. The Unit adopted the device of sending students a regular personalised text message. This went out every Sunday night 'I hope you had a good break, we look forward to seeing you next week. Remember to plan how you will get to your class.'

  This informal and seemingly minor prompt improved attendance and reduced the dropout rate by 36%. As with many behavioural insights this approach beat more conventional ones such as offering an incentive to turn up, or threatening a sanction.

- **Improving police diversity:** Only 40% of black and minority ethnic (BME) applicants passed the second 'situational judgment' stage of the Avon and Somerset police recruitment process. On the other hand, 60% of white, British-background applicants were successful. The nudge team changed the basic email sent to all candidates after phase 1. As before, it congratulated recipients on passing the first phase, but then included a request to 'Take some time to think about why you want to be a police constable.' They suggested the applicant did this before moving on to the next phase.

---

[10] Interestingly it is not clear why this specific proposition made a big difference. It could be that people realised the social impact of their failure to pay tax, or it could be guilt, or another reason. However, it is important to the say that this technique does not only work in a 'socialised' nation like UK. Guatemala is a nation where tax avoidance is almost endemic (as is mistrust of the government). Nevertheless, the Guatemalan Government adopted the same tactic, using a similar communication to tax avoiders. Tax receipts trebled. Whatever reason, this approach seems to work cross culturally.

This small change had no impact on white British applicants' performance in subsequent assessments. But 50% more of the BME candidates passed the exam.[11]

Even small gains from nudging are highly valuable—not least because they usually involve no, or very little, expenditure.

Improving Organ Donation

In 2012 over one million people registered to join the UK Organ Donor Register,[12] bringing the total to almost 20 million. Although this may seem like a lot, it's not enough. On average, three people die every day because there are not enough organs available.

This piece of data is generally widely available and understood. The message is underlined in popular UK medical dramas like *Casualty* where the plotlines not infrequently include desperate attempts to save someone who needs a transplant. Many people say that they would be willing to join the Register. But they fail to do so. Current UK opinion polls suggest that 9 out of 10 people support organ donation, but in reality fewer than 1 in 3 are registered. There is a significant gap between what people say they want to do and what they actually do.

The UK organ donation agency decided to try some interventions to close the gap, based on the 'nudge' heuristic. One intervention involved a series of online Randomised Controlled Trials (RCTs).[13] These trials compared the effectiveness of various nudges against the status quo.

---

[11] As with many behavioural insights examples it is not clear exactly why this works. Some follow-up research suggests it is because the BME candidates are encouraged to think more about themselves *in the role,* rather than trying to guess what the 'right' answer is. But the results are inconclusive. What is conclusive is the *impact.*

[12] The situation is different in Wales where an opt-out process has been adopted —transforming the availability of organs: http://www.bbc.co.uk/news/uk-wales-38144547. In fact, only 6% of people have opted out.

[13] According to Wikipedia: 'A randomized controlled trial is a type of scientific (often medical) experiment which aims to reduce bias [when testing an intervention.] The people participating in the trial are randomly allocated to either the group receiving the treatment under investigation or to a group receiving standard treatment (or placebo treatment) as the control. Randomization minimises selection bias and the

One trial tested the impact of including different messages on a high-traffic public webpage. People were coming to the website to sort out their car registration—so nothing to do with organ donation. But after completing their registration they were directed to another web page asking them to commit to becoming an organ donor.

Twelve different messages were randomly tested, each offering a different reason to sign up to be an organ donor. These ranged from self-interest: 'What would happen to you or your family if you needed a new organ or new organs?' to civic duty-style endorsements, 'This is a good thing to do for society.' Perhaps surprisingly, the best-performing message drew on ideas of reciprocity and fairness by asking people 'If you needed an organ transplant, would you have one? If so, please help others.'

The results were impressive, and could have a massive impact at scale. If this best-performing message was used over the whole year, and continued to have the same impact it would lead to approximately 96,000 *extra* registrations, saving perhaps 30,000 lives.

Default or Not Default?

The organ donor case study raises interesting cultural and ethical challenges. There are some countries where organ donation is an *opt-out* process not an *opt-in*. In Austria, almost everyone is an organ donor because they have an opt-out system. Whereas in neighbouring Germany, with its opt-in system, only 12% of individuals are registered organ donors. Though an opt-out system would clearly create more social benefit overall, it might be perceived as interfering with civil liberties or with cultural/religious preferences.

Three US academics: Mary Steffel, Assistant Professor of Marketing, Northeastern University; Elanor Williams, Assistant Professor, Indiana University and Ruth Pogacar, PhD Student in Marketing,

---

different comparison groups allow the researchers to determine any effects of the treatment when compared with the no-treatment (control) group, while other variables are kept constant. The RCT is often considered the gold standard for a clinical trial."

University of Cincinnati have undertaken some interesting research exploring how *awareness* of the use of defaults affects our attitude to them. The study below draws largely on their report.[14]

In a series of experiments, the three academics presented people with choices that were framed as either opt-in or opt-out. The team varied whether or not they told people about the purpose of the default. The subsequent analysis was designed to establish how knowledge of the purpose, or lack of it, influenced participants' attitudes and the actual decisions made.

In one experiment, participants were introduced to a new hypothetical social media site. The group being tested were asked two main questions:

• 'What kind of information—photos, age, background, education, etc.—would you be willing to share?'
• 'Who would you feel comfortable sharing the data with—from "friends of friends" to "advertisers"?'

The results were interesting. People were willing to share a third more data when they had to opt *out* of sharing various bits of information, than when they had to opt *in*. Perhaps more importantly, what these participants actually shared did not depend on whether they were explicitly told *why* the site had set the default the way it did, even when the site's goal was simply to get them to share more information with more people.

In a second complementary experiment, the researchers offered passers-by on a college campus free hot chocolate. Half were offered the chocolate with whipped cream on top—though they could choose to say 'no' to the cream. The other half were offered chocolate without the cream—though they could choose to have it.

Now comes the really interesting attitudinal issue. The proportion of people choosing to go *against* their offered default was 10%

---

[14] This section is largely a summary and edit of a fascinating article by the researchers. http://theconversation.com/default-choices-have-big-impact-but-how-to-make-sure-they're-used-ethically-65852.

in both cases. This was true even with the 50% of participants who were explicitly told the default had been set so that they were more likely to get a *healthy* drink (when they had to opt in) or an *unhealthy* drink (when they had to opt out).

In other words, disclosure that the choice was being shaped did not influence people's decisions. It did, however, affect how people *felt* about the default and the default setter. The researchers discovered in follow up interviews that participants in these and other experiments judged the use of a default to be more ethical and fair when the intention behind it was disclosed ahead of time than when it was not.

Participants also showed more interest in working with someone again in the future if that person was up front about how he or she was using defaults to influence their choices. The good news, then, is that you don't have to use defaults sneakily. Tell people what you have done, and the simple act of disclosing makes your action more acceptable to the target audience.

These effects were most pronounced when the default was designed to nudge people toward an option that was perceived to benefit society. But the advantages of transparency held even when the default was designed to nudge people toward an option that benefitted the default setter, and even when the default setter's motives were selfish.

The researchers summarise their conclusions, 'This is encouraging news for those who might be hesitant to disclose the intent behind defaults. It shows that default setters can create transparency by disclosing the nature and intent behind defaults without making those defaults any less effective. Disclosure may even improve default setters' reputations with consumers and lead to greater customer loyalty. But this is discouraging for those who hoped that disclosure might be an effective means of consumer protection. Defaults still guide choices, even when they are preceded by disclosure of their effects and the reason that they were instituted.'

De-Biasing Decisions

Steffel, Williams and Pogacar's conclusion is good news for we ethical nudgers. But the same may also be true for unethical nudgers. For example, companies who include a pre-ticked auto-renew on a subscription. So, what can we do to ensure that people, especially vulnerable people, are protected from exploitative defaults? (Assuming an outright ban is not advisable and would be difficult to police.)

Again, the team explored this issue in their study. Their view is that in order to protect people from defaults whose influence is exploitative, it is important to understand why these defaults work. A key reason is that they change the way we consider options.

The study, and others in the field, show that by making an option the default, most people tend first to consider reasons to *accept* the default. So, by implication, they start by putting aside any other options. Only if the default is transparently bad or difficult to do, do they seriously consider the alternatives. Another concern is that since people are often unaware of *how* any default is affecting their decision-making, the simple act of disclosure doesn't help. Essentially people don't know how to adjust their thinking to counter the influence of the default.

The research team decided to try to construct a way of reducing the influence of defaults, and get people to more actively consider any alternatives. They did so by shifting the focus away from the default and toward its alternative. They asked participants to:

- Think of reasons why the alternative might be a good option.
- List what were the Key Success Factors for them in the choice.

Both these approaches helped participants arrive at a more balanced view, whether it was choosing the default or opting for an alternative. A similar approach could be used by, for example, advice agencies helping an individual to decide how to deal with various options to handle debt. Or you could make *explicit consent* an aspect of any choice— though this doesn't guarantee the person will make a balanced choice.

The researchers suggest there may need to be legislation to avoid un-scrupulous companies taking advantage of individuals. In the UK, the Government has introduced legislation for charities; that means they have to seek explicit opt-in permission for specific communications. The effects are still being discussed as we write. But the expectations are that this legislation will make it harder to engage new supporters.

Nudging for a Legacy—Using Social Norms

Bequests or legacies are a key income source for many charities in the UK. They also make financial sense for a donor since current UK legislation means that inheritance tax is reduced for individuals who leave more than 10% of their estate to a charity.

And it would *appear* to be popular as a way to support causes people care about—around 35% of whom *say* they want to leave money to a charity.

But there is a problem. Only 7% of wills contain a charitable legacy—another example of a sizeable gap between stated behavioural intention and their actual behaviour.

The UK Behavioural Insights Team, mentioned earlier, explored how they might prompt or nudge more people to leave a charitable gift in their wills. Specifically, they decided to use an aspect of decision architecture called 'social norms.' (For more on this see **Chapter 10.**) The basic idea is that to encourage people to include a charity gift you should make it clear a number of other people similar to them have also left a charitable legacy.

To test the hypothesis, the BIT ran a large-scale experiment in association with a legal firm, Co-operative Legal Services, and an association of charities dedicated to promoting legacy giving called Remember a Charity.

By engaging a range of different charities, the team was able to ensure that any differences in behaviour were due to the nudge techniques employed rather than cause affiliation. Similarly, using an independent legal firm and their staff meant that there was no affiliation with an individual cause. The result, whatever it was, could be attributed specifically to the nudge adopted.

The experiment involved several thousand random legacy prospects recruited by adverts in the press. Individuals interested were offered the chance to have their will drafted for free. They were specifically invited to phone a helpline where they would be given advice by the partner legal firm on how to complete their will. It was made clear in the advert that when they called they would be able to discuss how to dispose of their assets—meeting the needs of family and friends—and also have the chance to discuss any charitable causes they wanted to support.

When customers called up for their advice they were routed at random to one of three groups of call takers. Each call taker was asked to use an exact script. After the 'formal' advice about how to handle bequests to family and friends, the call handlers offered one of three propositions.

- **Call Handler A 'No Ask':** Callers speaking to this person were not specifically prompted to make a charitable gift during the process. If they asked to do so, they were guided on how. These callers represented a *baseline*—that is, the behaviour to be expected in 'normal' circumstances.
- **Call Handler B 'Plain Ask':** Callers speaking to this person were specifically asked 'Would you like to leave any money to charity in your will?' This was classed as *plain ask*—that is, callers were encouraged to make a commitment in a gentle, general way. And no specific charity was mentioned.
- **Call Handler C 'Social Norm':** Callers speaking to this person were told 'Many of our customers like to leave money to charity in their will. Are there any causes you are passionate about?' These callers were encouraged to identify with their feelings, and with other people like them who were making their will—a *social norm*.

The results are illustrated below. Depending on the approach used by the call handler, there were large differences in the number of people who agreed to offer a charitable gift as part of their legacy, and also the size of the average donation. In each case the group who were prompted and were asked to identify with their feelings, and with others who shared those feelings, produced the highest result by a long way.

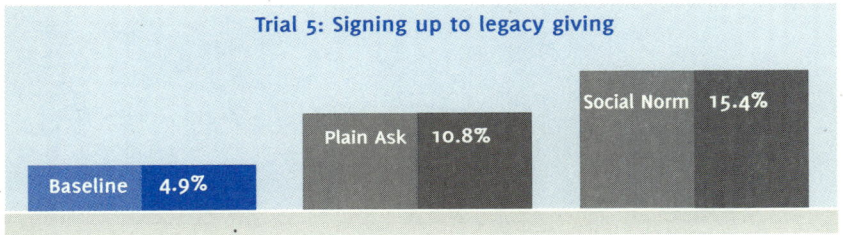

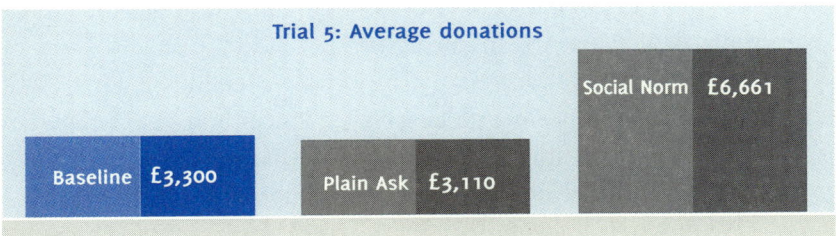

Source: The Behavioural Architects, www.thebearchitects.com

Using the *social norms* approach significantly increased the percentage of callers agreeing to leave a legacy, from 5% when no ask was made, to over 15% with the social norm prompt. It also doubled the size of contributions. The social norm group donated twice as much as the 'no ask' baseline group—a total of £990,000 from 1,000 individuals, which was £825,000 above the baseline group.

This approach has now been adopted by a number of charities in the UK including the National Society for the Prevention of Cruelty to Children (NSPCC). Working with the telephone fundraising agency ON Agency, they developed two characters, Pasha and Norm, who were used to inform the dialogues that call centre staff would use to engage with donors and prospective donors. Here's the staff guide:

According to Christopher Nield, Creative Director of ON Agency, in the first week of using this approach it led to 101 conversations about committing to a legacy, with zero complaints about the conversations, and a conversion rate of 46%.

An upswing in donations is also reported by Jen Shang, PhD, Research Director at the Centre for Sustainable Philanthropy at Plymouth University with a complementary approach that she used.[15]

Dr Shang describes a field experiment they organised during a direct marketing campaign for a faith-based organisation. The key change was to the classic response form used. The researchers changed the question respondents were asked immediately before they entered what their gift level would be.

Dr Shang explains: 'Depending on the condition, cash donors were asked to list three people "they know (or are known by)" or "they love (or are loved by)" most before they make a donation.'

'We then coded their listed relationships into either a horizontal (e.g. siblings or friends) or a vertical relationship (e.g. parents, children or mentors). We found that the increase in cash giving is higher in a "loving" and "horizontal" condition (about £4) than any other conditions (about £2) on an average donation of about £20.'

---

[15] Jen Shang quoted in www.charitychoice.co.uk/the-fundraiser/whats-your-favourite-lesson-from-behavioural-psychology-that/498

Yet again seemingly small changes in the dialogue, rather than massively different propositions, seem to be making a massive impact, in this case by asking donors to think of someone they cared about.

Health Nudging

An obvious area for 'nudgery' is health and physical wellbeing. And it has been applied to a number of health problems including smoking, alcohol misuse, obesity, diabetes, physical activity and sexual health.

One recurrent nudge strategy used is positive feedback. A nice example is The Didget blood glucose meter aimed at improving the desire of children with Type I diabetes to be more systematic in checking their blood sugar level. The Didget operates like any other blood-sugar meter, but with one important difference—it comes with a connection to an online space accessible only to Didget users, where children who use it can interact with other diabetes patients and play games.

Importantly The Didget connects to the hugely popular—social normative—Nintendo DS and DS Lite gaming platforms. The system awards points to those children who consistently test their blood sugar levels and meet targets. They can then use these points to unlock different levels in games online and through their Nintendo device.

Paediatric endocrinologist at Tallahassee Memorial Hospital, Larry Dee, who was involved in testing and developing the system, is clear about why this works. 'Kids don't exactly welcome the tests [of their blood sugar]. Diabetes is an incredible intrusion into a child's life, and it's an intrusion they really don't want, whereas children play games all the time.'

Local government in the UK is trying to use the nudge technique as well. In 2014 Stoke-on-Trent City Council undertook a pilot programme called Text4Change to send obese people, those with a Body Mass Index (BMI) of over 30, motivational weight loss texts. These were all pretty simple, such as: 'USE THE STAIRS MORE,' 'EAT FRUIT AND VEG,' and 'KEEP A CHECK ON SNACKS AND DRINKS,' to encourage them to lose weight. If people replied to the texts they were helped to set mini goals such as 'TRY NOT TO EAT PUDDING FOR ANOTHER 5 DAYS.'

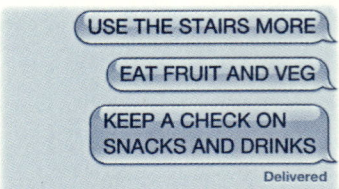

The council's aim was to cut the number of obese adults in the city. There were 70,000 adults who fit that definition at that time, and Text4Change helped make a dent in the £50 millon NHS bill for tackling weight-related illnesses.

As we write, encouraging initial results are being reviewed by Staffordshire University to see if the programme could be expanded and taken to scale.

The City That Lost 1,000,000 Pounds

One great example of nudging comes from the *City That Lost 1,000,000* campaign. On New Year's Eve in 2007, the mayor of Oklahoma City, Mick Cornett, announced that his city was going to go on a diet, and lose a collective million pounds. Two things had encouraged him to take this lead:

- The city he was mayor of had been named as one of America's fattest.
- By looking at a health website, he had discovered he was classed as obese.

He decided to go on a diet and to take his city with him. He identified that Oklahoma City, like many in the US, had been built around the car so there was little incentive to walk. Moreover, even neighbourhoods had poor 'walkability' for visiting neighbours, stores or local leisure facilities. In many cases developers had not even built pavements. He ordered a redesign of neighbourhoods based around a 'walkscore'—aiming to improve the potential to walk to places. This redesign, along with a website to help people with their individual diet and where they could record their collective weight loss, nudged the population towards the 1,000,000 pounds target.

And it worked.[16]

Gamification: Doing Good While Having Fun

Nudging is everywhere. Some hybrid cars display the fuel-efficiency of your driving patterns with different coloured images to reinforce 'good' patterns. The Lincoln MKZ hybrid car even has 'leaves' for short-term habits, and 'flowers', which are harder to earn, for long-term habits. This links strongly to the idea of gamification of nudges —where the change is presented as an entertaining distraction, 'doing good while having fun.'

A prime example is Amsterdam's Schipol Airport's 'fly on the urinal' image—below left. This encourages men to pee without missing or splashing, making urinals less unpleasant and saving time and cost in additional cleaning. In fact, this image, now adopted in various forms internationally, is reckoned to have saved up to 7% on cleaning bills.

The idea was taken even further in a Scottish urinal, below, where you can try to keep a small soccer ball moving.

---

[16] For more information, see www.thiscityisgoingonadiet.com.

Concerns About Nudge

The whole field of behavioural economics raises concerns about choice and the potential for manipulation. It raises issues about free choice.

Thaler and Sunstein don't ignore this.[17] They advocate the use of nudging for societal good. They maintain that having an ethical framework is essential for nudging professionals, whether public bodies or companies. They also point out that many for-profit agencies use nudging in a 'bad' way:

- Organising supermarket candy displays at child height to encourage children to pester parents for treats and bribes as they queue to check out.
- Offering 'meal deals' in take away restaurants that lure people to choose larger potions of unhealthy food.
- Clustering information on a web page that persuades people to choose an energy plan that is inappropriate for their needs.

[17] If you're interested to read more, try *Why Nudge? The Politics of Libertarian Paternalism*, 2014, by Sunstein. This is based on a series of lectures given at Yale University in 2012. In the book, Sunstein combines legal thinking with behavioural economics to explore the legitimate scope of government intervention, dealing with issues as diverse as obesity, driving, smoking and health care.

An ongoing example of unethical nudging we came across recently is the drink *Sunny Delight* being kept in a chill in a Spanish supermarket. The idea, we guess, is to suggest it is fresh, so making it more attractive to the busy shopper. This product can happily remain on an ordinary shelf for months.

Thaler and Sunstein use the term *libertarian paternalism* to outline what they believe should be the guiding ethos and values of nudgers. The key distinguishing factor should be that the result benefits the 'nudgee' not the 'nudger.' (In the for-profit examples the nudger, usually a business, is benefiting and the nudgee, the customer, is paying a negative price.)

They acknowledge that nudging necessarily involves paternalism but the two elements of the phrase are important and linked:

- **Libertarian** refers to the need for people to have freedom in making their own choices, and the need to protect free will.
- **Paternalism** means any individual or group's leadership responsibility for people and the planet.

Thaler and Sunstein are clear on the need for choice *'Nudges are not mandates.'*

Of course, there is an obvious concern here about *who* is making the judgment on what is appropriate and what is a better choice. Since Thaler and Sunstein are specifically concerned with 'social' outcomes, it raises some important ethical issues about 'manipulation,' and what is sometimes called nanny-ing. In general, nudging is considered most acceptable when it:

- Is intended for a good cause (e.g. quitting smoking).
- Doesn't limit the person's choices.
- Is transparent.

What Are the Lessons From Nudging?

In this chapter, we have focused on positive ethical nudges—those that guide towards a specific socially beneficial decision through reinforcement of a choice. There are other solutions that offer a different approach, see, for example, loss aversion discussed in **Chapter 5**. But overall:

- Nudging approaches help us identify the very subtle ways in which we can guide individuals and groups towards making appropriate decisions.
- Many of the most effective nudges involve small and seemingly irrelevant changes.
- Changes in communication or decision architecture—the way decisions are organised—can make a significant impact.

If you're keen to be a great nudger, there are some simple principles to observe:

- **Make less more:** People are confused by too much choice, so if you simply reduce the number of options, you make choosing easier. The key principle is 'less is more.' In a supermarket study by Boatwright and Nunes[18] fewer choices for specific products drove sales up.[19] For an online store a reduced choice set increased sales by an average of 54%. And interesting, 75% of their website customers spent *more* as a result of the reduced choice.
- **Be transparent:** By making any default option as transparent as possible you gain more credibility and acceptability with the audience you are trying to influence. This makes any individual

---

[18] Boatright and Nunes, 'Reducing Assortment: An Attribute-Based Approach.' http://journals.ama.org/doi/abs/10.1509/jmkg.65.3.50.18330.

[19] *Journal of Marketing*, Vol. 65, July 2001, pp. 50-63.

more likely to accept your suggestion or recommendation without conscious challenge.

- **Promote the popular**: There may be some occasions where significantly reducing available options is not possible or practical. In this situation promote a small sub-set of options likely to appeal to the average or new customer or service user. For example, promote one choice as being the most popular or favourite option by others.

- **Offer decision support**: Online interactive decision aids make people feel in control. The UK's USwitch website helps consumers choose an energy or mobile provider. The way the website narrows down your choices by asking questions helps consumers feel less overwhelmed by the choices. Deciding is made easier. Solar Aid have an online calculator that shows how much impact a specific donation level has. (https://solar-aid.org/online-impact-calculator.) And Islamic Relief have a Zakat calculator to tell you how much you should contribute to meet your religious duty.

- **Develop defaults**: Defaults help people to follow the simplest, easiest route to a decision. You see this at work on booking systems for airlines like EasyJet. You may think you've booked a flight but you can't actually progress straight to flight confirmation. Instead the site cheerily offers you the choice to select a hotel, rent a car, invest in cancellation insurance, pay a carbon tax, or make a donation to UNICEF. You have to consciously say 'no' to these options to progress to the final screen where you can confirm your ticket purchase.

Chapter 4

Find a Frame and Fill It

Summary

A key concept in decision science is the idea of *framing*. Framing, linked to priming and anchoring, involves putting any decision into a context which then impacts on the choice we make or how we make it. It also connects strongly to the idea of *bounded rationality*, explored in **Chapter 9**, our ability to process only so much of a specific kind of information in a given time.

Just as a physical frame can alter our perception of the painting or picture it surrounds, a conceptual frame makes us see information in a specific way. Re-framing can then change our perception of the same information. A simple example might involve a gym membership. Contrast the '£365 a year for gym membership' versus the reframing of 'less than the price of a coffee a day, for health.'

Frames are important especially when we are choosing between broadly similar choices. In this case the choice should, in theory, be driven by rational System 2. But a strong brand—a powerful frame— can make us feel very differently about two very similar products and services, such as the coffee from Starbucks or that from Costa Coffee.

We like simple frames, complex ones confuse us. And we like choices presented in a way that reinforces simple, relative comparisons and avoids extremes. If your roof needs a repair, you get three estimates ... and then choose the middle one because it 'seems sensible.' As is often the case in the world of behavioural economics there is no rational basis for this at all.

What we do when we make a choice in this way is to establish *comparative value*. This is an idea developed by Dan Ariely. His take on framed decision-making is that rather than making a decision based on pure value for investment (time, money, and the like), we factor in *comparative* value, that is, how much value an option *apparently* offers when compared to another.[1] (One of our favourite examples of framing as context is Rolls Royce deciding to promote their cars at yacht shows: compared to other cars, a Rolls Royce looks really expensive; compared to a yacht, they look like a bargain. The buyer can think 'I *saved* £10 million by not buying that boat; I can afford to pay £350,000 for a car.'[2])

Finally, we need to be aware of the uncomfortable reality that people prefer to frame their response to human suffering in terms of the impact on one person over the impact on many. This phenomenon, called *the identifiable victim bias* can mean that we ignore mass suffering in order to focus on an individual with a solvable problem.

Types of Frames

Framing can take different forms. Among the most common frames are:

- **Context:** The way we communicate—ideas, words, images—bears a cultural connotation. For example, if we tell potential donors that they're going to get a reward in return for donating, or they'll be entered into a lottery they might win, we are using a *commercial context*. They then might price the 'value' of the offer based on

---

[1] Note, though, that this response is tempered by our loss-aversion mechanism helping us to calculate the balance between cost and reward whenever possible. This mechanism is always vigilant, waiting on standby to keep us from giving up more than we can afford to spare. (For more on this see **Chapter 5.**)

[2] Our thanks to Meredith Niles for this example.

that context. Appealing to altruism in a *social context* 'Let's collaborate to save the whale,' attracts a different pricing model: 'How much is everyone else giving?' Or 'How much do I care about whales?'

- **Comparison:** Comparison or benchmarking is important in framing. Comparing the amount of money requested for a purchase or donation can alter how we feel about that amount. For example, comparing a charitable donation of £3 a day to the cost of a cup of coffee, something we buy every day without thinking about the price, makes it look like a small amount. But asking for £1,000 a year, essentially the same amount, might seem very high.

- **Re-framing:** A shower gel had slow sales as consumers felt the price was very high for a cleaning product, comparing it to a bar of soap. The company changed perceptions by moving the gel's position in shops so it was next to body creams. (See the discussion in **Section Three** on the importance of planograms in stores.) This change positioned the gel as a 'beauty care' product. The company then raised the price to match the creams. Sales improved. As many donors question the long-term impact of their donations, some organisations are re-positioning their requests as a *social investment* with long-term impact, not simple charitable *giving* addressing a current issue.

- **Branding:** People react very differently to exactly the same product when it is presented in branded and unbranded forms. At Christmas, in blind taste tests by experts, unknown champagnes from, say, discount supermarket Lidl, often beat high brand value marques at 3 or 4 times the price. But even when this information is published, consumers still seem to prefer the more expensive, recognisable, brands. (They may also want to experience luxury at Christmas, not value for money.) In fundraising, a strong brand is likely to generate more support than a weaker brand, assuming the same appeal/campaign. The message: build your brand.

- **Physical:** The way something is physically presented can make a significant difference. (See above on product classification.) A product placed on the middle of a supermarket shelf at eye level can hugely boost sales. And an unusual point of sale display can also drive increased engagement. The 'number of facings,' that is how many items of a product you can see, also has an effect on sales. Essentially, the more visible a product, the higher sales are likely to be.[3] Such thinking and understanding could help inform the way the goods in charity shops are laid out and the kinds of goods that are presented. Or even the way an ethical food coop helped promote healthy or fairly-traded products.[4]

And perhaps the most important one:

- **Gain vs. Loss:** With a toss of a coin you have a 50% chance of winning or losing. A doctor can tell his patient that the recommended surgery has a 90% success rate, or a 10% failure rate. Each frame, though exactly the same, results in a different perception, and possibly reaction. As explored below, losses or potential losses tend to have more impact than gains. See below for a further exploration of this. (And **Chapter 5**.)

Framing for Gain or Loss

A key frame consideration is whether an outcome is presented as having a positive or negative impact. Consider this thought experi-

---

[3] The product's location in an aisle is also important. Products placed at the start of an aisle don't sell as well as those in the middle. The thinking? A customer needs time to adjust to physically being in the aisle, so it takes a while before they can decide where to focus attention and what to buy. *https://theconversation.com/the-science-that-makes-us-spend-more-in-supermarkets-and-feel-good-while-we-do-it-2385*.

[4] See these reports quoted in *#Hooked*. Chandon, P., Hutchinson, J. W., & Young, S. H. (2002). *Unseen Is Unsold: Assessing Visual Equity With Commercial Eye-Tracking Data.* Working paper; Lindgaard, G., Fernandes, G., Dudek, C., & Brown, J. (2006), 'Attention Web Designers: You Have 50 Milliseconds to Make a Good First Impression!'; *Behaviour & Information Technology*, 25(2), 115-126; Carter, R., & Frith, C. D. (1998). *Mapping the Mind.* University of California Press.

ment offered in *Science*[5] journal that demonstrates the potential for changing decisions based on how positively or negatively choices are framed.

Imagine a given disease is expected to kill 600 people. Two alternative programmes are available to tackle the disease. Respondents in two groups have to choose between options. Here are the choices:

Group 1
- Programme A: If this approach is adopted, 200 people will be saved.
- Programme B: If this approach is adopted, there is a one-third probability that 600 people will be saved, and two-thirds probability that no people will be saved.

Group 2
- Programme C: If this approach is adopted, 400 people will die.
- Programme D: If this approach is adopted, there is a one-third probability nobody will die, and two-thirds probability 600 people will die.

Looking at these rationally, the options are identical. The key difference is that the options offered to Group 1, are framed by the number of lives saved, and those offered to Group 2, by the number of lives lost. Group 1's choice produces a 'reference state' for possible gains and Group 2's for possible losses.

In Group 1, 72% of participants chose Programme A. In Group 2, 78% chose Programme D. What does this experiment tell us?

- When it comes to gains, we prefer a sure gain (prefer programme A over B).
- When it comes to losses, we avoid a sure loss (loss aversion), and are willing to take a risk (prefer programme D over C).

---

[5] See 'The Framing of Decisions and The Science of Choice', *Science*, 2011, pp. 433-458.

The experiment and these broad results have been replicated with students, university professors and even doctors—confirming the importance of loss aversion as a frame preference over gain. See **Chapter 5**, for more on this, but the simple learning is to frame your message in terms of possible loss if you're looking for maximum leverage. ('These precious ancient objects could be lost forever if we don't organise the conservation programme now.')

There's more evidence on the importance of perceived risk avoidance and loss from a US credit card company's marketing team. They sent a message to a sample of 250 card holders explaining the benefits of using their credit cards over cheques or cash. 50% of customers received a negatively framed message, the other 50%, a positively framed one.

- Group 1: 'This means that paying by cash is not only less convenient, but also much less secure.'
- Group 2: 'This means that paying by *XYZ Card* is not only more convenient, but also much more secure.'

Each group was also given additional, differently framed, reasons for using the card. Group 1 was told about the *disadvantages* of using cash. And for Group 2 the *advantages* of using *XYZ Card*.

The results were significant: Group 1 with the loss-framed messages *doubled* their use of the credit card compared to Group 2.

This simple, seemingly irrational, change in framing—from positive to negative—produces better responses from consumers or service users. A promotion which stresses what users/customers are missing out on is more powerful than one emphasising the benefits to be gained.

For an Amazon rainforest campaigner there is an obvious implication: stress how the loss of the forest will reduce life expectancy for native peoples, kill off species and cause global warming. *Don't* focus on the possible life saving drugs that might be developed from plants, or the outstanding beauty of the landscape.

The 'Mystery' of the Meaningless Change

The framing differentiator doesn't need to be as stark as plus or minus. It can be quite small and subtle, since we are often concerned with comparative value. People will weigh two or more options against each other and a major part of their decision comes from how these choices are presented. (The values compared can vary—money, time, quality, or some other appropriate metric.) Dan Ariely's case study, explained below, demonstrates this.

A group of potential holidaymakers are offered the choice of one of two all-expenses-paid trips to places they had not visited: one trip is to Rome and one to Paris. Both cities, we think you'd agree, are wonderful, and fun to visit. But there are big differences in culture, sightseeing and food, so they are hard to directly compare. And they are especially hard to compare for an audience who has not been to either.

The choice offered to the test group of potential visitors was in one sense quite difficult—and in another there was 'nothing to lose' since both cities and holidays were fabulous and free.

Ariely and his team then slightly changed just one small element to the offer. They explained to the potential beneficiaries that the Rome trip would *not* include a morning coffee as part of the break-fast package. The implication is simply that the participants might have to pay €2–€3 extra per day for a coffee. Ariely and his team noted that suddenly the original Rome trip seemed less attractive in comparison to the Paris option. Participants preferred the Paris option in significant numbers.

There are several interesting implications here:

- The participants had almost certainly not considered that coffee was part of the 'deal' originally. So why did this small change make a very significant difference in terms of preference?
- In any event they were certainly not making a rational assessment. Even on an 'all-expenses' trip you might reasonably expect to pay for a cup of coffee. (And €3 is not a lot.)

• The choice between two great European cities could be made on many grounds, but the price of coffee should not be one. (And anyway, you should really be comparing espresso with café crème here.)

What is happening is that the Rome trip now 'dims' by comparison as a good deal. And this minor, really irrelevant, distinction has a powerful effect, with almost 70% of the holidaymakers opting for Paris.

The holidaymakers might seem very foolish, but all that is happening is the impact of the negative consequences and comparison heuristics kicking in. The implication for fundraising might be that if you are asking a supporter to choose between you and a similar cause or proposition to support, do not be afraid to make a lot of a small advantage or distinction. It might just tip the balance.

The 'Mystery' of the Meaningless Offer: the Decoy Bias

In contrast to the irrational decision-making of the holidaymakers, you might imagine readers of *The Economist* magazine are very rational people and closely in touch with their System 2 processing. They surely would not make the same kind of mistake as the naïve would-be tourists. Ariely decided to check this out using a test based around a subscription offer for *The Economist*.

He compared the take up of a real advertisement for different subscription options to a version that he invented. He was keen to see in what way what he called an 'apparently pointless and meaningless choice' affected potential subscribers' behaviour. The potential subscribers in question were a selection of MIT students—and you are supposed to be very smart to get into this prestigious US university.

The original advertisement had three choices, each given equal billing:

• Choice 1: Access a web-only version of the magazine for $59.

- Choice 2: Receive the print only version by post for $125.
- Choice 3: Enjoy the print and web version for $125.

Advert 1

Economist.com	SUBSCRIPTIONS

OPINION
WORLD
BUSINESS
FINANCE & ECONOMICS
SCIENCE & TECHNOLOGY
PEOPLE
BOOKS & ARTS
MARKETS & DATA
DIVERSIONS
	Welcome to
	The Economist Subscription Centre
	
	Pick the type of subscriptions you want to buy or renew.
	
	❑ **Economist.com subscription:** US $59.00
	One-year subscription to Economist.com
	    Includes online access to all articles from
	    The Economist since 1997.
	
	❑ **Print subscription:** US $125.00
	One-year subscription to the print edition
	of *The Economist*.
	
	❑ **Print & web subscription:** US $125.00
	One-year subscription to the print edition
	of *The Economist* and online access to all
	    articles from *The Economist* since 1997.

It's clear that one of these options is a really poor deal. And the choices made by the MIT students followed what you might expect. 84% chose the combination option at $125. And 16% choose the web only option—presumably since it was cheaper. No one chose what was obviously the 'bad value' print-only option at $125.

Ariely then removed the 'print only' option that had been rejected before and repeated the experiment, to a second group of 100 similar MIT students. In this case the results are different—more people opted for the web only subscription. (See next page for the comparison payoff table.)

Advert 2

Economist.com	SUBSCRIPTIONS
OPINION	**Welcome to**
WORLD	**The Economist Subscription Centre**
BUSINESS	Pick the type of subscriptions you want to buy
FINANCE & ECONOMICS	or renew.
SCIENCE & TECHNOLOGY	
PEOPLE	❑ **Economist.com subscription:** US $59.00
BOOKS & ARTS	One-year subscription to Economist.com Includes online access to all articles from
MARKETS & DATA	*The Economist* since 1997.
DIVERSIONS	
	❑ **Print & web subscription:** US $125.00 One-year subscription to the print edition of *The Economist* and online access to all articles from *The Economist* since 1997.

Comparison Payoff Table

	Subscribers to Advert 1: *with* the print subscription	Subscribers to Advert 2: *without* the print subscription
Web Subscription: $59	16	68
Print Subscription: $125	0	Not available
Web and Print Subscription: $125	84	32
Total Income	$11,444	$8,012

What seems to be happening here is that Advert 1, the third option, acts as a 'decoy' encouraging subscribers to prefer one of the other options more directly. That's a 30% difference in sales for *The Economist* by the simple and rationally meaningless device of using a *decoy* price of a print subscription. You can see similar effects in, for example, the way Apple prices different offerings: compare the way different iPhone memory configurations are priced. Some options are clearly decoys. You can see the same phenomenon in different mobile phone/gas/electricity tariffs.

For a simpler example, the next time you're out for dinner pay attention to the restaurant menu. You will notice they often have two 'outlier' items, especially on the wine list. One of these is very expensive and the other is very cheap relative to all the other items on the menu. The purpose of the outliers is to make the middle range of the menu appear more reasonably priced—because we prefer to operate in the middle.[6]

The decoy bias is a powerful effect. How might you use it in a social context? We have used it in creating donor superclubs—membership schemes for groups of supporters. Typically, such a club will have three levels—for example, Gold, Silver, Bronze—with different benefits and price points.

Below is an example, adapted for client confidentiality, we created for a visual arts gallery.

Picasso Club	• meet the artist dinners after openings • chance to sponsor education programmes • invites to organised trips to galleries abroad • original lithograph • private members bar hire opportunities	£2,500
Mondrian Club	• meet the artist functions/pre-openings • chance to sponsor literature about artists • invites to organised trips to UK galleries • signed print	£1,000
Magritte Club	• print of painting and certificate • invites to openings • shared membership of UK galleries	£750

---

[6] This is sometimes called the *decoy approach*.

Essentially this works the same way as *The Economist* example. The Magritte Club is a poor deal when compared to the others. But when you include it, the Picasso Club looks like an even better deal. The options were tested on potential supporters of a gallery. See below for the two payoff tables on this framework. Version 1 is obviously a better deal financially for the gallery.

Version 1: With decoy

17 Picasso members	@ £2,500	= £42,500
28 Mondrian members	@ £1,000	= £28,000
6 Magritte members	@ £750	= £3,750

Version 2: Without decoy

8 Picasso members	@ £2,500	= £20,000
42 Mondrian members	@ £1,000	= £42,000

Just Because It's Meaningless Doesn't Mean It's Not Important

'Meaningless' changes or 'framing' can have a powerful real effect elsewhere—as evidenced in the interesting world of placebo medicine research. According to Barden[7] clinical studies have shown that:

- The colour of a tablet or pill can make a significant difference to a patient's experience. Two entirely harmless but ineffective red pills are reported by patients as being more effective in providing relief for high blood pressure than one red pill. (And for those interested in semiotics or *The Matrix*, blue pills beat red pills in terms of perceived and spurious efficacy.)

---

[7] *Decoded*, Phil Barden, Wiley 2014, p. 182.

- Patients and doctors both report that a substantial number of patients given a placebo experience the typical side effects of the real medication where these are known to the patients. In one double blind randomised control trial on chemotherapy drugs,[8] 30% of patients, confirmed by doctors, reported hair loss, nausea, etc. This was despite the fact they were being give safe but ineffective saline rather than real drugs.

The implications are quite profound. A psychological effect can have physiological impact.

Comparing in One Dimension

The $125 'print only' option in the Ariely experiment above was logically irrelevant. But it clarified the distinction between the other two options, making the 'combination' choice seem more valuable ... when compared to online or print only.

Ariely argues that this highlights a bias we have, which is to focus on one particular value aspect or dimension and only use that to compare other options available. This means the choice is made *relative* to the presence of the key value in the other options, rather than the absolute value of the specific different proposition itself. The implication? Identify the key unique selling point of what you're offering and focus on that. We see this with a not-for-profit agency like CHARITY: WATER. They focus a great deal not on how effective their programmes are, or how wide their geographic reach is, but rather on the fact every cent of a donor gift goes to the field.[9] That's their differentiating Key Success Factor. Is there a subtle implication that other agencies spend some of their donor money on 'wasteful' administration?

---

[8] Randomised clinical trials, ideally double-blinded with a placebo control, have become the gold standard for clinical research. Importantly, this approach can separate specific effects of an intervention from those due to variation in the natural course of disease and from placebo effects.

[9] www.charitywater.org/donate.

'Just Right': The Goldilocks Effect

Pause for a moment and choose one of these circles.

We don't *know* which you chose. But most likely, it was the one in the middle. The great majority of people will choose it. This tendency to go for the middle option of three choices has been tested numerous times over a number of years.

In one deeply prosaic example a researcher at the University of Chester, Dr. Paul Rodway, organised identical pairs of socks in a line. He then asked people to choose their favourite. The majority chose the middle pair, regardless of whether the socks were laid out horizontally or vertically. He even repeated the experiment with photos of socks. The result was the same. Most people choose the middle sock option.[10]

In hundreds of tests and experiments people are consistently more likely to choose the middle option when presented with three choices, regardless of what is being offered. If it's of interest, contestants who stand in the middle of the contestants in game shows like *The Weakest Link* are more likely to win.

This preference is called the *Goldilocks Effect* or the *Centre Stage Effect*. It doesn't just apply to the physical arrangement of choices. Marketers use this bias to encourage us to opt for a specific choice in any range. An obvious example is the choice of coffee sizes you can buy. Most, if not all, of the big chains give you a choice of small, medium and large.[11] Just like Goldilocks in the fairy tale, our default

---

[10] Architects know that if they design the entrance of a large building with three ways in, the majority of people will opt for the entrance in the middle. There is a wider cultural reference set too. Think of Jesus in Da Vinci's *Last Supper* painting—and even the bride and groom in the middle position at the wedding reception top table.

[11] Some companies, like Starbucks, go further and use language to change the framing, with the grande, venti, and trenta. That means you can ask for any size with-

mind tends to assume the small will be too small and the large may be too much. The one in the middle, therefore, seems 'just right.'

Of course, 'medium' is a matter of opinion or perception. If a coffee shop changes the size of the cups so the medium is bigger or smaller than it was before, most people will still choose a 'medium' (middle) coffee. Whether it is 12oz. or 20oz. Essentially, if it is positioned in the middle of other options it will be the most popular choice.

Tim Horton's, the Canadian coffee chain, took advantage of this psychological preference. It changed the size and price of its coffee range—and added an even larger 'extra large' option, which served to make what had once been a 'large' coffee now merely 'medium.' As ever, customers continued to choose the coffee in the middle. But now the 'middle' had moved, and was more expensive. The result? Tim Horton's sold more coffee by volume, at a marginal increase in cost to them, and made more profit.[12] We wonder if an ethical agency trying to encourage more modest consumption could resize portions to reduce sugar or calorie intake.

---

out being classed as 'mean' (small) or 'greedy' (large). And you can sound pretentious without it being your fault.

[12] The same effect is found in fast food restaurants when options are offered for different sizes of a soft drink. Here's an experiment from researchers at Berkley. Consider two sets of drink portfolios, the first composed of a 12oz., a 16oz, a 21oz. and a 32oz. drink, and the second is similar except that the 12oz. drink is not available. If some consumers are averse to buying the smallest size we should expect some participants who bought a 16oz drink in a condition where a 12oz. drink was available to purchase the 21oz. drink when the 12oz. drink is dropped, since the 16oz. drink is now the smallest sized drink available. We find consumers tend to shy away from the smallest and largest sized options. Consequently, dropping a 12oz. drink not only results in most 12oz. drinkers purchasing a 16oz. drink, but it also results in many of the 16oz. drinkers moving up to a 21oz. drink. Likewise dropping a 44oz. drink results in some 32oz. drinkers decreasing their purchase amount since it is now the largest drink available.

Kathryn Sharpe, Richard Staelin, Joel Huber *Using Extremeness Aversion to Fight Obesity: Policy Implications of Context Dependent Demand.* http://groups.haas.berkley. edu/marketing/sics/SICS%202007%20Papers/revised%20paper%20for%20SICS%20 conference.pdf.

People's tendency to want to avoid extremes and jump for the 'reasonable' middle option works well in fundraising. Oxfam use this technique, offering donors a choice between three donation levels.

You'll notice that there are three distinct options here:

- The £25 choice on the left may seem like quite a modest gift.
- The £100 option on the right may seem like a lot.
- £50 sits in the middle and also has a very concrete payoff highlighted.

The Paradox of Choice: Too Much Choice Makes Us Unhappy

Not only do we like restricted choice, but having too much choice seems to make us unhappy or uncomfortable. This is the Paradox of Choice—so called since people *claim* to want choice, but actually have an ambivalent attitude to it.

Have you felt unhappy about your choice after a purchase, even if it is perfectly fit for the purpose? Maybe you subsequently searched the internet looking for a better price, or a negative review, on something you have already bought? If so, you are suffering from what's called *buyer's remorse*—an aspect of the *paradox of choice* at work. Even if our ultimate decision is clearly correct, when we have selected from a number of options, we are less likely to be happy with the choice we made.

When people eat out, they often wish, even as they eat, they had chosen another dish, or the dish of another diner. When you buy a house, you may worry about which of several hard-to-compare options are best for you, and might toss and turn over the decision. Lots of choices makes settling on the perfect one harder.

Part of the reason for this is we get confused easily when given too much choice. To demonstrate this psychologists Mark Lepper and Sheena Lyengar conducted an experiment in a supermarket.

They set up a stall with customer tasting opportunities for high-quality jams. There were two versions of the experiment: one with 24 jam choices and one with just 6. The results are in the table below:

24 choices of jam	6 choices of jam
• Attracted 60% of shoppers	• Attracted 40% of shoppers
• Shoppers sampled 2 flavours on average	• Shoppers sampled two flavours on average
• 3% of shoppers bought jam	• 30% of shoppers bought jam

Clearly the restricted choice option drives more sales, from fewer people, with the same level of interest. (See also **Chapter 9,** on the need to reduce choice in order to reduce the processing pressure on our brains.)

Happiness seems to be *reduced* when there is too much choice because:

- It takes brain effort to evaluate multiple options, and that can be stressful and taxing.
- Opportunity cost, which is hard to assess, affects the way we value items and we may not have enough data.
- If we choose, and choose poorly, we will have only ourselves to blame and we don't like that possibility.[13]

This same experiment was repeated with chocolate and even student essay topics, with the same result.

A good example of this response to 'choice overload' in campaign engagement comes courtesy of Paul Vanags, in charge of individual giving at Oxfam GB.

---

[13] Psychologist Barry Schwartz wrote a great book, *The Paradox of Choice*, 2004. He debunks the idea, implicit in Western society, that freedom of choice makes us happy. In Schwartz's estimation, choice has made us not freer but more paralysed, not happier but more dissatisfied. To follow his thesis, watch a TED talk he gave. http://www.ted.com/talks/barry_schwartz_on_the_paradox_of_choice.

Supporters were emailed to take part in a climate change campaign. When they clicked on a link they were directed to one of three test webpages with a choice of different engagement options:

- *Option 1* offered two ways to help.
- *Option 2* offered six ways to help.
- *Option 3* offered twelve ways to help.

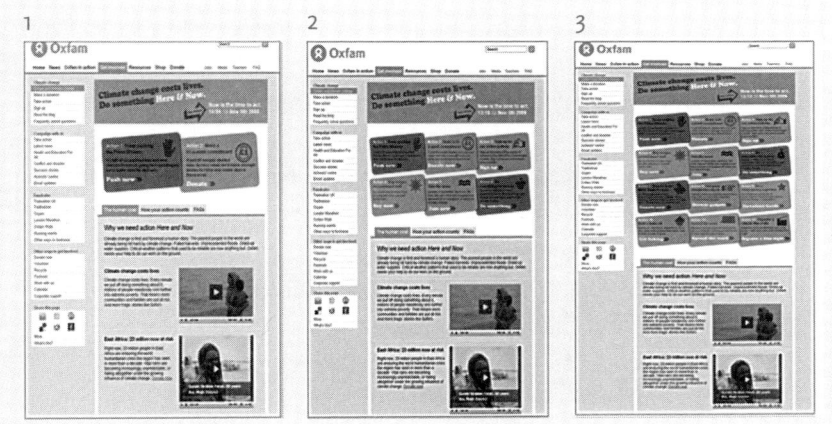

The Option 1, with only two choices, produced much higher response rates—almost three times as much as Option 3 and twice as much as Option 2. Why is this? In Option 1 the choices were more limited and so, easier. With less to choose from, responders felt more in control and satisfied with their choice. At the other end, 12 options was too many.

Psychic Numbing

Extreme comparisons can even trigger what is known as *psychic numbing* in potential supporters. This is especially important in fundraising or in campaigning, when the scale of the issues that you are trying to address is well outside the comprehension of an individual.

The idea of psychic numbing draws on a number of scientific studies on perception and response. (See on the next page) These have shown that we have a hard time detecting changes in stimuli when the stimulus intensity is very high. Put simply, when a problem gets too big we just can't process it. It is easier to notice differences when 'stimulus intensity' is lower. We can deal with topics or data that seem manageable to us. This in part explains why news broadcasters will often compare, say, flooding in Europe to 'an area the size of Wales,' or explain that the loss of rainforest in the Amazon as 'the equivalent of three football fields every minute.' Neither of the comparators is designed to do anything but make the facts more manageable for us to grasp.

This is very important in the public reaction to large-scale disasters. A very specific response seems to kick in as people assess the 'value' of saving lives. Distressingly, the broad principle is that the more lives that are at stake, the *less* valuable an individual life seems. The act of thinking about large-scale numbers of people suffering seems to reduce the strength of the emotional reaction we have. The experience of feeling overwhelmed by the scale of a tragedy then seems to reduce our willingness to donate or to act. We feel helpless, so we do less, or even nothing. We lack what's called agency.

Let's consider this in the context of fundraising. When we are confronted with a number of victims we may want to calculate the impact of any donation we might make in an objective and rational way—that is System 2 kicks in. But the impact on us of the tragedy is *lessened* when we cannot begin to imagine the numbers or scale of what has happened. So how do we begin to consider what it means to have 2.5 million refugees in Lebanon as result of the Syria crisis? That's too big a number for us to comprehend really. So we shut down some aspects of our response.

Partly this is because we don't deal with huge numbers on a daily basis. We might use System 2 to successfully hold a meeting with ten colleagues, buy five kilograms of apples, or manage 300 connections on LinkedIn. On the other hand, when presented with a manageable individual case that we can understand and address, we act in a stronger, more emotional way. In this situation System 1 kicks in and we connect through the identifiable victim effect.

A study on genocides by Paul Slovak, Psychology Professor at the University of Oregon, sheds some more light on this effect.[14] His study showed that increasing the scope of a crisis lowers the impact people *perceive* they can have by their intervention—hence they make lower donations. In an article for the American Psychological Society, Slovak studied the response to genocides on a community not directly affected—for example, exploring how US residents with no African connections responded to the Rwanda genocide among others. He noted that 'Most people are caring and will exert great effort to reserve "the one" whose needy plight comes to their attention. But these same people often become numbly indifferent to the plight of "the one" who is one of many in a much greater problem.'

The graphic below summarises this thesis. But it was maybe better summed up by Mother Theresa when she said: 'If I look at the mass I will never act. If I look at the one, I will.'

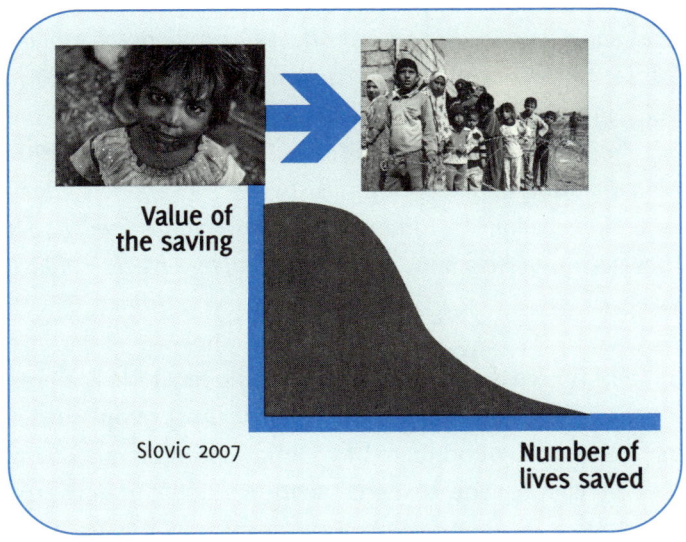

----

[14] For more on this visit http://www.apa.org/science/about/psa/2007/11/slovic.aspx.

Why We Want to Help Rokia, but Not All Her Friends

Other studies independently confirmed this finding. In one experiment for Save the Children two groups of similar potential donors were asked to support either a specific 7-year-old girl named Rokia who faced starvation in Zambia, *or* three million children facing starvation in the same country.

Here's the exact text for the two appeals. Decide which would be more likely to elicit a response from you—**A** or **B**?

A) *Any money that you donate will go to Rokia, a seven-year-old girl who lives in Zambia in Africa. Rokia is desperately poor and faces a threat of severe hunger, even starvation. Her life will be changed for the better as a result of your financial gift. With your support, and the support of other caring sponsors, Save the Children will work with Rokia's family and other members of the community to help feed and educate her, and provide her with basic medical care.*

B) *Food shortages in Africa are affecting millions of children. In Zambia, severe rainfall deficits have resulted in a 42% drop in maize production from 2000. As a result, an estimated three million Zambians face hunger. Four million Angolans—one-third of the population—have been forced to flee their homes. More than 11 million people in Ethiopia need immediate food assistance. They need your help now and by donating to Save the Children you can help.*

Which of these two appeals would you be most likely to respond to? You probably answered **A**. This is what most people did in this famous 'Rokia' study conducted by Deborah Small, marketing professor at Wharton. The research team working under Professor Small found that if organisations want to raise money for a cause, it is more effective in donation terms to appeal to the individual *heart* —and focus on individuals like Rokia—than to the mass *head*, which might say 'please help whichever person or persons is most in need.'

Perhaps more distressingly for those of us who are keen to win over hearts *and* minds, the Rokia study found that if a fundraising appeal highlighted Rokia *and* included data about overall need in the country, donors gave *less* than they did when the data was left out. (You may want to read that sentence again. It has some profound implications for anyone trying to change minds and behaviour.)

It gets worse. The real challenge of working too hard to get supporters to give with the head instead of the heart is most clearly illustrated in the final experiment of the Rokia study. This shows that simply activating logical, System 2, thought processes actually *reduced* charitable giving. When donors were asked to complete five simple logic problems- that is they were *primed* with a set of activities designed to stimulate rational thinking—*before* they were told about Rokia, they gave significantly less money. (For a more detailed explanation of this see **Chapter Nine**.)

The Rokia study points to a real challenge in initiatives to create 'educated' supporters and encourage them to give more and more rationally. Almost everyone in the field of fundraising would like to see supporters allocate their money based on a rational understanding of the size and relative challenge represented by the very considerable problems people face in different settings. Often this is presented as a desire for unrestricted money—'Give us support so we can put it wherever it is needed most.' (This is nowhere more evident than in the Syrian crisis.) But, sadly, what these studies tell us is that encouraging donors to consider their support in this rational way may undermine their 'natural' urge to give.[15] (For more on this see **Chapter 8**.) And if we share the *scale* of the challenges we're trying to address we may simply numb into inaction those we seek to engage.

---

[15] Reported in philanthropy.com/article/New-Research-Sheds-Light-on/163459. In another Slovic study, he found that people were more sympathetic to a single starving child than they were to two children facing the same plight. In the experiment, people were asked to give money to fight hunger overseas. In one scenario, the money would go to Rokia; in a second, to a boy, Moussa; and in a third, to both Rokia and Moussa. People gave equal amounts in the first two scenarios, but they donated less money to the two children combined.

Language and Framing

Previous studies have found that sections of the media systematically dehumanise refugees and other marginalized groups—partly through imagery, but also through language.[16] (The UK's *Daily Mail* and US *Fox News* are typical examples.) Sadly, it's not just the media. Former UK Prime Minister, David Cameron, for example, was widely quoted as referring to asylum-seekers in the Calais Jungle camp as a 'swarm.' Donald Trump was as bad—'Syrian refugees are Trojan horses.'[17]

Language can make a big difference in how situations and people are perceived. We've recently been working with the International Federation of the Red Cross and Red Crescent on helping change the language used to describe refugees. Some of the shifts are simple. In an experiment we conducted with UK donors, we asked them to support an online appeal across over 1,000 people using the phrase 'refugees in a group.' This produced many more positive responses, and higher gifts, than exactly the same appeal using the phrase 'a group of refugees.' A subtle language change seems to promote higher levels of empathy.

Of course, this doesn't just work with refugees. In a paper published in the *Journal of Experimental Psychology*, University of North Carolina Psychology Professor Kurt Gray looked at how subtle shifts in framing can alter the perception of groups.

His conclusion was that 'People generally perceive groups to have less "mind" than individuals.' His original experiment was carried out with participants being divided into three groups and asked to assess a group of accountants. The first group were asked about specified members of the firm and named individual workers. The second were asked about 'An accounting company comprised of 15 people.' The

---

[16] http://www.wired.co.uk/article/media-dehumanising-immigrants.

[17] https://www.nytimes.com/video/us/100000004648650/trump-likens-refugees-to-trojan-horse.html.

third group were asked to consider 'The 15 people who compose an accounting company.'

The participants asked to rate the three clusters on various measures, including ability to feel emotions. Respondents rated the 'people comprising the company' as equally capable of thoughts and decisions as the named, individual workers. They even rated them as more capable of experiencing emotion. This was in contrast to the group considering 'a company comprising of people.' Participants were much less likely to describe these individuals as capable of experiencing emotion.

Here's a reframing checklist you might find useful when appealing to supporters. It encourages you to consider whether the reframing should be cognitive, emotional or social.

Cognitive	Emotional	Social
• Change the measurement unit.	• Use powerful images to arouse feelings.	• Point out what other people are doing.
• Change the category definition.	• Tell an engaging and impactful story.	• Mention what people like your audience are doing.
• Change the values your offer embeds.	• Change the words or language used.	• Outline what aspirational figures are doing.
• Change the default option offered.	• Use a metaphor the audience can identify with.	• Refer to what experts are doing.

▶▶▶▶▶▶▶▶▶▶▶▶

Learning from Framing and Filling

By helping supporters make relevant comparisons we can guide them toward the key choices we want them to make. This fits into a broad behavioural framework or heuristic called *framing*.

We can influence people's decisions not only by giving them new information, but also by (re)framing the information. This framing can take a number of forms, and we need to choose the most appropriate.

People are highly sensitive to contextual and semiotic cues presented in communications. Changing a word or phrase here and there or representing the implication of an offer, or altering the colour of a product might seem tiny issues. But these changes are shown to have a measurable impact.

When we frame comparisons, we need to:

- **Understand the decision frame:** Many choices are not rational, and by trying to make them rational we may actually reduce engagement.
- **Create a frame:** That fits the cultural or social context of the supporter or person you're trying to influence. Don't make it complicated.
- **Prefer negative framing:** You get greater impact if you emphasise a potential loss. e.g. go on a diet to avoid the embarrassment of not fitting into your clothes.
- **Reduce risk:** Look for ways to implement a perception of reduced risk. e.g. for a non-profit emphasising how long you've been established, or your charity registration.
- **Re-frame value:** Breaking down an investment or a challenge into an understandable chunk can make it easier for the supporter to assess subjective value. 'It's as if *everyone in your town had diabetes*.'
- **Choose suitable comparisons:** Decide the comparison you want people to make—carefully selecting an appropriate metric. This can involve percentages or actual differences.

Don't give people too much choice, it's confusing, instead offer clusters of options to help. Maybe 3 or 4. Keep these to maximum and then if none of these options are attractive, offer a different 3 or 4.

Emphasise the individual or small group where their support can help them achieve agency. Be careful not to stun people with the scale of a challenge. 'Make sure Ashok is able to fulfil his musical potential.' Rather than '90% of children in UK state schools don't have music lessons.'

Be careful about the language you use—and do not be afraid to challenge language that reinforces stereotypes. Look for language that emphasises individuality and vulnerability.

Common sense suggests that emotions plus reason would have a stronger impact than emotions alone. But common sense is often wrong. Appealing to reason using facts and data will drive people to analyse and reflect and will block their emotional reaction. If you want people to think, appeal to reason. If you want them to act, appeal to emotions.

Chapter 5

Avoid Loss and Add Value

Summary

As indicated earlier, many studies suggest that the perception of *loss* —actual or potential—is more powerful, psychologically, than *gain*. This is so important it is worth exploring in more detail.

One specific implication is that someone who loses £100 in a transaction will experience a *decrease* in satisfaction *greater* than the same person will secure from a £100 gain. That's not logical but it is true. Nor is it a new observation. Adam Smith writing in 1759, showed he understood this: '*Pain ... is, in almost all cases, a more pungent sensation than the opposite and correspondent pleasure.*'[1] Apparently, we are programmed to avoid loss wherever possible.

The desire to avoid loss was identified by Kahneman and Tversky to explain the *endowment effect*. This effect suggests people place a higher value on something that they own, or that they helped create or add value to, than on something of identical objective value that they don't own or didn't add value to. As a result, we make irrational, System 1-based judgments on *perception*s of worth or value.

Loss aversion, plus the endowment effect, means that people feel more attached to current possessions than they rationally should. In a Thaler/Kahneman experiment, participants were given a mug, and asked what they thought it was worth. They were then told they

---

[1] Adam Smith, *The Theory of Moral Sentiments*, Edinburgh, 1759, p. 121.

owned it. Next, they were offered the opportunity to trade the mug for pens of equal value. Participants were reluctant. More than that, they asked for a premium in cash to swap the mug for the pens that was equivalent to *twice* the value they had put on the mug originally. The *perception* of ownership seemed to add significant value, and to give the mug up meant countering a perceived loss.

A related heuristic, *mental accounting*, creates separate 'budgets' in our heads. We seem to have virtual 'budgets' in our heads: typically one for entertainment, one for food, and a third for holidays etc. For each virtual budget we have a sense of how much we can, or should, spend. By understanding these budgets, and working across them, we can persuade people to buy more and perhaps donate more to different causes.

We Just Don't Like Losing

The documentary *The Armstrong Lie* opens with a tight close-up shot of the now notorious ex-cycling champion and cheat. He looks down at the camera and declares his philosophy. The slightly chilling verbatim quote is: 'I like to win, but more than anything, I can't stand this idea of losing. Because to me, losing means death.'

That quote explains a lot of about what Armstrong, and many athletes are willing to do for success. Now you might well look down on Armstrong and other drug cheats. But that basic philosophy is more widespread than we may care to imagine. Loss aversion can be summed up simply: we *like* to win, but we *hate* to lose.

Even something as simple as a coin toss can be used to demonstrate our widespread aversion to loss. Here's Kahneman's thinking:

'In my classes I say, I'm going to toss a coin, and if it's tails, you lose $10. How much would you have to gain on winning for this gamble to be acceptable to you?'

He goes on ... 'People want more than $20 before it is acceptable. And now I've been doing the same thing with executives or very rich people, asking about tossing a coin and losing $10,000 if it's tails. And they want $20,000 before they'll take the gamble.' To summarise, we're willing to leave a lot of money on the table to avoid the possibility of losing. And the same result seems to exist at scale.

Loss aversion isn't just confined to financial transactions. The basic principle applies more widely: in relationships, where we stay in failed marriages; in our cultural life, when we do not leave the theatre though we hate the show; and in business, carrying on with strategies that clearly are not working. What we are seeing here is a complementary anti-loss strand, the *sunk cost effect*, kicking in. With a revised decision comes the possibility that we'll make another wrong choice, or an even worse one. In contrast, sticking with the status quo feels much safer, even if we know it is not actually a good choice.

Like many decision heuristics, it is not clear *why* we have this aversion to loss. As we wrote in the opening pages of the book, this reluctance to take risks, some evolutionary psychologists believe, goes all the way to our early experience on the savannah. Loss aversion might confer a kind of evolutionary advantage. Perhaps we are hardwired to try and hold on to what we have.

Some behavioural economists, while recognising the original evolutionary advantage think it may hold less true now. In a fast changing world we as a species may need to be more risk-taking and more entrepreneurial—and more open to the possibility of loss. That may prove to be correct in the long term. But for the moment, the reality is that loss aversion is a significant powerful heuristic.

Framing for Loss in Marketing

The framing of any question can make a clear difference to whether it is perceived either as a loss or a gain. (Revisit **Chapter 4** if you need to refresh on *framing*.) For example, would you rather get a £5 discount, or avoid a £5 surcharge? Both outcomes involve exactly the same change in price when paying for a product or service. But the fact that they are framed differently has a marked effect on consumer behaviour. Which would you prefer?

Or think about this offer for Amazon gift vouchers. Which would you choose on first look, and which *actually* is the best deal?

Or consider these two

In some countries credit card companies insist petrol stations advertise their pricing policy as charging less for cash payment (gain), than charging more for credit card payments (loss). This way they encourage consumers to use their cards. And in a recent study of consumer reaction to price changes in insurance policies, researchers found price *increases* had twice the effect on customer switching, compared to price *decreases*. More evidence for the loss aversion preference.

A variation on loss, potential loss, is also found in the influence guru, Cialdini's work, mentioned in **Chapter 7**. For him 'scarcity' is a key influence principle. He demonstrates that things—service, goods, opportunities—are more attractive when their availability is limited, or when we stand to lose the opportunity to secure them on favourable terms.

For example, we might buy something that otherwise we would not, if we are told that it is the last one, or that a special offer will soon expire. We can see the impact of this thinking across a range of marketing messages: 'Book now and avoid disappointment.' 'When it's gone it's gone.' 'Only five seats left at this price' etc. Here is an example from Expedia online.

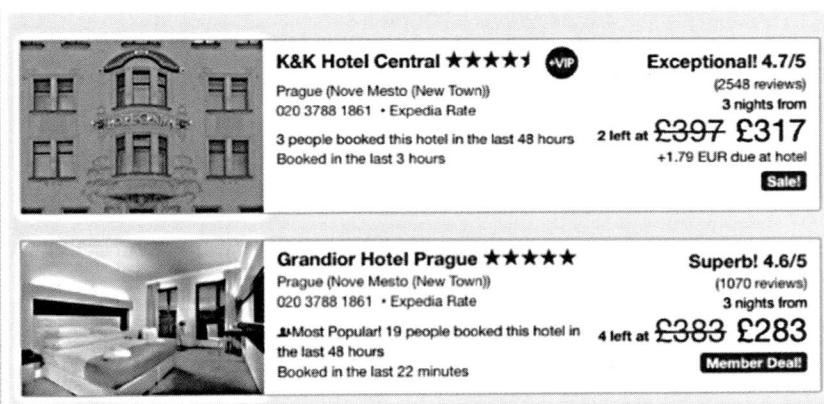

There are, in the original web version, little messages in red and green designed to make you act … before the hotels are gone! You would hate to miss out on this opportunity, even though, logically, it means you might miss out on the *next* opportunity.[2]

And in Life

There are other examples of the effect from everyday life. You're at a film and after ten minutes you decide you don't really like it. But you decide to stick it out for the whole two hours, every minute hating it more and more. Why do you behave like that? Decision science suggests that as you have paid for the ticket, you do not want to 'waste money' by not seeing the film. Logically this doesn't make

---

[2] Note also the semiotics of the colours of the information. Green to say 'go' and red as a 'warning.'

sense. You won't get the ticket money back by staying, so why do you feel like you have to?

Economists refer to this variation of loss aversion as the *sunk cost fallacy*. Sadly, we're inclined to throw good money after bad when we have committed to a specific action. (The alternative would be to admit that we had lost the money or time invested. And by implication that we had made a poor judgement.)

Governments, companies, and, sadly, charities too, very often continue policies or strategies when they are clearly not working. Gamblers carry on gambling to avoid acknowledging what they've already spent or lost. We carry on driving along a route that almost certainly is wrong in the hope it might work out right.

Generally, we are prepared to carry on with a plan, hoping for a gain, even if this might involve a bigger loss in the long run.

As you can see loss aversion neatly complements the *endowment effect* heuristic—the tendency for people to place a higher value on something they own than on an identical thing that they do not. (See **Chapter 4** for more on this, and below for the *IKEA* effect variant.)

Fundraising and the Threat of Loss

In a fundraising setting you can see the effects of loss aversion as a driver of behaviour very clearly. At The Management Centre (=mc), Bernard and his colleagues are proud to have worked with The Dian Fosse Gorilla Fund for a number of years, helping them to secure the future for the world's gorillas.

By testing a number of different approaches, we have learned that stories like the one below, which emphasises the *threats* to gorillas and their habitat, have a much more powerful impact than ones which stress the real *progress* in saving the gorillas that has been made.

Helping people. Saving gorillas.™

PROGRAMS   WAYS TO GIVE   GORILLA BLOG   LEARNING & FUN   DIAN FOSSEY   NEWS & EVENTS   ABOUT US

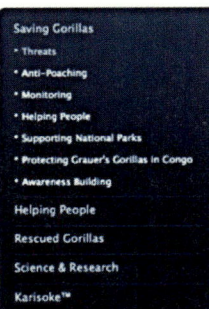

Saving Gorillas
- Threats
- Anti-Poaching
- Monitoring
- Helping People
- Supporting National Parks
- Protecting Grauer's Gorillas in Congo
- Awareness Building

Helping People

Rescued Gorillas

Science & Research

Karisoke™

Where We Work

Threats to Gorilla Survival and Conservation

All types of gorillas in Africa are endangered, primarily due to human activity such as poaching, disease transmission, and habitat destruction.

Ultimately, human poverty is the greatest threat to gorillas. They live in countries in Africa with some of the highest population densities and lowest adult life spans, literacy rates, and standards of living in the world. The challenges that such intense poverty brings to gorilla conservation vary depending on where in Africa the gorillas live. Western gorillas, which inhabit 11 west African countries from Nigeria to Angola, are primarily threatened by illegal hunting for food, habitat loss from logging,

You can also see a similar impact for other agencies and sectors:

- World Wildlife Fund (WWF) asking us to 'save the last few' rhinos or elephants alive in Kenya or Zimbabwe'.
- Greenpeace seeking support to save the Brazilian rainforest which is disappearing at a rate of two football fields a minute.
- The National Gallery in London seeking support to ensure a painting is not 'lost' to a gallery in the USA.

Marketers exploit our awareness of loss aversion and try to engage us by finding ways to mitigate it. For example, offering 'try before you buy' periods and 'risk free returns.' In addition, these techniques make use of a consumer's preference to value any product or service *more* after they have acquired it, the endowment effect, and made it part of their status quo.

In the not-for-profit world you see organisations like CHARITY: WATER, mentioned in the previous chapter, offer a guarantee to supporters that '100% of your donation goes to the cause,' implying that no money will be 'lost' in administration. In fact, they simply have a restricted fund led by a small group of donors that meets these administrative costs. The implication is the total amount that goes to the cause, and the amount that goes to beneficiaries, is the same. Again, this is not logical but many supporters find this 'all your cash goes to the cause' framing compelling.

Bad News Beats Good News

An insightful and challenging blog by leading fundraiser and marketer, Jeff Brooks, explains yet another dimension of loss aversion. The blog begins with this great headline, and follow-up.

'I Have Terrible, Awful, Unbelievably Horrible News'

'Did I get your attention?'

'I think so. You could hardly help but take notice, because your brain is wired to pay more attention to negative information.'[3]

Brooks goes on to report on a Welcome Trust funded study from the Institute of Cognitive Neuroscience at University College London run by Professor Lavie and a team of colleagues. The team showed fifty participants a series of words on a computer screen. Each word appeared for only a fraction of a second—at times only one fiftieth of a second. This is too fast for anyone to consciously read and understand the word.

The words were either *positive* (e.g. cheerful, flower, peace), *negative* (e.g. agony, despair, murder) or *neutral* (e.g. box, ear, kettle). After each word, participants were asked to recall whether the words they were shown were neutral or 'emotional' (positive or negative), and how confident they were of their decision.

The result was they more accurately recalled clusters of negative words. Even though they didn't consciously see any words at all. It seems we pay more attention, even subconsciously, to the negative.

---

[3] Jeff Brooks' blog post is here. http://www.futurefundraisingnow.com/future-fundraising/2016/02/why-bad-news-works-in-fundraising.html.

Maybe this isn't surprising. Evolutionary psychology tells us we need to be able to respond super quickly to information. As Brooks says, 'We can't wait for our consciousness to kick in if we see someone running towards us with a knife or if we drive under rainy or foggy weather conditions and see a sign warning "danger."'

Those of us involved in social change need to note that people respond more strongly and quickly to problems and negative situations than they do to positive, unthreatening messages. This is challenging news for many agencies who prefer to share positive images of what might be, and seek support for that. For example, many INGOs have strict guidelines about the kind of images they will use to portray children—in particular, they want them to be positive representations of the people they work with. But there is a huge weight of evidence that negative beats positive in fundraising terms. This is a conflict.

UK readers might recall the poor fundraising performance of the *Lift Lives Up* campaign, which showed positive images of the very real good that Oxfam's support had done. The campaign was well executed, but it did not key into this powerful heuristic.[4]

Brooks summarises the fundraising learning from his experience, 'If your fundraising message is: Everything is great! Please give to keep it that way!' You're swimming upstream against basic human psychology. Instead, he says, 'make your message: Problem! Help solve it!' Just to be clear—we don't like this reality, it's just true.

Mental Accounting

Mental accounting helps us understand another interesting aspect of loss aversion. In 2006, psychologists at the University of Pennsylvania ran an experiment in a US apartment block. It was an upscale

---

[4] To find out more on this case study see http://www.campaignlive.co.uk/article/oxfam-launches-lift-lives-good-fundraising-campaign/1225720, and to see an example of the adverts try https://www.youtube.com/watch?v=n2zymuD83aM.

building where most people were wealthy and would have no problem buying everyday products or services.

One day, the researchers left out a bowl of M&M-type sweets in the reception area. Beside the bowl was a small scoop. At the end of the day the researchers noted how many sweets were taken. The next day they refilled the bowl with the same sweets. But this time they placed a much larger scoop alongside.

Just like Brian Wansink's ice cream experiment outlined in **Chapter 3**, when the scoop size was increased, people helped themselves to more sweets—in this case on average 66% more.

Of course, residents could have taken just as much on the first day by taking additional scoops. But in the same way that larger serving sizes, as promoted by McDonald's and fast food chains, encourage people to eat more, the larger scoop encouraged the residents to take more.

The experimenters were clear from follow up research this was not to do with people simply being greedy. Part of the explanation is that it is simply *easier* for our System 1 brains to count 'scoops' and use that as the measure, rather than trying to work out the total weight of the sweets taken. Scoops act as a kind of mental accounting unit and that neatly sidesteps the real issue of the number of sweets, or calories, eaten.

Richard Thaler explored the consequences of this kind of systematically irrational behaviour in his book *Nudge*. (See **Chapter 3**) It was he who coined the term *mental accounting*. He thinks the scoops of 'M&Ms' are part of a system people have of specific accounts that relate to different parts of our lives. We have an account for health, one for holidays, one for philanthropy etc. These kinds of accounts tend to help us think a little faster, and therefore seem more efficient to our System 1 brains. But they also distort our decisions.

Businesses sometimes try to deliberately confuse us and our budgets. If you go to a casino you have to play with plastic chips, designed neither to look nor feel like real money, but rather to appear like a child's counters. We are less reserved about using the 'toy money,' which comes from our mental play/entertainment budget —and so may overcommit ourselves financially.

Thaler came up with two experimental scenarios that elegantly demonstrate further examples of our flawed mental accounting at work:

Q1: Imagine you have decided to see a movie and have paid the admission price of $10 per ticket. As you enter the theatre, you discover that you have lost the ticket. The seat was not marked, and the ticket cannot be recovered. Would you pay $10 for another ticket?
46% of participants said they would buy another ticket. He then asked:

Q2: Imagine you have decided to see a movie where admission is $10 per ticket. As you enter the theatre, you discover that you have lost a $10 bill. Would you still pay $10 for a ticket to the movie?
The scenario is exactly the same in terms of outcome, but he got a very different response—88% of participants said they would buy a new movie ticket.

This is clearly not rational. The *loss* in both situations is the same—$10. So why the big change? According to Thaler, we see going to a movie as a *transaction*—ticket price in exchange for film. But buying a second ticket to replace the lost one, he says, makes the mental cost of the movie too expensive, since a single ticket now 'costs' $20. It *feels* as if we have bought two tickets for the same seat. If, however, we lose *money* to the same value as a ticket, we don't post the 'loss' to the movie mental account, and therefore we don't mind finding another $10.

Of course, this is neither logical nor even consistent behaviour. These contradictory decisions, Thaler says, violate an important principle of classical economics, that money is fungible: a dollar, pound or euro is always a dollar, pound or euro. (But because the System 1 brain engages in mental accounting, we end up thinking about money very differently.)

In another experiment, when Thaler asked people if they would drive 20 minutes out of their way to secure a $5 discount on a $15 calculator, 68% said 'yes.' However, when he asked whether they would drive 20 minutes out of their way to secure a $5 discount on a $125 leather jacket, only 29% said they would.

Clearly the decision about the level of effort required to secure a $5 discount was not dependent on the *absolute* amount of money being laid out. The decision depended on the particular *mental profit & loss account* that the decision would be posted to.

In the case of the inexpensive calculator, it appears the savings to be gained activated a mental P&L which made people inclined to make the journey. But that same $5 seems to become irrelevant when framed in the context of a much larger purchase. This phenomenon links strongly to *framing*, discussed in **Chapter 4**.

Organisations often fall victim to mental or 'depart-mental' accounting when they run short of money in one area while under-spending in another. Because of mental accounting they are not able to transfer the money to where it is needed.

But some social agencies like Kiva (www.kiva.com) or Lend with Care (www.lendwithcare.com) have turned mental accounting to their advantage. They describe your contribution as a 'loan,' not a 'gift' or 'donation.' This allows you to contribute to the cause from your mental loan or investment account, rather than your charitable giving one. The implication? It is worth spending some time thinking about the different accounts your supporters have and how you can engage them.

Phone Philanthropy

Text-to-donate is a popular and powerful way to collect cash and contact details for a range of charity causes. Donors send a short code text message and a fixed amount—£5 or £10—is taken from their mobile phone account and transferred to the charity.

Research suggests that this approach is popular partly because it is easy, but also because, as with Kiva or Lend With Care, the donation comes out of a different mental account. When you text, a gift comes from the phone bill account rather than your philanthropy account. It also doesn't reduce the amount of money in your wallet, purse or pocket which is what happens when you take actual cash out to donate to a collection pot.

Moving mental accounts can be useful to secure funds, especially when the 'account' doesn't seem to involve cash or near cash.

More recently, partly to get around the challenge of people having less cash on them these days, a number of UK charities have begun to use electronic collection boxes—using contactless technology instead of static collection boxes for cash. Some of these boxes have been placed next to the regular contactless machines in cafes, making the process of donating effortless.

Hertzberg, Donors, and Loss

You may be familiar with Herzberg's ideas on hygiene factors and motivators in social psychology. Bernard and his colleagues in =mc have adapted this model for fundraisers, as it's ideal when considering the issue of *possible loss* for donors. We have seen this work particularly strongly with HNWI. Hertzberg's model describes two important clusters of drivers:

Hygiene factors: These are factors which if not present cause dissatisfaction or unhappiness. In a work setting the lack of proper equipment, or poor administrative systems or a lack of a formal performance management system, will often be a *hygiene factor*. Herzberg's research showed that if these elements are *missing* there will be unhappiness, but if they are *present* they simply take an individual to a point of neutrality.

Motivators: Hertzberg's research shows that there is another cluster of activities or factors—*motivators*—that cause feelings of positivity or engagement, taking you beyond neutrality. Again, in a work setting, these might include praise from a senior staff member, bonuses for work done exceptionally well, etc. It is these factors that help change behaviour. In general, they are distinct from the hygiene factors.[5]

Applied to fundraising the parallel is obvious.

Hygiene factors are those that ensure a donor—and particularly a major donor—feels that an agency will safely use their money. These might include: a strategic plan, a governance structure, clear and positive accounts, a stewardship model etc. None of these things will *motivate* a donor to offer support. But if missing they might *discourage* a donor.

These factors when present make the supporter feel neutral towards the cause. We need to draw on a different cluster to drive change.

Motivation factors are those that ensure a donor—again, more particularly a major donor—feels engaged and excited. This list includes a personal commitment to the cause, the possibility of personal or family advancement, a sense of affinity with a group, a sense of personal spiritual reward, etc. When present these will *motivate* a supporter to engage.

When you are trying to engage a potential supporter you need to be clear about what their personal hygiene factors and motivators are.

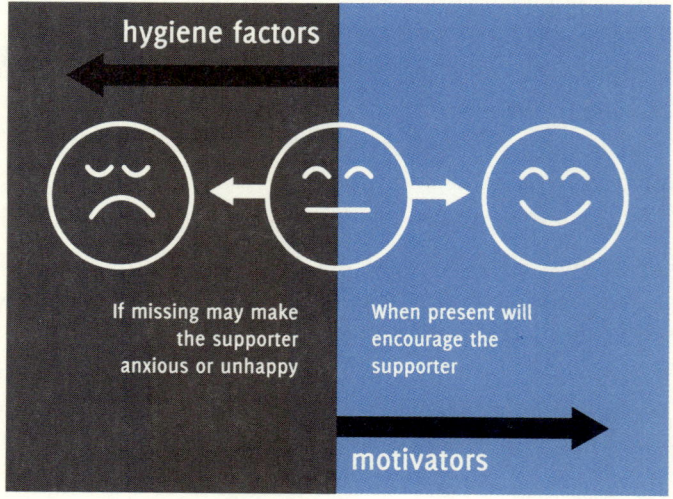

---

[5] Applied to consumers you might see an endorsement by an accrediting agency or a well-established track record as hygiene factors, and a high performance product or a guaranteed result as motivators.

Major donor fundraisers also know that many HNWI are keen not just to give money to a project but to be involved in developing and even implementing a solution. This may be closely related to people's strong desire for control.

Donating Through Denial

Control could be seen to be an important part of popular charity campaigns to give up or reduce the intake of alcohol or chocolate. These can be seen to go back to the ancient Catholic tradition of Lent where believers give up something for a period of 40 days. A number of these campaigns in the UK focus on the healthy desire to reduce alcohol intake e.g., Go Sober for October, Dryathon, and Dry January.[6]

Meredith Niles, Executive Director of Supporter Engagement and Fundraising for Marie Curie in the UK, has an interesting take on the desire for control and the popularity of 'self-denial' campaigns. She thinks the popularity of these campaigns is less filling a desire on the part of the supporter to exhibit control over themselves and more about the 'martyrdom effect.' Doing something painful is more likely to inspire others to donate than doing something perceived as easy.[7] See later in this chapter for more on this.

Whatever the precise driver, going back to the experiment at the start of this chapter, people are more willing to take a bet on a coin *they* flip, than on a coin *someone else* flips.

---

[6] There has been an increase in the number of 'self denial' campaigns that have successfully taken off in recent years. If you're looking for more information http://fundraising.co.uk/2016/02/24/10-self-denial-fundraising-campaigns-2 has insights on how charities have worked to involve supporters in giving up chocolate, alcohol, treats, and even coffee.

[7] For more on Meredith Niles' view see this useful and relevant piece of research. https://www.ncbi.nlm.nih.gov/pmc/articles/PMC3613749/.

Donate More Tomorrow

Those clever people at the UK's Nudge Team, BIT, used a nice variant on loss aversion to help charities. They worked with a large retail chain called Home Retail Group—which owns a number of major UK stores such as Argos and Homebase—and the Charities Trust, a donations management agency. The aim of the joint project was to identify a new way of encouraging charitable giving in the workplace using a process known as auto-escalation.

The approach was based on the well-established US scheme called Save More Tomorrow (SMT), discussed in **Chapter 2**. This scheme encourages individuals to be proactive in saving for their retirement. It uses a simple mechanic of asking them to save more ... but not until they get their next pay rise.

Note that people have an interesting attitude to time—especially the difference between our current and future selves. For example, when offered snack choices, three-quarters of Danish workers chose fruit over chocolate for the following week's delivery, but the majority opted for chocolate *now*.

The link to 'loss aversion' is that if you ask people to save more *today* they are immediately and concretely aware that they will have less in their take-home pay—a loss. But a general commitment to save more *tomorrow* offers a lesser sense of pain, or at least pain postponed. And by committing to an increased contribution—auto-escalation—when we secure a wage rise we experience no perception of immediate loss. The whole process seems easier and less painful.

The BIT team adapted this model. They asked company employees to commit to auto-escalation of their payroll-giving in the workplace to specific charities. The target was to persuade individuals to commit to an increase of 3% a year.

As is often the case with real world situations, the scheme did not immediately work. The initial take-up was low—only 10% of new donors opted in. So, the BIT team changed the scheme. This made automatic enrollment to the scheme the default option. But, of course, employees were able to opt out. The donation rate with this default approach rose dramatically by 49%. BIT estimated that this approach could raise an extra £3 millions a year for charities if it was adopted across all existing payroll giving schemes.

The auto upgrade technique in the charity world is, however, controversial, especially when not made completely transparent. In 2012 World Vision Canada[8] attracted a storm of criticism from the media and some supporters when they automatically upgraded donations from regular supporters on annual renewal. In fairness, they had sent a letter explaining this would happen. But the notification was 'buried' in a host of other information. The technique worked in terms of income growth, but the media controversy caused bad PR. World Vision apologised and promised to be more transparent the in future.

There is a distinct difference between a deferred conscious 'loss,' even one that benefits a good cause, and one where the customer or supporter is not clearly aware of the implication of the auto-upgrade.

The IKEA Effect

The *IKEA Effect* is the name given to a version of the endowment heuristic in which we value something more if we have had a hand in 'making' it. The value we perceive is increased out of all proportion to the objective value our efforts contribute. The first experiment to demonstrate this effect was undertaken and published in 2011 by Dan Ariely, Michael Norton and Daniel Mochon, of Duke University, Harvard Business School, and Yale University respectively. The experiment is discussed in the box below.

---

[8] You can read a full account of the controversy here http://agentsofgood. org/2012/04/opt-inopt-out.

The IKEA Effect: DIY as Added Value

Dan Ariely and his colleagues were keen to find out the extent to which people would see added value, and pay a higher price, for products that involved them in self-assembly. They conducted three separate experiments as part of a series to explore the *added value through assembly* hypothesis.

The first experiment gave the project its name. Participants were asked to put together some pieces of IKEA furniture. The experimenters then priced the pieces the subjects had made, as well as some pieces which had been assembled separately and professionally. (Some of the self-assembly pieces, as you might imagine, were not very well put together.) Subjects were offered an opportunity to buy a piece from either the ones they had made, or those professionally put together. The result? They were willing to pay more for items they assembled themselves, regardless of the technical quality of the assembly.

The second experiment involved origami. One group of amateur 'makers' were asked to fold origami frogs or cranes. They were then asked how much they would be willing to pay for their own creations.

Another group, 'buyers', who had not taken any part in making the origami creatures, were asked how much *they* would be willing to pay.

Finally, both clusters were asked a follow-up question about how much they would be willing to pay for a similar origami creature made by an origami expert.

As you might expect the 'buyers' group, acting more objectively, were willing to pay more for the expertly built piece than the 'makers.'

The original 'makers' group were then asked to review a display. The display consisted of the set of origami figures they had made themselves and the set that had been made by experts. These subjects were asked to bid on the different 'expert' and 'amateur' made origami. As you might expect, the amateur 'makers' valued the origami they created as highly as the, objectively rather better, ones created by professionals.

The IKEA effect might not strictly seem at first to be an aspect of *loss aversion* since it 'adds' value. But we believe it is a complementary heuristic that links strongly to endowment.[9]

---

[9] This connects to a further significant body of research in motivational thinking which suggests that people actually *like* work rather than disliking it. (More in line with what is called Theory Y management thinking.)

The effort that people add doesn't need to be substantial. There are some nice commercial examples that reinforce this. For example, when 'instant' cake mixes were introduced in the 1950s they were expected to be an overnight success. (This was part of a general move to make 'domestic' work easier and more fun by reducing the effort involved.) The Betty Crocker Company even introduced mixes where you simply had to add water to the mix and put in the oven. Et voila, perfect cake!

The target market though—mostly American housewives—was slow to take up the product, and sales were weak. Research showed consumers recognised the all-in-one mix made baking easier and almost idiot proof. But it was almost too easy and standardised. This had the effect of making the consumers' skill and effort seems less valuable. Responding to a desire from the target market to appear like a real cake maker, the solution from the manufacturers was to change the recipe so that users were required to do *more*–to add an egg. This relatively minor 'effort' by the cake maker improved sales. People felt they were *really* baking.

In the same irrational vein, the Build-a-Bear Workshop offers people the 'opportunity' to construct their own teddy bears. And the store is able to charge a premium over ready-made bears for doing so. How odd. In a business setting you might imagine that if you ask people to contribute labour to a service or product they would expect a discount. In fact, there's some significant evidence, this example included, to suggest that, within reason, asking someone to add their own labour and giving them some agency[10] actually *adds* value to an experience for them.

Many charities recognise that active volunteering, as well as fundraising, is a vital and valued part of their supporters' experience.

---

[10] Agency can be created really simply. In one experiment, mentioned in *Hooked*, researchers at the University of Toronto assigned participants to one of two experiments. In Experiment 1 participants were given word pairs that either rhymed or were linked, like *sweet-sour*. In Experiment 2 participants were given word pairs where one of the words was fully spelled out. Following this both sets of participants were asked to recall the word pairs. The Experiment 2 participants scored on average 85% for recall. Those who were 'given' the words scored 69%. We like to do a bit of work!

In The Management Centre's recent work on the global engagement strategy for the International Federation of Red Cross and Red Crescent Societies the focus has been on creating opportunities for three kinds of engagement from supporters:

- **Time:** Asking supporters to volunteer providing services such as first aid, counselling, charity-shop volunteering.
- **Treasure:** Asking supporters to give money in various forms, cash, bequests, shares, etc., to the cause.
- **Talent:** Seeking ideas and advice from supporters to improve delivery.

The thesis here is that supporters feel more engaged when charities combine these three elements and enable them to add value in different ways.

In other charity or fundraising contexts people enjoy a range of opportunities to 'take part' which involve effort. For example, one of the largest UK charity events is the Macmillan Coffee Morning where people try their hand at baking, many for the first time, to raise funds for this cancer support charity.

Supporters seem to *enjoy* the extra work involved in making and selling their baking efforts for a good cause. Moreover, participants often demand, and attract, a premium price when they sell their baked goods precisely *because* they are homemade. (Bernard made a rather sad-looking pizza. It was not technically worth the £1.50 a slice he charged for it at the coffee morning we organised in our office. But he was determined to charge it, and people seemed happy to pay.)

This is just one example of a growing baking phenomenon. According to research by the Charities Aid Foundation (CAF), the *Great British Bake Off,* a popular UK TV show, inspired an estimated six million people to take part in charity bake sales in 2015. Based on a survey of a representative sample of more than 1,000 adults, the research found that:

- In the previous 12 months 8% of people baked for charity and 30% bought food from a charity bake sale.
- Baking for charity was most popular among 25-34 year olds, with 13% of them baking for a good cause.
- 63% of respondents agreed that raising money for charity is a good reason to do something they enjoy.
- 58% of those surveyed agreed that bake sales and charity bake offs make fundraising fun.
- 20% of respondents even agreed that cake 'tastes better' when it has been baked for a good cause.

The overall result was that in 2015 bake sales in the UK helped raise an estimated £185 million for charities.

Why does it add value to ask people to do more? According to Dan Ariely, quoted in *Decoded,* 'Our prehistoric ancestors spent much of their waking hours foraging for and consuming food, and that instinct obviously paid off. Today this instinct is no less powerful, but for billions was it satisfied in the minutes it takes to swing by the store and pop a meal in the microwave? With our physical needs sated and time on our hands, increasingly we are finding psychological outlets for this drive by seeking out and consuming concepts.'

By asking service users or customers or supporters to do extra or to contribute in a practical way to a project, we can add value for them, and create extra value for our cause. If you're not sure if your supporters are ready to volunteer take a look at TripAdvisor—despite being a transparently commercial service it has 200 million reviews on it from 300 million visits by 'volunteers' every month. That's cyber activism!

Doing Good ... While Feeling Pain

Researchers are looking increasingly closely at how different aspects of human behaviour can contribute to philanthropic or supportive feelings and action. Christopher Olivola, a graduate student in psychology at Princeton, has suggested that fund-raising events that involve pain, such as marathons or even walks across shards of glass or burning coals, might sometimes spur bigger gifts than pleasurable events, such as picnics or dinners.

In one study Olivola compared the actions of two sets of participants in a group decision-making activity. One group had to put their hands in freezing water before contributing to a cause. And a second group were simply asked to donate. The group who went through the 'ice cold pain trial' gave more than those who did not suffer. Olivola suggested the reason for this was the *martyrdom effect*. 'When you have to work hard and suffer for a cause, then you become more involved and more motivated to help that cause.'

Consider how this insight informs campaigns like the Ice Bucket Challenge, involving pouring ice cold water over yourself—or any endurance events that seem to involve more pain than is strictly necessary to deliver a charitable result.

It is All About Engagement

The Red Cross and Red Crescent, Macmillan and others may be onto something important about engagement, informed by Minjung Koo and Ayelet Fishbach's research work on linking generosity and your sense of self.[11] Their work suggests generosity and commitment to causes improves when giving is personal and involves multiple touch points.

---

[11] Minjung Koo and Ayelet Fishbach, *Giving the Self: Increasing Commitment and Generosity Through Giving Something That Represents One's Essence*. Social Psychological and Personality Science 1948550616628607, first published online February 2, 2016.

In a series of elegant linked studies, psychologists Koo Graduate School of Business (SKK) and Fishbach (University of Chicago Booth School of Business) explored the impact of various types of giving on the giver themselves. These included:

- Contributing to an endowment
- Anonymous vs. personalised notes to people with disabilities
- Donating blood vs. money
- Signing a petition for future giving

The researchers' positive conclusion is summarised by Koo, 'Giving something that represents the self, such as one's own blood, signature, or possessions, will lead the giver to perceive herself as a more generous and committed person, compared to giving that is less associated with the self, like monetary giving. This change in self-perception has an important implication: The giver is more likely to give again in the future.' Put simply, the more ways someone supports an organisation, and the greater their active multi-point engagement with the cause, the more loyal they become.

These are the experiments underpinning this:

- **Let it go:** In their first study, the research team explored the impact on 'givers' when they gave up an item they believed they owned long-term versus those who believed the offer was a short term 'chance to use.' (The study group was 50 South Korean students.) 50% of the participants were told at the start of the study they could keep the pen they had been given at the end of the experiment. The other 50% were told they had to return the pen. At the close of the session all participants were, in fact, asked to donate the pen to a good cause. Those who gave up the pen for the cause, having 'owned it' reported feeling more generous and committed than those who expected to only temporarily use it. In line with Ariely's 'IKEA effect' the group who had briefly owned the pen also perceived it as more valuable.

- **Blood is thicker than money:** The research team ran two complementary studies comparing the feelings associated with donating blood and donating money. The target group was 80 US workers who were already blood donors. The volunteers were offered two scenarios. In the first, they imagined giving blood or donating money. Those who imagined giving blood reported feeling more generous than those who imagined donating money that would pay for an equal value of blood. They also reported feeling more commitment to the cause. In the second scenario, participants were allowed to choose whichever they felt was 'easiest'—donating blood or money. The resulting *feelings* were the same.
- **Claim the name:** In two final studies, the research team wanted to explore the impact of persuading people to physically sign something with their name. The research showed that those who signed a donation form felt more engaged and generous than those who gave without being asked for their signature. (We know from our own work that a pledge card signed by a donor at the end of a special event has a much greater likelihood of converting to a gift than a simple verbal promise.)

Koo draws an interesting general conclusion here: 'Across these studies, we find self-giving does not need to be public, effortful, or tangible; the only requirement is that giving is associated with the self.' A question for you might be how often do you create that sense of self-association in your engagement programme?

Learning from Avoiding Loss and Adding Value

Avoiding loss in its various forms is a powerful driver of behaviour —much more powerful than potential gains. This overall preference seems to be hardwired into our DNA. At the same time showing guaranteed added value through the endowment effect can prove a significant motivator.

We can see this in fundraising stories, and how they deal with the positive vs. negative loss vs. gain issue. We're familiar with the story of overcoming the odds. The set-up shows someone in a tough or even tragic situation, in dire need of support, or they may suffer significant loss. Then the story tells of the incredible transformation that the supporter's help can deliver. The story will have positive and negative aspects, their balance depending on the real-life situation (sudden disaster, such as an earthquake or outbreak of war) and the desired supporter action (immediate emergency donation, on-going regular donations).

Linked to this is a *present bias*, leaving *rational decisions* for the future ('I'll eat fruit next week') and *emotional/impulsive choices* for the present ('but right now I want chocolate.') Thinking about the future leads to different decisions than thinking about the present.

For people we aim to influence we need to:

- Clarify the loss that is possible, and frame it clearly and compellingly. Consider whether to show the loss as one that will happen now or in the future.
- Don't be afraid to emphasise the loss, and don't try to balance it with rational + and −.
- Understand and respond to the irrational rules of mental accounting which people apply—find out about their internal budgets. Decide which to target.
- Play to the *IKEA Effect*, encouraging people to add value through their own efforts so they want to avoid losing that investment.
- The *IKEA Effect* also implies that the supporter should be the hero, not the organisation.
- Help to magnify any impact by using social media-sharing and co-creation opportunities as digital forms of the *IKEA Effect*.
- Work to create engagement opportunities that impact on supporters' sense of self.

Chapter 6

Be Social and Reciprocal

Summary

A key part of our decision-making framework centres around us as fundamentally social animals. This ability to be part of a social group made evolutionary sense. Sticking to the clan or tribe[1] increased our chances of surviving natural disasters, animal attacks, and conflicts with other tribes.

Imitation of others in the group, especially the more successful ones, not only increased our chances of survival, it also reduced shame and guilt in case of failure. Social conformity also saved cognitive energy. Those with social skills survived. Others perished.

This chapter, like **Chapter 8** on *Emotions*, is different from the others which focus on very specific cognitive techniques you can apply. The social dimension applies right across the field of behavioural economics and decision science. Here we examine some specific aspects of the way we interact with others, which are worth considering in terms of how to change behaviour.

Two key principles that are enormously useful in the social space have been elaborated by Robert Cialdini[2] and his team at Arizona University. These principles are *social proof* and *reciprocity*. *Social*

---

[1] See also the discussion on *in-group versus out-group bias* in **Chapter 8.**

[2] Robert Cialdini, Professor at Arizona State University has contributed significantly to the understanding of social decision-making though his six key principles of persuasion outlined in his book *Influence.*

proof is the idea that we can influence the beliefs or behaviours of others by showing that individuals with authority—or that the target audience can relate to—hold a particular belief or act in a particular way. *Reciprocity* refers to the feeling we have that we should try to 'repay' what another person has provided to us.

Other important principles here include the ideas of *imitation* and *social contagion.*

Imitation is about copying the behaviour of others. We see this in many social situations where couples or groups mirror or match each other. Such mimicry also makes good survival sense. As social networks expert Duncan Watts explains, 'The world is too complicated for each individual to be able to solve problems on their own. We rely on information that is encoded in our social environment. We assume other people know things we don't.'[3] (For more on this see **Chapter 10.**)

Social contagion explains how ideas seem to take off—increasingly important as we think about social media driving successes like the 'ice bucket challenge' or 'no makeup selfie.' Note, though, that social contagion does not just take place online. Indeed, throughout history there are many examples of this phenomenon.[4]

Make 'Em Laugh

There is a mystery around the canned laughter often used in TV shows. All audiences claim they dislike it. But the research results are quite clear, canned laughter makes people laugh. It gets worse. Experiments have shown that canned laughter encourages an audience

---

[3] Quoted by Michael Bond in *The Power of Others*, Oneworld Publications, London, 1988.

[4] For example, consider how tattoos, spotted by sailors in the British Navy when visiting Polynesia with Captain Cook in 1773. Within 2 years of this first contact almost 85% of sailors in the UK navy had a tattoo and the Admiralty were worried some secret society was being set up. So tattoos were banned for a time. Think of the challenge to get this shared information around at that time.

to laugh longer and more often during a comedy show. And they rate the material presented as funnier. Perhaps most frighteningly, there's evidence that canned laughter is most effective for poor jokes.

The big question for decision scientists is: *why* does it work, especially when people say they hate it? Cialdini's answer is the *principle of social proof*. 'One means we use to determine what is correct is to find out what other people think is correct. We view a behaviour as more correct in a given situation to the degree that we see others performing it.'[5] We laugh *because* others do.

Social proof works in personal *and* professional settings. The next time you're in a meeting or at a dinner party, notice that people unconsciously look around quickly when something happens, to see what the appropriate response is. If others are laughing, they do too. And if others are scowling, they fall in with that.

For those of us working in social change, social proof is a powerful shortcut we can apply to persuade others to adopt a particular behaviour or belief. Take, for instance, the UK Government's social proof strategy for recovering unpaid income tax, outlined in **Chapter 3**. Or the energy company in the US, which found that by sending bills that showed other residents in the area were using less electricity, many consumers reduced their own use to bring it closer to the average.[6]

For another practical charity example of social proof, on Macmillan's Cancer Support website, when you are offered choices about making a regular gift at different levels, they tell you how many people are currently giving at that level. Follow this url to check it out https://www.macmillan.org.uk/donate. Camfed, a great girls' empowerment and education programme, actually names specific recent donors at the bottom of their donation page, again encouraging us to do as others do. https://camfed.org/donate.

---

[5] Cialdini quoted in http://www.blockshelf.com/influence-robert-cialdini.

[6] The impact of showing images/sharing case studies can be magnified if they can be matched to the donor. For more on this see Shang and Croson, *A Field Experiment in Charitable Contribution* http://econweb.ucsd.edu/~jandreon/PhilanthropyAndFundraising/Volume%202/27%20Shang%20Croson%202009.pdf.

Social proof is increasingly important in marketing/fundraising/ sales because there's some evidence people have lost trust in brands. Increasingly they are more likely to trust information from 'peers' even when these people are strangers—for example, on Trip Advisor. The annual Nielsen *Global Trust in Advertising* surveys demonstrate how much more we value 'word of mouth' and other 'peer recommendations' over constructed brand messages. Interestingly, there is some evidence we prefer products with lots of reviews over ones with fewer but better reviews. The implication seems to be that even if the reviews aren't all good, if a product has lots of them, it must be popular.[7]

Be Careful if You Make 'Em Cry

Our tribal sense doesn't allow us to treat all social proof equally. The more relevant or connected people are to us, the more likely we are to do the same as them. ('Relevant' or 'connected' people may be people like us, or in our situation, people we aspire to be like, or perceived experts and authorities on the matter.)

This tendency for connected behaviour, even without direct connection, has some very distressing implications. David Philips explored suicide statistics in the United States from 1947 to 1968. He established that 'Within two months after every front-page suicide story, an average of fifty-eight more people than usual killed themselves.' He also established that most of those suicides happened in or near the geographical location where the original suicide event had been most widely reported. This effect is now called the *Werther effect*, after the unhappy suicide hero in Goethe's novel *The Sorrows of Young Werther*. And, of course, we are sadly all-too-familiar with the idea of copycat killings where a murderer repeats a similar style or act of violence having heard about it. What seems to happen is that a certain extreme behaviour becomes normalised be-

---

[7] For a more detailed exploration of this see *The Love of Large Numbers: A Popularity Bias in Consumer Choice,* Derek Powell, Jingqi Yu, and Melissa DeWolf, http:// journals.sagepub.com/doi/abs/10.1177/0956797617711291?journalCode=pssa.

cause someone else exhibited it and it was publicised. (For more on the worrying implications of normalization see **Chapter 10.**)

A more positive implication of the power of group behaviour is documented in one scientist's research into phobias.[8] Albert Bandura established that children who were afraid of dogs quickly learned to overcome their fear by watching another child playing happily with a dog. They could even learn to overcome their fear by watching a video of 'unafraid' behaviour by other children.

What's the key implication of social proof for agencies involved in change for good? By demonstrating that your proposition or campaign is valued and endorsed by other people whom the prospect can relate to, you can lower reluctance or anxiety to join in. Social proof may even increase a potential audience's confidence in your ability to deliver a service or even succeed in a campaign.

Social Proof in Action

Evidence for social proof goes back as far as one of scientist Stanley Milgram's less controversial experiments.[9] A researcher, posing as a regular bystander, stopped in a New York street and looked skyward for 60 seconds. Almost everyone simply walked past the man without noticing that he was there, far less glancing up to see what he was looking at. The experiment was run with a range of individuals assigned to stop and stare. The result was the same with different genders, heights and ethnic origins. However, when a group of three or more researchers posing as 'normal' pedestrians stopped and looked up together there was a differ-

---

[8] https://en.wikipedia.org/wiki/Albert_Bandura. Bandura is a Professor Emeritus of Social Science in Psychology at Stanford University. For almost six decades, he has contributed to the fields of education and psychology.

[9] Milgram is perhaps most famous for his controversial experiment in which a group of subjects give what they believe are increasingly brutal electrical shocks to individuals behind a glass screen. The subjects are told to do this by someone dressed in a lab coat and acting with authority. This troubling experiment suggests that individuals can be convinced to undertake unpleasant, and even what they would normally consider immoral, acts when encouraged by someone in perceived authority.

ent impact. The number of passers-by who stopped and joined in, looking to see what was happening, increased by a factor of four.

In this example, the reason people stop to stare is because 'enough' other people were doing it. With social proof, there is often a *critical mass* after which people are likely to adopt the specific behaviour of wearing A, eating B, demonstrating against C, signing a petition on D, donating to E, etc. Charities and businesses alike want their campaigns to have this traction. This is what seems to happen when campaigns 'go viral.' (For an interesting exploration of how the Ice Bucket Challenge, and its variants came to be, see this article in Slate. http://www.slate.com/articles/technology/technology/2014/08/who_invented_the_ice_bucket_challenge_a_slate_investigation.html.)

UK readers over a certain age may remember the impact of Comic Relief's first, pre-internet, *Red Nose Day* in 1988. The starting point was asking people to buy a red plastic nose to wear to work on 5 February to show their support for the charity and its work. The campaign began slowly, but through TV and media exposure, gradually gained more and more traction. Then as the actual Red Nose 'Day' came closer everyone who *didn't* have a nose was desperate to get one—worried they might not be seen as part of the 'in' group. (At one point Comic Relief was scouring the world for supplies of red plastic to meet demand.) You can see the same process of people seeking the joining in 'badge' for Poppy Day in UK, Irish Cancer Society's Daffodil Day in Ireland, and even Orange Eating Day for Terre des Hommes in Switzerland.[10]

You can see the *social proof* approach being consciously used by agencies you interact with in quite subtle ways:

When it has only just opened for the day, if you go into a Café Nero or Costa, on the counter will be a half full jar with money in it marked 'tips.' The money has of course been placed there by the staff before any customer has actually left a gratuity to encourage you to think that tipping is normal and something others do. And by implication, so should you.

---

[10] For more on Terre des Hommes Orange Day see here. https://www.tdh.ch/en/orange-sale.

Watch a charity telethon and you will know the hosts read out the names of others who are giving, and how much they gave. And, of course, they indicate the fact that celebrities we know are doing it too. You may remember the celebrities who stepped forward at the 2014 opening of the Commonwealth Games to make a text donation to UNICEF. They gave, and then asked us to give—to join them in a group activity.

If you go into a not-very-busy restaurant the maître d' or server will normally place you in the window table where you can be seen by passersby if the rest of the restaurant is empty. They are doing this to make the restaurant appear popular to any potential customer, encouraging them to come in.

Some nightclubs keep a queue at the entrance when they don't really need to—indeed, some pay people to stand there in a line. The clubs are keen to create a sense of popularity and scarcity that will encourage others to join the queue.[11]

Putting Social Proof to Work

If you're keen to show social proof at work for your organisation or cause, then you should try some or all of the following:

Tactic	Implication
Share *case histories* from some of your most engaged donors or supporters, explaining how they benefit from their involvement. Do the same thing for service users—e.g. typical substance abusers who have benefited from your programme. In both cases your programme or agency will have more credibility.	Credible case histories can be more impactful on changing opinions than impressive statistics. Build cases into all your communications. And as indicated earlier, match them, by gender, location etc., to the donor.

---

[11] Charities sometimes do it, too! See this example of a *Save the Children* charity clothes sale http://www.mirror.co.uk/3am/celebrity-news/save-children-charity-sale-supported-5920610.

Tactic	Implication
Show *images*, especially videos of people making use of your offering or service. Ideally, name the person involved —though that may be difficult in some settings. If you have to anonymise the person, then give them a typical name and age—'June, 31' or 'George, 55' 'seen here seeking advice at the centre.' Even imaginary personas seem more real.	Seeing others taking part in an activity makes it real for us. This can be used to encourage supporters to come on board—or to encourage others to make use of the service. (Be careful, though, of normalising bad behaviour.)
Use an *impressive number*. Mention how long your agency has been around. Or the number of donors you have, or service users you have helped. If appropriate, maybe even mention the number of women, children under 10, Asian origin individuals, etc. Remember McDonald's built their reputation by signs showing a running count of burgers served.	These numbers become a measure of success. Share your 'best' numbers, and think about how you present them. Which is more powerful? '1 in 5 children in this town can't read' or '10,000 children in this town can't read'?
Show *important or well-known people* using your product or service. This makes use of what is called the *halo effect*. Do make sure, though, that the person is someone whom the target market admires or respects.	Here you borrow the positive feeling people have towards the celebrity named. Of course, this can change when negative revelations come out about these celebrities—e.g. Bill Cosby, Rolf Harris, etc.
Report if your agency or service is mentioned in *respected media*: 'As featured in *The Economist*/on the BBC/in an NPR documentary.' Where possible pull out and use a specific quote. And if an esteemed correspondent is involved mention them, too.	This represents an associated approval and endorsement of your agency, offering or service. The more prestigious the media the better. Again, consider who the target market would respect and what will offer reach to that market.
Mention your charitable not-for-profit (NfP) status. If possible display a *seal of approval* by an independent rating organisation	This puts an official stamp—called an imprimatur—from an external approval system.

[12] How often have you bought a bottle of wine in a supermarket attracted by its gold medal label, and believing that it has won the first prize in a contest? In fact, many 'contests' where awards are given are not contests at all. Producers are given a gold

Tactic	Implication
like Charity Navigator. Finally, a prize or award can help especially if it is seen as objective and authoritative.[12] When MSF and Amnesty won the Nobel Peace Prize it lifted both supporter numbers and income.	Note there are many prizes and awards. And they don't need to be especially rigorous. Look at how many bottles of wine in the supermarket have won prizes. Are they all good. See below for an expose.[13]? But don't be afraid to enter contests to try and win—there are awards in almost every area of non-profit activity.
Warn supporters about *limited opportunities* to take part in an offering due to demand—'Only 5 guaranteed places left for London Marathon runners through our charity golden ticket.' This also works well on crowdfunding sites where there may be a limited number of fulfillment opportunities at any specific level	This approach combines the social proof of *popularity* plus another strong influence principle developed by Cialdini—*scarcity*. (It also links to the idea of *loss aversion* discussed in **Chapter 5**.) By encouraging potential supporters to believe that the chance to support you is popular and scarce you have the perfect storm for engagement.

Emotional Contagion

There is a variation on social proof called *emotional contagion*. We can see this at its most extreme in crowds. People in crowds define themselves according to who they are with at the time—anti-war protestors, fans of a particular football club, feminists, environmental activists. This transient 'social identity' determines how the crowd behaves.

---

medal for entering and fulfilling some very basic criteria. But marketeers know the power of a perceived award—and especially the power of a 'gold' award. http://www.dailymail.co.uk/news/article-3721006/The-truth-wine-awards-used-marketing-bottles.html.

[13] The UK's Daily Telegraph exposes the wine awards racket in this article. You may need a stiff drink afterwards. http://www.telegraph.co.uk/foodanddrink/wine/11617630/The-truth-about-wine-awards-why-medals-dont-mean-great-bottles.html.

There have been some extraordinary examples of emotional contagion in recent years. For example, the mass display of grief when Princess Diana died. After a quiet start, hundreds of thousands of people, many of whom had been indifferent to her while she was alive, turned out to mourn her death.

We see similar reactions at pop concerts when emotional pleas are made from the stage to support social causes. (Many charities, including Greenpeace and Oxfam use specialist recruitment teams at events like Glastonbury Festival to recruit supporters caught up in the emotion and excitement. The STOP AIDS NOW charity in Holland tries to persuade everyone to take a condom at festival and concerts.)

On a microscale, emotional contagion may explain why many couples who have been together for years begin increasingly to resemble each other as the years go by. They have unconsciously mimicked each others' expressions and mannerisms so often that even their lines and wrinkles have started to match. (Recent insights into the emotions of animals and humans suggest this might also apply to dogs and their owners.)[14]

One thing that makes human behaviour difficult to decipher or predict is that it involves certain paradoxes. We are, at the same time, individualistic and self-seeking *and* collaborative and caring about the interests of the group. The group could be our sports team, fellow volunteers, work colleagues, or humanity at large. Both the context and our mental state determine how we react in a given situation. And the form and timing of any communication can influence both the context and mental state. Think how easy it is to be swept up in both commercialism *and* altruism at Christmas.

---

[14] Dogs look like their owners—it is a scientific fact. BBC, http://www.bbc.com/future/story/20151111-why-do-dogs-look-like-their-owners.

We Don't Believe Our Own Eyes

Solomon Asch's classic line experiment provides some interesting insights into the power of social proof and contagion over solid data.

A number of unsuspecting individuals were placed in a larger group who had been primed to drive a misleading conclusion. The unsuspecting subjects were invited to take part in an experiment on visual perception. Along with the 'in-the-know' group, they were shown a series of lines. All the participants were asked to say which of the three lines on the right—A,B,C—was the same as the one on the left.

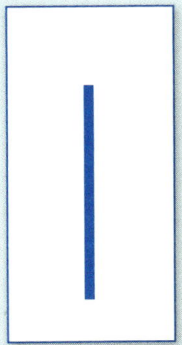 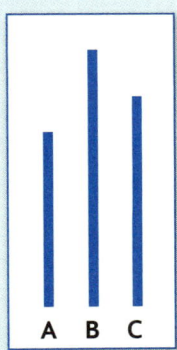

The primed individuals declared one by one that line B was equal to the one on the left, despite the clear visual evidence to the contrary. Almost all of the subjects fell in with the declared, 'primed', group view. Despite the evidence of their own eyes they conformed to the (incorrect) majority opinion. The experiment was repeated a number of times with different subjects. Over the 12 critical trials run by Asch on average 32% of 'innocent' subjects agreed with the transparently wrong answer given by the other group members.

Asch was disturbed by these results, 'The tendency to conformity in our society is so strong that reasonably intelligent and well-meaning young people are willing to call 'white' black. This is a matter of concern. It raises questions about our ways of education and about the values that guide our conduct.' We share his concern, but believe that the issue here is perhaps less about the quality of education and more about those hard-wired conformity rules we feel the need to respond to: social proof simply trumps our rational mind.

Decisions, Decisions

To save mental energy, people resort to one of three broad decision-making strategies:

- Mental short cuts or heuristics (what's an easy cue to make this decision?)
- Emotions (how do I feel about this decision?)
- Social reference (what do other people, like me, do?)

The social factor is important for another reason. As we highlight throughout the book, we largely make decisions based on mental short cuts and emotions, usually operating on a sub-conscious level. So, what is the role of reason? Social justification. According to Hugo Mercier and Dan Sperber in their book *The Enigma of Reason*, and others, the main purpose of reason is to justify to others the decisions we made subconsciously, driven by our biases and emotions. We make our decisions in a fast, intuitive and emotional way (System 1), and then we rationalise (tell rational lies) those decisions (System 2).

Imagine you are making a business decision on the launch of a new product, or a personal decision of choosing your life partner. You may be satisfied with your decision and not seek a rational explanation for it. But if you have to justify your decision to others, you cannot say 'Oh, I just feel like it.' That's where social justification comes in.

We also seek rational explanations in order to maintain our rational self-image, but self-image and social-image are closely connected.

When to Use Social Proof

The *social proof* rule is most effective under two main conditions, *uncertainty* and *similarity*.

Uncertainty: social proof will have most impact when the group or individual you are trying to engage is unaware or *uncertain* about your proposition, brand or agency. If you are a completely unknown or new charity, for example, social proof could help you reassure or secure new supporters. But if you are already a well-known brand name, such as Red Cross, it is unlikely social proof would engage supporters more. Where it might help is if you want to introduce your target audience to a new offering that they don't associate with you, such as corporate sponsorship of refugee camps. ('You might not think that as a charity we do ABC ... but I'm delighted to announce that we're launching a new scheme next year, following a trial with these great commercial partners ... XYZ.')

Similarity: the principle of social proof, according to Cialdini, 'operates most powerfully when we are observing the behaviour of people just like us.' This accounts for the great number of testimonials or endorsements by 'ordinary' people in press, TV and radio advertisements. Sometimes these people are real. More often they are actors playing the role of being 'an ordinary mother looking to feed the family quickly,' 'a young man keen to be attractive so using X deodorant,' 'a couple looking to save for retirement and choosing Y pension scheme.' (Consider the great success of the Dove *Campaign for Real Beauty* showing ordinary, normal women using their products.)[15]

The audience should be able to recognise the similarity and say, 'Yes, those people are like me and they are using that product or service or supporting that campaign or agency. Therefore, I'm the type of person who would use it or support it.' You can see the power of this in the explosive growth of websites where consumers can report on their experience. Amazon and TripAdvisor offer you the opportunity to comment on and rate experiences or products. Both these agencies exert enormous power over subsequent purchases by recording the feedback and promoting to customers the most popular choice of hotel or the most highly reviewed model of headphones. Also note how both these sites 'reward' those who post comments

---

[15] See the Guardian article 'Real women' ads do wonders for Dove figures', https://www.theguardian.com/media/2004/jul/29/marketingandpr.advertising1 and the discussion in **Chapter 10**.

and ratings—and influence others—with status markers: 'trusted reviewer,' 'top 10 restaurant reviewer,' etc.

What would happen if someone set up a TripAdvisor for NGOs, where donors, or even beneficiaries, could feedback directly on their experience of the agency?

Similarity is strongly related to the notion of *in-group* versus *out-group* explored in **Chapter 8**.[16]

'After You' the Diffusion-of-Responsibility Effect

Social proof can be shown to work most effectively when there is a clear transaction—as when you are trying to persuade someone to buy something. (The transaction involves money in exchange for a clear benefit or payoff.) Demonstrating that 'appropriate' others have already said 'Yes' encourages the same response in the prospect. ('9/10 users report a decrease in visible lines using this face cream.')

However, when you ask a potential supporter for help while mentioning others there might be a challenge. You may have to manage what's called the *diffusion of responsibility effect* which can work against social proof. If the prospect's System 2 kicks in, they may respond: 'There are *lots* of others helping here, so my contribution is not valuable or needed.'

There are several ways to tackle this:

- For *public situations*, such as an event, a crowdfunding site, or telethon, you need first to point out how many others are taking part, *and* how important each individual contribution is in making up the whole. You could also explain how a specific supporter's gift directly supports one child or one family in need.

- For *personal* situations where others are also being asked, as in a solicitation by phone or mail, emphasise first, the difference that person's help

---

[16] For most of our history we have lived in small groups of 10-1000 people. The people we knew were all relatives or friends. Those we didn't know were enemies. This created a strong *in-group versus out-group bias*. In today's world, most people we deal with are not friends or enemies, they are strangers or acquaintances. Yet, our *in-group versus out-group bias* is still deeply ingrained in our psyche.

will make, and *then* point out how many others are also helping. Some
agencies report greater success by mentioning that the person they spoke
to immediately before the current supporter made a gift of £X. It may also
help to let the supporter know that someone respected is helping.[17]

- For *major gift personal solicitations*, saying nothing directly about the number of others helping may be best. It's probably more important to single
out the prospect in terms of their specific ability to help to bring others
onboard. 'Only you can provide leadership at this level—and that will be a
signal to others in the community to come on board.' This is asking *them*
to be the provider of social proof: their leadership will drive followership.

The Bystander Effect

People are most in need of social proof when they are most uncertain—for example, when it is unclear what is happening. This is ex-
acerbated when *everyone* in the group is uncertain. At that point all
of those engaged can be looking around for clues as to what is the
most appropriate response.

When there are no clear signals on appropriate action the result
can sometimes be what Cialdini calls *pluralistic ignorance*, or the
bystander effect.

---

[17] In their study 'How Can Bill and Melinda Gates Increase Other People's Donations
to Fund Public Good' (2014), John A. List, Chairman and Homer J. Livingston Professor,
Department of Economics at the University of Chicago, and Dean Karlan, Professor of
Economics at Yale University, explored the impact of naming the matching donor, the
Bill and Melinda Gates Foundation (BMGF), versus not providing the identity of the
matching donor. The sample consisted entirely of individuals who had not previously
donated to TechnoServe, a charity headquartered in Washington, D.C., that focuses on
international development and poverty reduction. They found that the 'quality marque'
of naming the Gates Foundation as the source of matching funds significantly increased
the average gift per solicitation. In fact, it raised it by 51%. Moreover, the mention of
Gates as a matching donor increased the probability of an individual making a donation
by 26%.

As an example of this phenomenon he quotes the distressing 'Failure of entire groups of bystanders to aid victims in agonising need of help.' One famous case is the murder of Catherine Genovese in New York in 1964. This young woman had just arrived back from work when, over a period of 35 minutes, she was stabbed to death. According to various accounts the attack was witnessed by between 12 and 38 neighbours and people in the street. Yet none of them telephoned the police until after the woman stopped struggling and was dead. The local and national media characterised the lack of action by the witnesses as heartlessness, the result of a failure in contemporary society to care or even to get involved.

Researchers followed up the story and established there were two reasons no one helped. First, no one had helped *precisely* because there were so many observers. With so many people watching, all the witnesses assumed that someone else had already contacted the police. Second, and connected to the first, there was no clear 'rule' for what to do—and no clues from others as to what was the right thing to do. In fact, each individual saw others doing nothing and assumed that doing nothing was the right thing to do—a vicious circle. In the state of *pluralistic ignorance* if no one else is acting, everyone else interprets the situation as a non-emergency, and they don't take action.

Subsequent research has proved the broad principle that people are generally less likely to receive help as the number of bystanders grows. For example, in a follow-up experiment, also in New York, a college student who appeared to be having an epileptic seizure was offered help 85% of the time when there was a single bystander. But only 31% of the time when there were five bystanders present.[18]

---

[18] This experiment was conducted by Bibb Latane and John Darley. They watched students respond to the perceived choking of a fellow student in a nearby cubicle. When the test subjects felt they were the only other person there, 85% rushed to help. When the student felt there was one other person, 65% helped. When the student felt there were four other people, the percentage dropped to 31%. Information and chart from https://blog.bufferapp.com/6-powerful-psychological-effects-that-explain-how-humans-tick. There are a number of YouTube videos sharing examples of this experiment. One of the most shocking is a video of a woman being assaulted in a park. Only 1 in 10 people stops to help. https://www.youtube.com/watch?v=zNOTWjIJ58E.

Bystander Effect: Likelihood of Helping Someone in Need

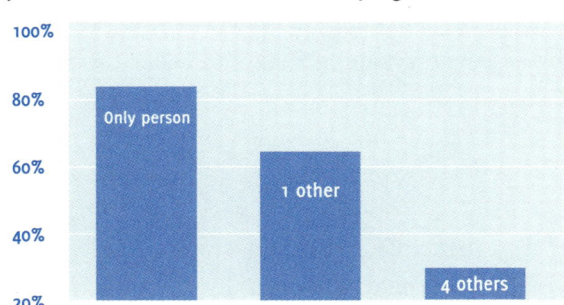

The key to pluralistic ignorance is uncertainty. If you are in need—whether as a result of illness, from an attack, or trapped somewhere—the most effective way to get help is to ask a specific individual, and to ask in a very specific way. Research shows that in such a situation people are normally very responsive. Individuals understand there is an emergency, and that their particular help is needed. The inaction response results when they see bystanders standing around not acting—and they then decide 'nothing' is the right thing to do.

This heuristic has been used by the British Red Cross in a recent advert to encourage people to overcome their natural inclination to step away from challenges. Here the message is designed to address—and overcome the bystander effect. (We're grateful to Meredith Niles for the example below.)

BYSTANDER EFFECT
BRITISH RED CROSS

In partnership with **TOYOTA**

The *bystander effect* can be reduced by using the *observation effect*. When we feel we are being observed by others, regardless of whether this is the case, we modify our behaviour to make it socially acceptable.

Reciprocity

The second key principle that Cialdini identified as important in influence and decision-making was that of *reciprocity*. This is based on the idea that as people, we aim to return favours to those who do them to us, paying back a real or perceived debt. Simply, if someone does us a favour, we think we should do one in return. If someone gives us a birthday present we believe we should also remember their birthday. If we are invited round by a couple to dinner, we must invite them to our house for dinner—even if the first dinner was a truly terrible experience. Anyone who breaks this rule feels awkward and uncomfortable.

This fundamental behaviour was clearly very useful to early humans in tribal settings. ('I will share the results of my hunting today so that you will share yours tomorrow.') In a contemporary setting, if a colleague helps you when you're busy with a last minute project, you might well feel obliged to support her ideas for improving marketing when they are discussed. Reciprocity remains part of our psychological makeup today. We don't like 'social loafing' and will punish those who practice it.

Reciprocity: The Mexican Mystery Solved

Cialdini discussed one of our favourite examples of reciprocity. In 1985 Ethiopia was gripped by an enormous famine. Millions of people around the world saw the haunting pictures on TV, and maybe remember it as perhaps the first and most powerful experience of what unrelenting drought, war and starvation meant.

Cialdini learned from a newspaper article that in that same year $5,000 was sent from Ethiopia *to* Mexico. At first, he was puzzled, thinking there must have been a mistake and that the people of Mexico had sent the money to Ethiopia. But Cialdini researched further and identified some officials from the Ethiopian Red Cross who confirmed that, despite the extraordinary privations of their nation, in that year they had indeed sent $5,000 to Mexico. (1985 was the year Mexico City was hit by a terrible earthquake.)

But why, Cialdini asked, had the Ethiopian Red Cross chosen the Mexico disaster to support? The answer is hugely revealing about the rule of reciprocity *and* the extraordinary humanity of individuals. The Ethiopian Red Cross officials explained that in 1935, almost 50 years before, Mexico had sent aid to Ethiopia when it was invaded by the Italians.

'The Mexicans helped us the when we needed help and so it was right that we should help them when they similarly needed support.' Even 50 years later, and in the midst of their own disaster, the folk memory of the need for reciprocity was buried deep in the psyche of the Ethiopians.

Reciprocity exists in many circumstances in our lives:

- A manager who goes out of her or his way to offer to help a team member—for example by offering to run them to the doctor if they are feeling unwell—might instil a sense of social obligation. The manager may hope they can call on this social obligation at some point in the future.
- Waiters often give you a small sweet with the bill and some leave a note or draw a smiley face on the print out. There is a reason for this. By adding that sweet *and* the note to the bill, they are giving you both a physical and psychological gift. And it can increase their tips by up to 14%. (In fact, the highest tips come to waiters who give more than one sweet, explaining at the same time 'I liked you as customers, so I brought you an extra chocolate/mint.' For more detail on the example see **Section Three.**)
- Marketing companies often offer consumers a 'free sample' when they launch a new product or start a new campaign. This creates a feeling of obligation in the consumer 'They gave me a product for free, I should buy their product, at least once.' The MAC cosmetics

company offers 'free' make-up sessions to customers ... encouraging participants to feel obligated to buy products subsequently.

- Charities often enclose small gifts or premiums in the direct mails they send to donors to encourage them to sign up. While these do not work for everyone, many recipients feel that if they use the gift, whatever it is, they have a social obligation to make a reciprocal gift, a donation, to the charity. The gifts can be quite involved even if not expensive. A recent recruitment direct mail pack from the British Red Cross to one of us, included a lapel badge, two coasters, some address stickers, a pen, and ... a teabag. We are reliably assured this is their very best 'acquisition' pack and plays exceptionally well with the target market of older women.[19]

- Charities often use the idea of matching gifts, where a $100 donation from an individual is matched by an additional £100 from another donor, such as an employer or major donor. The thinking is that it is motivating if we know that someone else has pledged to match our gift. It becomes a kind of virtual reciprocity. This technique is successful—but interestingly it only seems to work up to a point in terms of the scale of the match.[20] See the further explanation below.

Not Too Much Matching

As indicated above, matching donations increases the likelihood of securing a gift. But many charities, and fundraising experts believe

---

[19] A 2005 study by Armin Falke http://www.ucl.ac.uk/~uctpshu/falk.pdf offers evidence from a field experiment of the importance of reciprocity for charity fundraisers. In collaboration with a charity the researchers sent three variant appeals to a dataset of 10,000 potential donors. The researchers randomly assigned the variants. One third contained no gift, one third had a small gift and one third had a large gift. The results confirm the importance of gift-exchange. Compared to the 'no gift' option, the relative frequency of donations increased by 17% if a small gift was included, and by an impressive 75% for a large gift.

[20] It's worth noting some research suggests that matching gifts are powerful but 'seed money' can be even more powerful. http://www.nytimes.com/2008/03/09/magazine/09Psychology-t.html?_r=1&st=cse&sq=what+makes+people+give&scp=1&oref=slogin.

that the greater the ratio of the 'matched' donation, the more effective it is at persuading others to donate. (Will the donation be matched 1:1 or 1:2 or even 1:3?) For example, in Dec 2016 we received a series of emails from Planned Parenthood of America offering not just a 1:1 match but 1:3.

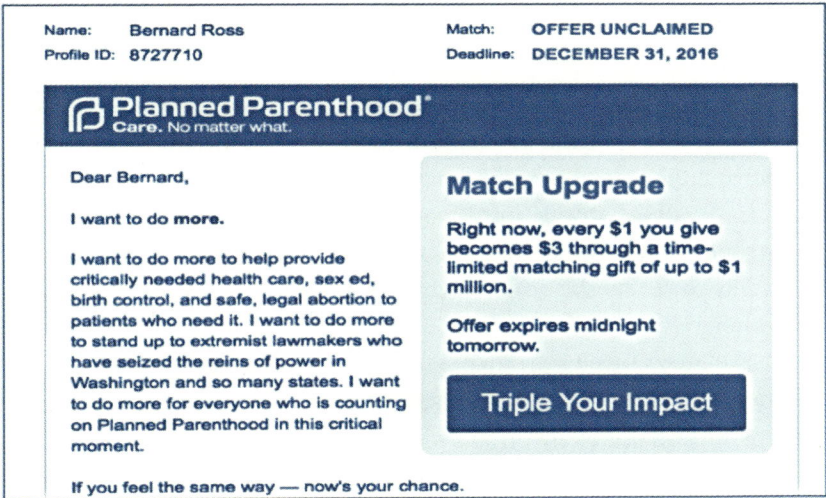

Clearly Planned Parenthood, and the generous donor behind the offer, believed that a 1:3 ratio would make a significant difference to gift levels, which would seem to make System 2 logical sense.

But where is the data to show that this actually works? Through a series of field experiments two philanthropy researchers, Dean Karlan and John List (see footnote 16) decided to check if there was real empirical evidence for this.[21]

Working with a well-established, 'liberal' political organisation in the US, they tested the impact of different offers on 50,000, already committed donors. They found that matching 1:1 did indeed have a significant impact on both the response rate and the amount donated. But increased matching ratios—2:1 or 3:1—had no extra impact.

---

[21] *Effect of Matching Ratios on Charitable Giving in the United States,* Dean Karlan and John List https://www.povertyactionlab.org/evaluation/effect-matching-ratios-charitable-giving-united-states.

Specifically, for 1:1 ratios, the probability that an individual would donate increased by 22% and the donation level rose by 19%. But at 2:1 or 3:1 incentive rates there was *no* additional effect.

Using the matching gift model undoubtedly works to encourage potential donors. But make sure you don't 'waste' the matching cash.

What About the Impact of Lead Gifts?

While we're exploring various forms of 'match' funding it's worth exploring the reality behind the impact of a lead donor whose funds are used to meet the administrative costs of an organisation. This approach is used by a number of agencies—famously charity: water— as a way to tackle the concern that some supporters have about the 'overhead' in charities.

Uri Gneezy[22] and a group of colleagues set out to explore whether embedding in an appeal various options—a lead donor, a matching donor, or lead donor covering overhead—impacted on donation rates.

For their study *Avoiding overhead aversion in charity* they created four options to share with a cluster of existing supporters:

A *control* option: 'Our goal in this campaign is to raise money for the projects. Implementing each project costs $20,000. Your tax-deductible gift makes a difference. Enclosed is ...'

A *seed money* option: 'A private donor who believes in the importance of the project has given this campaign seed money in the amount of $10,000. Your tax-deductible gift makes a difference. Enclosed is ...'

A *matched gift* option: 'A private donor who believes in the importance of the project has given this campaign a matching grant in the amount of $10,000. The matching grant will match every dollar given by donors like you with a dollar, up to a total of $20,000.'

---

[22] Uri Gneezy *et al.*, *Avoiding Overhead Aversion in Charity*, http://rady.ucsd.edu/docs/Science-2014- Gneezy-632-5.pdf.

A *seed money to meet the overhead* option: 'A private donor who believes in the importance of the project has given this campaign a grant in the amount of $10,000 to cover all the overhead costs associated with raising the needed donations.'

Each of the options produced a significantly different response.

Option	Response rate	Income per piece
Control	3.36%	$.80
Seed money	4.75%	$1.32
Matched gift	4.41%	$1.22
Meet overhead	8.85%	$2.31

The implication? It seems that having a supporter meet 'overhead' costs makes it more likely that another supporter will contribute to a campaign and that they will make a higher gift. (The editors of The Agitator blog http://www.theagitator.net/uncategorized/matching-gift-facts-and-insights who first shared this research suggest that the authority and social proof heuristics combined to deliver this result.)

'The Coke Experiment' Disguised as 'The Arts Experiment'

Matching a promised gift might seem obvious. But how about making an upfront gift with no promise of return? Is that a sensible strategy? To find out, Robert Cialdini explored the impact of offering help or a 'gift' in advance in a situation where you want to exert influence. The gift need not be tangible. It could be in the form of a compliment or offering help to an individual—but without immediately or obviously looking for a return. His work suggests this initial investment may well have a subsequent payoff.

Psychologist Dennis Regan, a peer of Cialdini, conducted an experiment in 1971 confirming this thesis. Individuals were asked, in seemingly random pairs, to take part in an art appreciation project. One of each pair was a genuine participant. The other—let's call him Joe—was an assistant pretending to be an ordinary participant.

There were two versions of the experiment.

Version 1: With an Upfront Gift After discussing the art together with his partner, 'Joe' would leave the room for a few minutes saying he was going for a toilet break. When he returned he brought two bottles of Coca-Cola, explaining he had asked the experiment manager if he could get himself a drink while out. The manager had said it was okay, and Joe had decided to buy one for the other person.

Version 2: Without an Upfront Gift Joe behaved exactly the same way as in the first part of the experiment. As before, he left for a short toilet break and then returned—but without the Coca-Cola offer.

The experiment, in both versions, then moved on to a second phase. On his return, in both cases, Joe asked the subject to do him a favour. He explained he was selling raffle tickets as part of a draw for a new car. He further explained that if he sold the most tickets, which were priced at 25¢ each, he would win a $50 prize. His final nudging sentiment was 'Any [number of tickets] would help, the more the better.'

Obviously the most interesting part of the experiment is how the reciprocity set up with the Coke affected the other person's response. The result was clear. When the subject had been given a free Coca-Cola first, they bought twice as many tickets as those who had not been given any favour.

In an interesting follow-up to the study the 'genuine' participant was asked whether they liked or disliked 'Joe' as a personality to see if this impacted on the number of raffle tickets bought. Perhaps surprisingly, liking or disliking Joe had no effect on the number of tickets they bought. The major driver was whether or not they had been gifted a Coke.

This experiment suggests that reciprocity works on the subconscious level and is disconnected from 'liking.' One practical implication is that medical charities, for example hospitals, could ask those who have benefited from care or from research to support the charity financially in order that they can help others. Some agencies are already doing this. For example, Johns Hopkins in the US and Kings College London in UK both have specialist teams who approach patients or their families to seek support after they have been 'gifted' medical support. Another implication might be that a care or even probation worker might buy a coffee for their client and then ask them for some changed behaviour—being on time for the appointment, taking medication as agreed, etc. It's important to stress that this is not the same as making a 'deal'—'I'll do this, if you do that.' The psychological contract is implicit not explicit: it is driven by System 1 not System 2 thinking.

Doctors Do Believe in Free Lunches

In general, US doctors earn pretty good salaries. Even fairly humble general practitioners earn more than $200,000 a year, and more specialist clinicians can earn up to $500,000 if they are well known and skilled. But a recent and quite troubling study demonstrated that these well-heeled professionals are not only easy, but also inexpensive to influence—specifically in terms of the drugs they prescribe for patients.

A team of researchers studied the prescribing behaviour of 279,669 US doctors—a huge data set. All these doctors had been regularly bought relatively cheap meals—salads, sandwiches, wraps, pizza—by pharmaceutical representatives while sharing information about their brand name products.[23] Astonishingly even *very* inexpensive meals, average cost less than $20, had a strong correlation to the same doctors prescribing more of the associated brand-name prescriptions rather than generics.[24] Just a one-time meal 'gift'

---

[23] For more on this see: *Even a few cheap meals changed prescription-writing by doctors*, http://pic.twitter.com/NXruaWQvLp.

[24] Brand-name drugs are, of course, usually much more expensive than their generic exact equivalents.

had strong positive impact on prescribing promoted products for the company involved.

The researchers concluded that '[receiving sponsored meals was associated with] an increased rate of prescribing the promoted brand-name medication to Medicare patients.' When a number of the doctors were asked if they felt they had been influenced in a follow-up interview, they absolutely denied any effect whatsoever on their prescribing habits. It does, however, seem that the impact of even small acts of reciprocity can be enormous. And importantly, they are subconscious.

Don't Over Think:
Marketing Lessons from 419: Nigerian Scammers

As social marketers we may laugh at the efforts the of so-called 'Nigerian' scammers—sometimes called 419-ers.[25] We spend ages carefully crafting our communications to make them seem as credible and desirable as possible, using techniques from decision sciences in subtle and sophisticated ways. So how on earth do the scammers who send out badly spelled and improbable emails make any progress? (e.g. 'My uncle was the oil minister of Nigeria and deposited $20 million in a foreign bank account. Because of government controls, I can't access the cash. But, if you help, I'll give you half of the money we recover.') Microsoft researcher and cybercrime expert, Cormac Herley, has studied the scammers' techniques. His conclusions represent a 'dark side' of decision science application. He identifies three key principles that the scammers apply that makes their seeming incompetence actually quite subtle.

- **Lose the Critical Thinkers Early On:** Scammer job number one is to 'turn off' *unlikely*, more critical prospects. By mentioning

---

[25] The name '419' actually derives from the section of Nigerian law that con artistry and fraud comes under. Hence the association with Nigerians.

Nigeria, making the rewards improbably big, having misspellings in emails etc. the critical thinkers who receive the email will usually choose to drop out.[26] At that point the scammers are left with really gullible, and vulnerable, people.

- **Help the Most Gullible Self-Select:** This is the obvious complement to losing the critical thinkers. A scammer is looking for two kinds of people to actively respond to their email. The first is people who do not notice the poor spelling and grammar, and have no real sense of whether this is a realistic deal or not. The second is people who do spot the mistakes but believe they are then dealing with someone who is him or herself gullible. These individuals think they can outsmart the scammer.

- **Encourage the Targets:** To make money the scammers have to convince their targets, 'marks', to share personal details, keep the arrangement secret, and eventually send cash or give the scammer access to their bank account. This means they need a lot of love and attention. The marks will probably get a little bit suspicious at some point, and many will drop out of the process. The scammers, therefore, have to give likely marks individual attention—lots of personal emails, phone and Skype calls, etc. These take time and energy.

By applying these three principles, the scammer does not waste time on unlikely prospects, can identify and engage more victims, and so maximise Return on Investment (RoI). Even if a few good prospects are lost through the less plausible initial pitch, the higher ratio of victims in the revised customer set makes the process more profitable. Herley says, '*By sending an email that repels all but the most gullible the scammer gets the most promising marks to self-select, and tilts the true to false positive ratio in his favor.*'

Why should you care about scammers? Well often fundraisers and campaigners spend lots of money and effort looking for the

---

[26] Also, the critical thinkers might try and report the scammers to the authorities, making it difficult to carry on with business.

widest possible supporter cluster, or trying to convince the sceptical to engage. The answer might be to focus on the easiest and most readily committed. And then give attention to them. That way you lose the inefficiencies as soon as possible. And good decision science, in a general sense, is science that is effective. Incidentally scammers are undoubtedly effective. One estimate puts their global earnings in 2016 at US$12.7 billion.[27]

Learning from 'Be Social'

We humans are fundamentally social animals. We are heavily influenced by how those around us act and what they say. So we reuse our hotel towel to help save water when we know that other guests are doing the same. We are more likely to take the stairs rather than the lift when our work colleagues do it.

But this is not just done in a vacuum. We pay attention to ratings on TripAdvisor or Amazon, and we like to add to those ratings. We like it when we can gain public recognition for our efforts. To succeed as decision scientists we need to ensure that we offer the right level and form of recognition.

If someone gifts us a favour we feel obliged to return the favour. If someone sends us a Christmas card, we feel obliged to send them one too. When someone helps us at work we want to help him or her in return. When people pass us food at the table we pass them food back.

By knowing how social influence operates—with social proof and reciprocity—we can include key triggers into decision-making frameworks:

- To help people use the behaviour we want.
- To encourage people to take action.

---

[27]   http://www.geektime.com/2014/07/21/millions-of-victims-lost-12-7b-last-year-falling-for-nigerian-scams.

Note that these processes are happening at a subconscious level. They are not part of a 'deal' we make. Making any deal explicit might engage System 2 and encourage people to consider 'Is this worth it?'

Finally, learn from the scammers. Focus on the key audience you want to engage, and work to send the communications they want or prefer to help them self-select into your cause.

Chapter 7

Tell Powerful Stories

Summary

This chapter explores the importance of stories in decision-making and the science that underpins them. It is not strictly devoted to one defined heuristic like a number of the other chapters, instead it shows how and why stories work in the context of decision architecture and influence.

Storytelling is our most human and ancient way of communication. But stories are rarely simply a way to share a narrative about something that happened or might happen. Whether historical or contemporary, stories often share something about *us*, whether it is to others or ourselves. They offer events and experiences from an individual's point of view. When done well they make us engage with the protagonist, share their emotions, and understand their strengths and weaknesses. These protagonists need not be positive or heroic —many novels (such as, Dostoevsky's *The Brothers Karamazov*) are written from the point of view of the villain. Heroes can even be a bit stupid and vain—like Dickens' *David Copperfield*. The key here is empathy, we want to understand them and feel what they feel.

From a decision science perspective, stories serve another purpose. They give us a sense of completion and put our brain at ease. We tell stories and remember them because they help us make sense of the world in a System 1 way. Stories are our most effective way of conveying motivation.

You can share your brand as a story. Many of the most famous and effective brands have great anecdotes about them that reinforce their key messages and positioning.

Storytelling can persuade people to take action. For individuals and agencies involved in social change they can help:

- Individuals in a safe European home understand why some people are refugees.
- Men to understand how offensive it is to negatively stereotype women.
- Smokers to be inspired to give up smoking.
- Donors to feel their small gift can make a worthwhile difference to a big disaster.

> It is said that people can go forty days without food, three days without water, and about thirty-five seconds without finding meaning in something.
>
> *Wired for Story*, Lisa Cron[1]

[1] Cron, Lisa. *Wired for Story: The Writer's Guide to Using Brain Science to Hook Readers from the Very First Sentence.* Ten Speed Press, USA, 2012.

What is Storytelling?

> *Stories are a particular type of human communication designed to persuade an audience of a story teller's worldview. The storyteller does this by placing characters, real or fictional, onto a stage and showing what happens to these characters over a period of time. Each character pursues some type of goal in accordance with his or her values, facing difficulty along the way and either succeeds or fails according to the storyteller's view of how the world works.*
>
> *Winning the Story War,* Jonah Sachs

Definition

Humanoids appeared around 200,000 BC and for most of our history, we lived in small communities, bands, and tribes. We communicated verbally, and conveyed our stored wisdom to new generations through stories. Telling and listening to stories is deeply ingrained in our psyche. The first human writings go back only 5,500 years. For centuries the dominant form of communication was oral—and many great literary classics probably began life as oral traditions. It is likely Homer's *Iliad* was handed down as a song for generations before being captured by a scribe. The printing press was introduced to the world around 1440, allowing the wider transmission of books. Over time we have evolved and now stories exist in many media including the web.

Today, we still tell stories, many of them based on the myths of the ancients: the movie *Jaws* is basically the same story as the ancient poem *Beowulf*—a reluctant hero battles against the evil sea monster, saves the village and in doing so becomes a more mature person.

Stories can serve a number of functions. The parables in the Bible are a way of explaining and sharing key philosophical ideas to create what many social activists would now call a movement. Other stories, like Aesop's fables or Japanese Zen stories contain important knowledge about a shared culture or contain advice on how to behave. As individuals involved in social change we need to tap into the purpose and structures of stories to help convey information and ideas in a powerful memorable way.

World Bank and Knowledge Management Through Stories

Steve Denning was a senior manager at the World Bank in charge of their knowledge management programme. He became a firm advocate of stories as a way of sharing knowledge rather than their traditional dry 'facts and data' approach.

In the middle of the global financial meltdown, September 1998, Denning was called into a meeting with the President and the senior management of the World Bank. He had been asked to make a presentation on 'The status of the knowledge management program.' His audience expected to hear him explain how the bank was focusing on data analysis and creating benchmarks for recovery etc. Instead he told a five hundred word story.

The Pakistan Highways Story

'Let me tell you,' I said, 'about something that happened just a few weeks ago to a World Bank team in Pakistan.

Just a few weeks ago, on August 20, the Government of Pakistan asked our field office in Pakistan for help in the highway sector. They were experiencing widespread pavement failure. The highways were falling apart. They felt they could not afford to maintain them. They wanted to try a different technology, a technology that our organisation has not supported or recommended in the past. And they wanted our advice within a few days.

I think it's fair to say that in the past we would not have been able to respond to this kind of question within this time frame. We would have *either said we couldn't help, or said to them that this technology was not one that we recommend, or we might have proposed to send a team to Pakistan. The team would look around, write a report, review the report, redraft the report, send the report to the Government, and eventually, perhaps three, six, nine months later, provide a response. But by then, it's too late. By then, things have moved on in Pakistan.*

What actually happened was something quite different. The task team leader in our field office in Pakistan sent an e-mail and contacted the community of highway experts inside and outside the organisation (a community that has been put together over time) and asked for help within forty-eight hours.

And he got it. The same day the task manager in the highway sector in Jordan replied that, as it happened, Jordan was using this technology with very promising results. The same day, a highway expert in our Argentina office replied and said that he was writing a book on the subject and was able to give the genealogy of the technology over several decades and continents. And shortly after that, the head of the highways authority in South Africa—an outside partner who is a member of the community—chipped in with South Africa's experience with something like the same technology. And New Zealand provided some guidelines that it had developed for the use of the technology.

The task manager in Pakistan was able to go back to the Pakistan government and say: 'This is the best that we as an organisation can put together on this subject, and then the dialogue can start as to how to adapt that experience elsewhere to Pakistan's situation.'

And now that we have realized that we as an organisation know something about a subject we didn't realize we knew anything about, now we can incorporate what we have learnt in our knowledge base so that any staff in the organisation anywhere at any time can tap into it. And the vision is that we can make this available externally through the World Wide Web, so that anyone in the world will be able to log on and get answers to questions like this on which we have some know-how, as well as on any of the other myriad subjects on which we have managed to assemble some expertise.[2]

---

[2] http://www.creatingthe21stcentury.org/Steve6-Pakistan.html.

To summarise, his argument was that the key resource in the World Bank was the *people and their connections* who could organise wisdom and knowledge into a story. As a result, the bank developed a whole programme around storytelling as a way to explain and share complex data and solve challenges. This approach is now central to their work. And if stories can work for the World Bank then they can certainly work for you.

The Need for Closure

There is a trend in contemporary storytelling—in movies, literature, and theatre, from *Waiting for Godot* to the movie *Inception*—for stories to have more ambiguous endings. This may be 'cool' but it is not helpful overall. Arie Kruglanski, Professor of Social Psychology, is an exponent of the *need for closure*. He defines closure as a 'desire for a definite answer on some topic, any answer, as opposed to confusion, and ambiguity.' Today's deluge of news, information, figures, and half-finished social media conversations can often leave us uncertain and frustrated. Stories with closure give us meaning.

As you know, our brain—equal to 2% of the total body weight but consumes 20% of its energy—seeks a level of comfort and energy saving in line with the *law of least effort*.

One way it saves energy is to 'bring things to a closure,' so that they don't have to keep exerting the mental effort of thinking about them. That is why many of us do not like books and movies with open or ambiguous endings. And why the internet is full of people asking, 'But what did it mean?' when TV series like *Twin Peaks* and *Life on Mars* finish with no obvious conclusion. it is also why a riddle, a crossword clue, or a quiz question that we cannot answer can drive us crazy until we find the solution and can put our brain in rest mode.

We Even Invent Stories Where There are None

There are not many weeks, it seems, when we don't hear about someone discovering the face of an iconic figure in a fruit or vegetable, or on toast, or some other bread product. Below on the left is an example of the face of Jesus 'found' in a piece of toast. In the middle is 'the face of Jesus' digitally printed onto toasted bread. On the right is a piece of atheist toast.

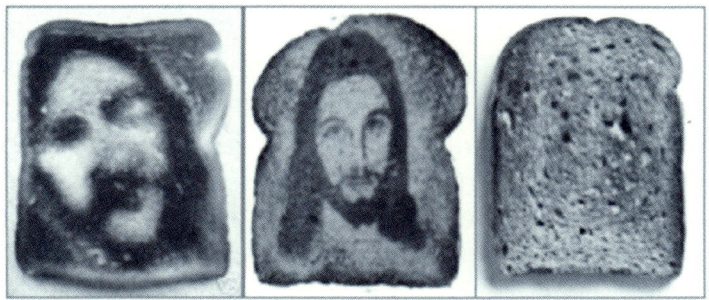

With very little provocation, our brains automatically look for patterns or narrative to bring sense to what we are seeing and to close down speculation as quickly as possible. These become stories.

Now take a moment to watch a short movie available on the internet, ideally with a friend. You should be able to find it at https://www.youtube.com/watch?v=1pMgry05WJg or, if not, try goo.gl/sZS0we.

Now reflect on what happened. If you watch it with someone else explain to them what you saw. And ask them to explain their perception.

This video is a version of the classic *Heider and Simmel* experiment. In this, subjects were shown this two-and-a-half-minute video clip of moving geometric shapes. This is a still from the animation.

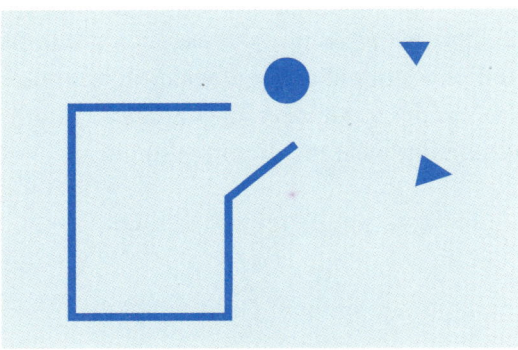

If you watched the animation, you will have seen a rectangle with a 'door' that is opened and closed as a small triangle, a larger triangle, and a circle move around it.

When you fed back to your companion, if you explained something along the lines of 'the circle and the triangle were having a fight and then the smaller triangle helped ...' etc. your response has been to tell a story. And that's what people normally do. People describe different perceptions but nearly all involve the idea that there's some kind of narrative. In fact, the movements are random.

In the original experiment subjects were asked to 'Describe the content of the movie in a few sentences.' Most did not limit themselves to describing geometric shapes moving randomly either, but instead constructed stories that explained what they thought was the relationship between the different actions. For example, some saw the big triangle as chasing the little circle, while the small triangle tried to save the circle. Subjects also gave vivid descriptions when asked to describe the 'personality' of the shapes. Obviously, this is all imagined. The shapes simply move. There is no 'story' but we *need* one to make sense of the actions.

The conclusion of the Heider and Simmel experiment is that an audience will not only invent a story, they will interpret any story or stimulus in their own way. (Think, for example, of any news story that promotes controversy. Did Trump standing behind Hilary Clinton in the Presidential debates show his eagerness to contribute, or a misogynist desire to unnerve? It depended on how you wanted to frame that data as a story.) For those of us involved in social change, this means it is vital that we know how our audience thinks about the topic we are telling a story about, and what their mindset is, so that our message has the desired impact. In communication, what matters is not what we say, but what the other person hears.

Why Are Stories so Important for Social Change?

Stories make us feel something, and unless we feel, we won't act. (The clue is in the word *e-motion*.) In our experience of working with stories in fundraising and campaigning we have found that, if used correctly, stories have seven powerful payoffs in social change.

1. Stories are memorable. In one of our workshops we discussed the global water problem. We showed data on population trends, water consumption for drinking, irrigation, and sanitation, as well as the number of people suffering from lack of water. Lots of people nodded at each graph and chart.

We then told the story of Rachel, who died tragically, aged nine, and her continued legacy of providing clean water to people who need it by her gift to charity: water. (You can find out about Rachel here. www.charitywater.org/rachels-gift.)

A few slides later, we asked our audience what they remembered about the water problem. No one could remember any numbers or facts. Everyone recalled Rachel's story.

2. Stories are personally relevant. When we follow a story, we can often see ourselves in it, usually as the hero or heroine. That is why many strong stories do not portray a perfect hero/ine who always gets it right. They show a good person with noble intentions, but who makes mistakes or has certain weaknesses, just like us. The hero/ine often goes through a transformation through which s/he overcomes the challenges s/he is facing. This is the inspirational part of the story that gives us hope in becoming our better self. It also explains why you don't need to portray your organisation as perfect—explaining that you make mistakes and then rectify them can make you more credible and engaging, see below.

3. Stories build trust. Telling stories about yourself, or your organisation, helps build trust between you and your audience. Interestingly, even stories that recount our failures can build trust. (See *They Call Me Naughty Lola*, below.) Once this trust is established, your audience will support you of their own volition. People often use the story as a form of proof to themselves or others. Stories or case studies can be a much stronger behaviour changer than other forms of persuasion. (Like the examples on weight-loss programme websites. They are almost exclusively anecdotal, but concrete, case studies of transformation: 'Like Jim you could lose 10 kilograms in just 10 weeks' rather than '90% of people on our XYZ programme lost an average of 20% of body weight in 12 weeks, reducing their BMI to 21.')

They Call Me Naughty Lola[3]

They Call Me Naughty Lola is the title for a collection of real dating advertisements originally published in the *London Review of Books*. The adverts below were among the most successful in attracting dates. What's interesting about these successful ones, is that they show people being quite ironically negative about themselves, generally in a humorous way. This signals that honesty, or even a little self-deprecation, is a great way to attract a partner. And maybe even something NGOs could learn from in terms of attracting supporters?

---

[3] *They Call Me Naughty Lola, London Review of Books*, Reprinted by Simon & Schuster, Inc.

Adverts by men

- Bald, fat, short, and ugly male, 53, seeks short-sighted woman with tremendous sexual appetite.
- Mature gentleman, 62, aged well, noble grey looks, fit and active, sound mind and unfazed by the fickle demands of modern society ... Damn it, I have to pee again.
- Unashamed triumphalist male for the past 46 years. Will I bore you? Probably. Do I care? Probably not.
- Bastard. Complete and utter. Whatever you do, don't reply—you'll only regret it.

Adverts by women

- Eager-to-please woman, 36, seeks domineering man to take advantage of her flagging confidence. Tell me I'm pretty, then watch me cling.
- Blah blah, whatever. Indifferent woman. Go ahead and write. Box no. 3253. Like I care.
- Your stars for today: A pretty Cancerian, 35, will cook you a lovely meal, caress your hair softly, then squeeze every damn penny from your adulterous bank account before slashing the tyres of your Beamer. Let that serve as a warning. Now then, risotto?

4. Stories normally create a sense of balance at the end. Think of Greek tragedies where the Eumenides have to restore moral order at the end of the play, or Grimms' *Fairy Tales* where everything turns out right. Stories most often have a happy, fair, and positive ending that helps us make sense of the world, and give us hope that we can create a more just place. Many charities base their campaigns on stories that look as though they could go wrong, and ask us to make the story different, better or fairer.

5. Stories bind us together with a common narrative. One of the pleasures of watching a movie together, or reading the same novel, is the discussions that follow. Many watercooler conversations on a Monday morning are about a show or film that people may have seen, and a discussion of the shared reactions.

In both fundraising and campaigning, it is important to create stories that others want to share. Often stories give individuals permission to share their experience. When the UK's child protection charity, the NSPCC, ran its famous its *Full Stop* campaign, designed to raise awareness of cruelty to children, it not only provoked a strong philanthropic reaction, but also gave 'permission' for many adults to share and talk about their personal experience of child abuse.

6. Stories fit with how our brain works. They link strongly to ideas of personalisation and completion. Our brains are used to '… this, and then that …' thinking, or cause and effect. This is how stories work. We feel stressed with random occurrences, disconnected facts, and the apparent meaninglessness of many of life's events, including our own. (That is also why we often assign human attributes to animals and objects to avoid a sense of meaninglessness.)

Stories balance the new and the familiar. They tell us about situations and feelings we are familiar with 'That's exactly how I feel when …' But they also tell us things we do not expect. That is why we describe some books as a 'page-turner' or 'unputdownable.' 'Page-turner' stories play on our need for closure. When a chapter ends with a statement like 'He opened the door and couldn't believe his eyes' or 'She wondered what to expect as she opened the envelope' we cannot wait to know what was going to happen, and we say to ourselves, 'OK, one more chapter, then I'll go to sleep.'

7. Stories are useful. While many of us read fiction for enjoyment, stories have a practical value. They make us more emotionally intelligent, familiar with a broader range of emotions, and relationships. Studies show that those who read more fiction are better able to identify the emotional states of others, and empathise with them, than those who don't read fiction. Stories enable us to think differently about many topics: ethics, gender, violence, politics, sex, relationships, class, and more.

We pay attention when people tell stories, and much of what we learn is through stories. In an increasingly globalized world, stories can cross the borders of language, culture and age. And in a time of information abundance and attention scarcity stories illuminate complex truths. They can also build a sense of community and common purpose. They connect in the brain and make data more meaningful.

The 7 Basic Story Plots[4]

Earlier we mentioned how common the 'brave hero tackles monster' story line is—from *Beowulf* to *Jaws*. Many charity stories have different specific details or narratives but share the brave hero/ine framework. For example, MSF describing a nurse's courage in the face of the monster Ebola, or Malala the Nobel Peace Prize-winning young woman, as a child seeking education and standing up to the tyrannical Taliban monster. In both cases there is even more resonance—an evil force attacking peaceful innocent people and threatening their lives. In this situation traditional solutions don't work, and unusual and heroic action by an ordinary person is needed. We like it when ordinary people do extraordinary things and overcome the odds. They change the world and make a difference. In the process, they are also transformed. And we see the possibility for ourselves to be transformed and to create transformations.

---

[4] It is important to distinguish between the narrative and the story. The *narrative* represents how you deliver your main message.—'Good always defeats evil, but only after paying a price.' 'The hero will always face a challenge, will suffer setbacks, but with perseverance and help from his mentor, s/he will reach her/his goal.' The narrative involves the archetype of a hero, mentor, rebel, ruler, sage, etc. The *story* is the specific execution of such a narrative—it might take place in a different environment, and with different personalities representing the narrative's archetypes.

Despite the fact there are many millions of narrative variations, stories have very few basic plots. The 18th Century Italian playwright Carlo Gozzi declared there were 36 possible plots. Two hundred and fifty years later, author Christopher Booker claimed there were only seven. How many of your favourite films or books draw on these basic plots?

1. **Overcoming the monster** (*Beowulf, Dracula, Star Wars.*)
2. **Rags to riches** (*Cinderella, Aladdin, David Copperfield.*)
3. **The valiant quest** (*Iliad, King Solomon's Mines, Indiana Jones.*)
4. **Voyage and return** (*Alice in Wonderland, Gulliver's Travels, Apollo 13.*)
5. **Redemption through comedy** (*Much Ado About Nothing, Bridget Jones, Four Weddings and A Funeral.*)
6. **Tragedy: The fall from grace** (*Macbeth, Carmen, Moby Dick.*)
7. **Rebirth and transformation** (*The Frog Prince, Beauty and the Beast, The Snow Queen.*)

When shaping your story for your campaign or message, it is worth considering how you might use these story archetypes to frame or structure it.

Brand Narratives and Fundraising Stories

Successful and sustainable brands manage to strike a balance between consistency over time, and freshness in-line with societal changes and the need for innovation. Apple tells a *Think Different* narrative in a variety of stories. Nike asks us to *Just Do It* in many different ways. Or for a more more prosaic example, in 2012 the UK snack bar Twix, which consists of two separate chocolate biscuit bars—began a series of adverts which created a fake backstory about how the two halves were made by different rival factories. According to Patrick Fagan 'The campaign was a smash: the UK sales volume grew by 37% and household penetration by 4.3%.[5]' Before the story this was just one biscuit among many, After the story it was a brand with character.

---

[5] *#Hooked*, Patrick Fagan, Pearson 2017, p. 16.

The James Bond movie industry is an almost perfect example of balancing brand consistency and freshness—apart from *On Her Majesty's Secret Service*, which went way off brand with a Bond who was a romantic, went shopping, got married, etc. Audiences did not like it, and the producers learned not to make the same mistake again.

Similarly, Coca Cola, having maintained its consistent brand identity for nigh on 100 years, made a short-lived mistake with the launch of New Coke in 1985. And its less successful arch rival, Pepsi, has been through 11 major logo changes since 1898.[6]

Thinking about charities–how many would you say have maintained and updated their brand identity with the same consistency as the Bond franchise or Coke? UNICEF? MSF? Red Cross/Crescent?

What Kind of Hero is Your Brand?

Linked to the idea of story archetypes is the idea that brands represent themselves as specific kinds of heroes. This builds on work in *The Hero and the Outlaw* by Margaret Mark and Carol S. Pearson.[7] They developed a model that suggests there are twelve archetypal 'heroes' used in fiction and drama, and brands can also use to position themselves. Here are the twelve, each shown with a commercial brand that might commonly be associated with them.

The Innocent (Innocent)	The Adventurer (GoPro)	The Sage (The Economist)	The Hero (Nike)
The Outlaw (Harley Davidson)	The Magician (Apple)	The Regular Guy (PG Tips)	The Lover (Chanel)
The Jester (Ben & Jerry's)	The Caregiver (Heinz)	The Creator (Lego)	The Ruler (Rolex)

(With acknowledgement to Patrick Fagan, *Hooked* and http://visionone.co.uk/consumer/brand-research/brand-archetypes-2.)

---

[6] For some interesting insight on this see http://www.brandinfection.com/2009/07/31/evolution-or-revolution-what-branding-strategy-pays-off-the-cola-wars-of-pepsi-vs-coke.

[7] McGraw-Hill Professional (2001).

What brand archetype does your organisation currently represent? What archetype would you *like* to be identified with? Does
that suit your supporters and the direction of your campaigns? What
stories do you have that would support that brand positioning?

Brands and Storytelling

A brand is what an entity (person, product, service, organisation)
stands for in people's hearts and minds. New brands become popular
when they offer their target audience a proposition that is useful
and engaging. The newness of the organisation, service, or offering
can add appeal to the proposition. The brand then faces a dilemma.
On the one hand, the brand may want to repeat what has worked so
far. On the other hand, simply repeating what you've done in the
past is a recipe for consumer boredom and failure. The challenge for
brands is to strike a balance between familiarity and newness.

From a brain point of view, we know that the brain feels at ease
with the familiar because it is risk averse, and fears the unknown.
However, if a signal is simply repeated continuously, it does not
arouse our interest. In economics, this is known as the *law of diminishing utility*. In psychology, this is known as *habituation*.

In a world where about half of the 100 largest economies are
corporations, not countries, many of the stories shaping our world
today come from commercial brands. And these corporations spend
money sharing their brands' stories, spending over $400 billion on
global advertising.

When an audience listens to a brand story, they want to see their
own realities and values reflected in it. Whether you are an NGO or a
business, you should start with your audience and its needs and desires.
Then introduce the brand as a catalyst that can help the hero (the
supporter, donor, consumer, volunteer) meet their needs and achieve
his/her goal. In storytelling terms, when a brand tells a story, the
brand is not the hero. The ordinary person is the hero, and the brand
is the mentor who helps the hero achieve their goals.

Three Common Errors in Brand Storytelling

- *Not being true to the brand, making false promises that cannot be translated in reality.* VW's dishonest covering up of emissions was a massive cost to their integrity. Scandals involving dishonesty, cheating, breaking promises, covering-up, and lack of transparency, damage trust—and trust is any brand's most valuable asset. Recent scandals involving UK charities and exploitative fundraising methods have had a significant impact on donations and income levels.

- *Portraying the brand itself and what it does as the hero.* This self obsession shows a lack of understanding. An audience or the people who deliver the service need to be the heroes. In Médecins Sans Frontières (MSF) communications, the doctors *and* the donors are the complementary heroes. In our work with the International Committee of the Red Cross (ICRC), we've struggled with the 'neutrality' mandate and branding—which may mean it is seen as less attractive by private donors.

- *Relying on facts alone, and forgetting about emotional connections.* Many climate change organisations focus on the science. Look at the two images below. Which is likely to attract greater engagement? One of our colleagues, working on an environmental campaign website, suggested replacing the image of a map showing the impact of global warming on the Arctic with the polar bear on melting ice. This attracted five times more traffic and involvement. The map is too abstract. The polar bear picture suggests a story.[8]

---

[8] Note the bear picture is clearly photoshopped. It's not meant to be realistic, but rather to suggest an archetype of the situation.

The Long, the Short, and the *Very* Short of It

When we think of stories, sometimes we think of *Hamlet, War and Peace, Les Miserables, Lord of the Rings*, or *Harry Potter*. All successful, but all very long and detailed. Using these as a model would make your fundraising or campaign appeals a bit heavy. But you don't have to use thousands of words to convey your message. You can use just six.

Ernest Hemingway was approached by a man while drinking at his favourite bar, La Floridita, in Havana, Cuba. The man told him he knew Hemingway was a great writer, but he was busy and did not have the time to read Hemingway's sophisticated long works. The man challenged the author to write a short story overnight, and laid a significant bet the author couldn't do it. The next day Hemingway read his challenger the story he had written. We reprint it in full below:

'For sale: Baby shoes, never worn.'

Those six words are very clever and very moving. They convey the potential for a host of interpretations—inspiring *our* imaginations to create different stories. Note how important it is that we fill in much of the information. The learning is 'don't tell your story in too much detail.' Allow others to do some work and add some value.

This event and the six-word story sat in the realms of literary history for some time until a BBC World Service programme repeated it, and asked listeners to send in their version. This subsequently started a worldwide six-word story trend, with both famous authors and the general public sharing their work. Collections were published, and there is even a website devoted to six word stories.

Here are some of our favourite stories from the website:

- *I still make coffee for two.*
- *Never should have bought that ring.*
- *Mistakes were made, but smarter now.*
- *The light that night was perfect.*
- *After Harvard had baby with crackhead.*

- *Wasn't born a redhead. Fixed that.*
- *Well I thought it was funny.*

And here is our six-word summary of this chapter:

Stories deliver emotional and social impact.
Could you tell your organisation's story in six words? Try it. It's not easy but powerful to do.

HAI's Value Proposition

One of our favourite INGOs is Health Action International (HAI), based in Holland. The CEO, Tim Reed, does not quite manage six words but he has distilled HAI's value proposition in 4 × 6 words:

- 350 medicines cure 90% of global diseases.
- These are denied to 1.2 billion people.
- They're too expensive or not available.
- HAI ensures people can get them.

Two Very Different Examples of Storytelling in Digital Fundraising

Stories can fulfil different roles in fundraising, and can work in different modalities and formats. Coming up are two contrasting examples of this. One is a very 'spare' but powerful Direct Response TV (DRTV) advert in which Doctors Without Borders/MSF create a simple engaging story in 59 seconds. Almost everything here is an archetype, allowing you to fill in the details. The other involves the use of very specific concrete background stories linked to low-cost, second-hand goods to drive engagement. (This one links to the *IKEA effect*—discussed earlier.)

Doctors Without Borders (see it here https://www.youtube.com/
watch?v=Tm9D3MatgKw or goo.gl/vIsprG)

In this advert, the camera moves from above to what looks like a
generic 'African landscape.' A small van is rushing a child to a modest
health centre, where the doctors and nurses go in to action immediately and with a strong sense of urgency. There is no dialogue, but in
the background there is 'discordant' music, maybe in an African register, but not clear. We also hear stressed breathing, from the child
or his parents is also not clear.

As the doctors begin their work, the lights in the operation room
start flickering. The doctors look worried, for good reason, as the
power then goes off completely. Now we can only see a glimmer of
light, and hope, in the boy's eye.

We then cut sharply to a very brightly lit bank in a generic 'developed country', where a young woman goes to place a regular giving
standing order to donate to MSF. The moment her order is approved,
and we hear the sound of the teller's stamp, the light goes back in
the operating room.

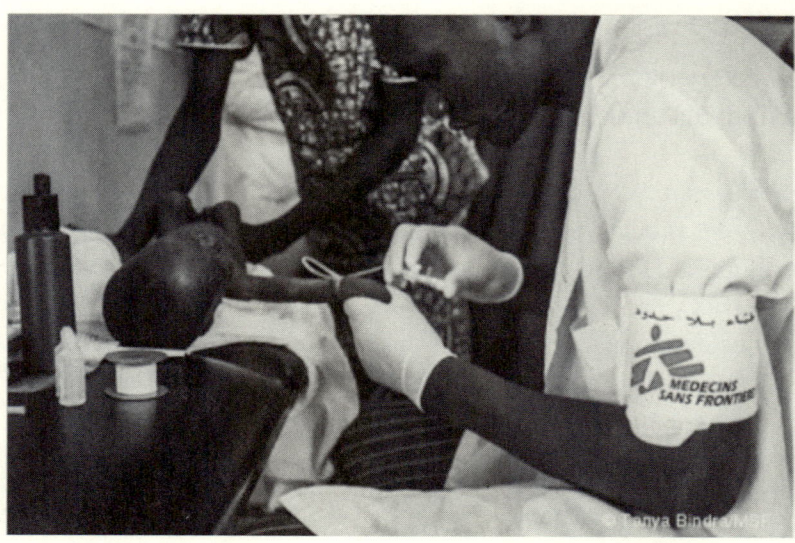

This is a powerful, emotive story that draws the viewer in from the first moment, wanting to know what is going to happen next. It has little detail, but there is a clear structure. It has a beginning (boy being rushed to a health centre), a middle with conflict (the doctors are performing a surgery in the operation room, but there is a sudden power cut), and an ending (when the donor signs off a donation, in another country, the electricity goes back to the operation room), and presumably the surgery is completed successfully.

The story is told in images and sounds but without words, and saying very little about the organisation MSF. Importantly the hero is the donor who helps the doctors and the child. The tangible and immediate impact the donation makes is highlighted dramatically in the way the light switches back on in the operation room as soon as the donation form is stamped.

Oxfam Shops: 'Find Out More Here'

The international development charity, Oxfam, has a major network of charity shops in the UK. In 2010 they wanted to see if they could sell more donated goods if customers to the shop knew the items' back stories. They spoke to donors and attached labels with their stories to a small number of the goods for sale.

While the experiment was not wholly successful—it did not directly lead to an increase in sales, it *did* make supporters and potential supporters feel more positive about their experience of the shop. Possibly a version of the added value engendered by the *IKEA Effect?* We also love this example from another UK charity shop.

Here the price is connected to an outcome.

The Power of Words in Stories

Roger Dooley is a neuroscientist and blogger who drew our attention to an interesting paper in *The Journal of Consumer Research.*[9] Dooley points out most of the time we do not consider the name of an offering or product in category terms. For example, toothpaste is pretty much toothpaste, milk is by-and-large milk, and a charity shop is broadly an 'under-a-fiver' charity shop.

However, what many restaurants do know is that what you call something affects its appeal and subsequent sales. In one test, people were more likely to order food described as 'Traditional Cajun Red

---

[9] Caglar Irmak, Beth Vallen, and Stefanie Rosen Robinson. 'The Impact of Product Name on Dieters' and Non-Dieters' Food Evaluations and Consumption.' *Journal of Consumer Research,* October 2011.

Beans with Rice' than 'Red beans with rice.' And in a follow up experiment, those who ordered the same dish but this time called 'Ma's Recipe Traditional Cajun ...' rated it as tastier! Just a few words help to create a 'back story' and higher emotional engagement in a product.

You might think System 2 would kick in for anyone on a diet as they carefully look at calorie counts and assess if a food is healthy or not. But food marketers are able to exploit our System 1 language preferences. In particular, unhealthy dishes that dieters might well want to avoid can be made more appealing. Relabel potato crisps as 'veggie chips,' and make a pasta-vegetable combination appear healthier by calling it 'pasta salad.' Sugary drinks become 'sparkling fruit-flavoured water.' And a stand-out example for Dooley, and us, is the renaming of 'cake' as a 'muffin.' No one would sensibly order calorific carrot cake and a strawberry milkshake for breakfast, but what about a nice 'healthy' carrot muffin and a fruit smoothie to start your day?

The study named above shows that dieters, or those trying to eat healthily, will avoid some foods by name. So, they will skip the associated-with-calories 'milkshake,' but will still happily order the healthier-sounding, but exactly the same, 'smoothie.' Another test showed that subjects ate more 'fruit chews' than 'candy chews,' even though the product was exactly the same.

You can achieve the same impact with other senses. Think about colour. Light blue in Europe and North America is seen as a low-calorie colour; think of Ribena and light Ribena, compare Cup a Soup or Slim a Soup, or consider low-fat Ambrosia Rice pudding versus the 'normal' kind. All use the blue identifier to signal low-calories. In fact, there's often little difference calorifically between these products.

This phenomenon may even go further, to the point where as Maya Angelou said 'words are things.' They can impact our sense of smell. In a study[10] *'Reading Cinnamon Activates Olfactory Brain Regions'*, a research team showed subjects a list of words, some of which

---

[10] To read the full study see www.ncbi.nlm.nih.gov/pubmed/16651007.

connected to smells. (Words like 'cowshed,' 'garlic' and 'cinnamon' with strong associations to smell were tested against words with lesser association.) The participants had to rate words 1-7 based on a scale for strength of the association. While the association was being made the participant's brains were scanned using MRI.

What the scan revealed is that when words with a strong smell association were recognised they stimulated an area we know to be associated with strong smells anyway. Implication: the word itself can stimulate the experience of the smell. In the language of neuroscience 'What wires together, fires together.'

The simple implication is that you want your language and stories to have impact in a way that's concrete and stimulates all of the senses: colour, smell, taste, touch and sounds. ('The cruel disease of cancer', 'the smell of refugee camp poverty') The more specific the better. In this way, you can engage the brains and hearts of supporters with strong associations.

Beyond Food

Changing the words used can help distinguish a similar product, or make people feel OK about something that rationally might be bad for them. Similarly, changing the language you use about your organisation might allow supporters or even non-supporters to think differently about you.

We have already looked at Kiva and Lend with Care, who talk to supporters about their financial commitment as an 'investment' not a 'donation.' By *reframing* the language, they broaden the pool of supporters to include individuals who do not necessarily agree with the idea of charity, but like the idea of helping people to become self-sufficient.

We could consider changing language elsewhere. Should campaigners talk simply about 'vaccines' or change it to the more powerful 'life-changing vaccines'? Or about 'social disadvantage,' or 'grinding poverty'? Don't be afraid to use strong language.

Learning from Storytelling

In this chapter, we have analysed how stories work—their definition, origin, and structure. We have touched on the evolutionary psychology, neuroscience, and behavioural economics behind stories. We have also looked at how words are a powerful ingredient to an engaging story—and how you can think about your charity brand as a story.

In the context of social marketing, campaigning and fundraising we know that:

- An individualised *story* has more impact than a big number. People are moved to act by personal stories, not statistics.
- A consistent narrative for your brand, *and* keeping it interesting with fresh story updates is a powerful draw and a source of security.
- You should develop a relevant archetype for your organisation that is true to the brand, distinctive against other organisations, and relevant to your target audience.
- A story where the central plot is 'overcoming the odds' has a special power. It strikes a balance between positive and negative communication. You need to be David and find your Goliath
- If you can create a story where the supporter is the hero, this unlocks a powerful response. Your organisation should be their enabler. Do not try and make the organisation the hero.
- To succeed a story must follow a consistent structure. Bring your story to a clear end, ideally with a call to action.
- Don't overshare or give too much information. Offer a broad framework and ideas tied to characters. Allow the supporter to fill in the details and complete the story.
- Don't tell a perfectionist story about your agency or its work, admit to failings or imperfect results. Ask people to help you become better.
- It is important to pay attention to story execution and narrative. Choose your words and images carefully, and manage them according to the different cultural norms you are working with.

Chapter 8

Touch with Emotions Not Data

Summary

Emotion and motivation share a common Latin root word *movere* which means 'to move.'

In other words, if we *feel* nothing, we *do* nothing.

In this chapter we start with a moving and shocking case study from the recent past, and explore the impact and implications for humanitarian work through the lens of behavioural economics. The story also reintroduces us to the *identifiable victim effect*—discussed in **Chapter 4**—a strong emotional heuristic that anyone involved in tackling issues of social justice needs to be aware of and to work with sensitively and ethically.

To successfully use emotions for social change it is important to understand what they are, from both an evolutionary and neuroscientific perspective. We describe the most basic and relevant emotions, with an emphasis on how they link to empathy.

We also explore how the identifiable victim effect is linked to the idea of *in-groups* and *out-groups*. It is much easier to promote empathy, and associated action, if we can ensure our target market identifies closely with the individual or small group for whom we are trying to secure support.

Counterintuitively, it seems we can *reduce* the effect of what we are trying to do by mixing individual emotional stories with facts and data. (For example, 'Jim is 18 and has nowhere safe to sleep tonight in London despite freezing temperatures. [individual + emotional]. He is one of 10,000 young people in London who are homeless tonight and every night, 20% of whom are likely to be assaulted.' [group + numbers.]) By mixing emotion and facts our brains are torn between System 1 and System 2 processing. If the System 2 approach takes over, then we may withdraw or reduce our support, worried that we cannot make a real difference.

The science of emotions helps explain why they are quite so important in decision making—for both businesses and not-for-profit organisations. Interestingly Harvard scientists have managed to work out a monetisable value for different levels of emotional engagement—even on products as prosaic as washing up liquids.

In the world of campaigning, fundraising and advocacy, understanding how emotions work can help us convey messages that trigger the desired emotion, and enable us to establish strong connections with our supporters.

Aylan Kurdi: The Boy on the Beach

In spring 2011, the conflict between the Syrian regime and its opposition turned into a civil war. By April 2014, the United Nations estimated that 8,803 children had been killed. The Oxford Research Group estimated that 11,420 were killed by late November 2013. By January 2015, the total estimated child deaths ranged between 140,220 and 330,380. This is in addition to many hundreds of thousands of killed or injured adult civilians, and some millions of refugees. Despite this heavy and sad humanitarian toll, media, public, and political attention has been disappointingly low. Most humanitarian charities have had difficulty raising money for Syria, despite the huge number of casualties. We are sure you will agree this is appalling. And we are equally sure that by the time you have finished reading this paragraph, you will have already forgotten all the numbers mentioned in it. Let's try a different tack.

On Wednesday 2 September 2015 the world finally seemed to pay attention to the Syrian tragedy.[1] The body of 3-year-old Aylan Kurdi was discovered by a police officer off the coast of Turkey's Bodrum Peninsula. Aylan's small body was washed up on the sand, face down. He was wearing a red t-shirt, blue shorts, and black shoes.

Aylan was one of 12 people who drowned while trying to reach a Greek island from Turkey on a rubber raft. His 5-year-old brother Galip, also dead, washed up on another part of the beach.

Nilüfer Demir, a photographer working for the Turkish agency Doğan Haber Ajansı (DHA), took Aylan's picture. It was picked up and spread like wildfire to people all over the world. Nilüfer was horrified even as she took the picture. In an interview some days later she spoke about the impact on her of the experience.[2] *'I almost felt paralysed when I saw the child's corpse. Later, I learned that he was just three years old. At the same time, as a photographer I have a task that does not allow time for second guessing, for freezing. So, I took the pictures.'*

Asked how she felt about the picture reaching the world so quickly, she replied *'On the one hand, I wish I hadn't had to take that picture. I would have much preferred to have taken one of Aylan playing*

[1] There is a very interesting and exhaustive discussion of how the image grew in impact on social media and how it changed the conversation about refugees online here http://research.gold.ac.uk/14624/1/KURDI%20REPORT.pdf.

[2] https://www.vice.com/en_uk/article/zngqpx/nilfer-demir-interview-876.

on the beach than photographing his corpse. What I saw has left a terrible impression that keeps me awake at night.'

'Then again, I am happy that the world finally cares and is mourning the dead children. I hope that my picture can contribute to changing the way we look at immigration in Europe, and that no more people have to die on their way out of a war.'

The conflicting emotions of Nilüfer were mirrored by many others in both the mass and social media. One media observer remarked *'If these powerful images of a dead Syrian child on a beach don't change Europe's attitude to refugees, what will?'* The Executive Director of the *New York Times* said, *'We debated it, but ultimately we chose to run ... this photo because it brings home the enormity of this tragedy.'* The Assistant Managing Editor of The *Los Angeles Times* expressed the shocking influence of the photo saying, *'We have written stories about hundreds of migrants dead in capsized boats, sweltering trucks, lonely rail lines, but it took a tiny boy on a beach to really bring home to those readers who may not yet have grasped the magnitude of the migrant crisis.'*[3]

But why then? Why did the world not react equally strongly when we read about the millions of Syrian refugees and the thousands of deaths? Because when we can give misery a name—Aylan —we experience the *identifiable victim effect.*[4]

> *A single death is a tragedy: a million deaths is a statistic.*
>
> Stalin

---

[3] Some media, it must be said, were against publishing Aylan's picture, seeing it as a violation of his dignity since he could not consent to becoming a symbol. However, the overwhelming sentiment was that publishing was morally the right thing to do.

[4] It is not unusual for humanitarian organisations to struggle to raise money for situations like Syrian refugees. The Syrian crisis is considered a result of war and is 'man-made,' as opposed to 'natural' disasters, such as earthquakes, hurricanes, or tsunamis. 'Man-made' disasters are harder to raise money for, even when they last longer than natural disasters, or have more victims, which they often do. Victims of 'man-made' disasters are often blamed for their situation 'They brought it on themselves,' while victims of natural disasters are not—'It could have happened to us.' Yet, this distinction collapses when the story of a single person is told, especially that of a child.

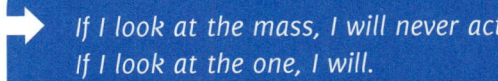

If I look at the mass, I will never act.
If I look at the one, I will.

Mother Teresa

Focus on the Identifiable Victim

Probably the most intimate connection we can make is to identify with one other person, an identifiable victim. The identifiable victim is a population of one. And when we help that person we are helping *everyone* there is to help. *We* feel that we can solve the problem. Our impulsive and intuitive System 1 is activated.

As part of System 1, emotions work primarily on a subconscious level. The language of the subconscious is mainly stories, metaphors, images, music, and other subtle codes.

As a campaigner or fundraiser, you might believe that you have to appeal to supporters' emotions first to capture their attention and then it's essential to back this up with facts and figures to put the problem in context. *But,* and it is a big but, the evidence tells us this is not how people work. (This challenge to common sense is part of the beauty of the behavioural economics and neuroscience approach.) When we present an identifiable victim proposition we activate System 1, resulting in a strong, fast, intuitive and emotional reaction. However, adding data, numbers, and facts to the story is likely to activate the slow, deliberate and analytical System 2. Also with larger numbers, System 2 asks us to explore the scale of the challenge against the scale of the resources we can contribute. And at that point we risk diluting the fierce emotional reaction and then deciding to do nothing.

This psychological conflict is elegantly summed up in a set of experiments conducted by Paul Slovic and colleagues, where he compared the impact on donations for what he called *identifiable* and *statistical* victims.[5] (These experiments further explore and quantify the broad conclusions of the Rokia example we discussed in **Chapter 4**.) Below we explore the results and implications of several of these experiments.

Experiment 1: Two groups were presented with different propositions—one with an *identifiable victim* proposition, and the other with a *statistical victim* proposition. The group looking at the identifiable victim proposition gave much more than the group with the statistical victim proposition, broadly repeating the Rokia result.[6]

Experiment 2: Two groups of similar participants read a summary of the identifiable victim research. They were then asked to contribute financially to either the identifiable victim proposition or the statistical victim proposition, depending on which group they were in. This was obviously meant to create informed advocates; the activist's dream audience that both understands the challenge *and* supports the cause with a gift.

In fact, the shared research insight had an adverse effect on donation levels from the *identifiable victim* group. But had no effect on the *statistical victim* group. The subjects in identifiable victim group, having had the 'emotional' nature of what would have been their typical reaction pointed out to them, seemingly behaved in a much less generous way, perhaps more 'rationally.'

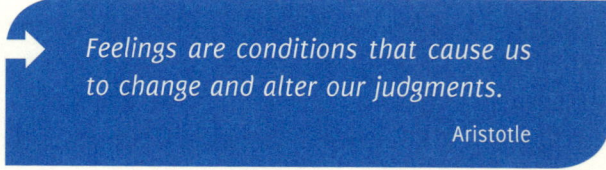

Feelings are conditions that cause us to change and alter our judgments.

Aristotle

[5] Paul Slovic (ed.), *The Feeling of Risk: New Perspectives on Risk Perception*, Routledge, Ch4, *Sympathy and Callousness: The Impact of Deliberative Thought on Donations to Identifiable and Statistical Victims*. Small, Lowenstein and Slovic.

[6] The differences in figures are quite significant, and if scaled up across a mass audience could represent a sizeable difference in income. The average amount donated to an identifiable victim proposition was $2.38. For a statistical victim proposition it was $1.14. The average for an identifiable victim followed up by statistics was $1.43.

The behavioural economics model suggests that when you activate System 1 with emotional messages, you shouldn't confuse those you are trying to influence with data. Otherwise you risk their switching to System 2 mode and so *reducing* their strong emotional reaction to your message. However, if you are already activating System 2 with statistical-logical reasoning, it won't matter if you add *more* rational information.

Experiment 3: In this variation, two groups of subjects were *primed* in either a general logical or emotional way. Group 1 was primed to induce a 'calculating' mode. They were given tasks that needed them to deliberately answer logical arithmetical problems such as:

Q. If an object travels at five feet per minute, then by your calculations how many feet will it travel in 360 seconds?
A. _____ feet.

Group 2 was primed with 'feelings.' Subjects were asked to base their answers on the feelings they experienced. They were asked questions such as:

Q. When you hear the word 'baby' what do you feel?
A. Please use one word to describe your predominant feeling _____.

This general emotional priming resulted in a much higher average donation than the calculation priming in the context of the identifiable victim ($2.34 vs. $1.19), but not in the case of the statistical victim ($1.45 vs. $1.34).

This experiment set suggests that consciously engaging *either* System 1 or System 2 modes of thought helps drive support. However, activating the fast, emotional System 1 leads to a stronger, more positive reaction to donating or supporting. Rational thinking before or after activating System 1 invites the slow and analytical System 2 to take over. At best you risk slowing down the more powerful emotional reaction, at worst you may eliminate it altogether.

The researchers summarise it objectively: 'Deliberative thinking reduces the reliance on sympathy when evaluating an identifiable victim.' Their assessment is that data leads people to think their feelings are less relevant to the decision they are about to make. And as we said at the start it is *feelings* that drive action.

It's probably not surprising that people want to give money to identifiable victims like Rokia rather than unnamed and generalised famine victims. But there are some wider implications from the research related to sympathy and how it connects to charitable giving. For example, the research team found that 'if people are told about the *inconsistent* levels of sympathy evoked by identifiable and statistical victims, people reduce their giving to identifiable victims, but don't increase their giving to statistical victims.' So, they become more consistent, but in a downward direction. The normative heuristic unhelpfully kicks in.

The study makes the fairly obvious point that the overall level of giving bears no clear relationship to the likely social payoff of the funds raised, nor indeed to the amounts needed. For example, there have been a number of well publicised cases where very different sums were donated to help very different identifiable victims. In 1987, Jessica McClure, then an 18-month-old toddler, fell into a disused well near her home in Texas.[7] She was rescued 58 hours later, with some non-life threatening injuries. Despite the relatively positive outcome the worldwide media attention for 'Baby Jessica' drove almost $1 million, at 1987 values, in public donations. In another case, during the invasion of Iraq, American missiles landed on 12-year-old Ali Abbas' home. The missiles killed his parents, including his pregnant mother, his brother, and 13 other family members. Ali himself lost both arms and had third-degree burns on 35 percent of his body. His cause drove around $550,000 in donations, only half as much, and mostly from Europeans. Even animals, when identified as individuals, can also generate significant sympathy. In 2002, donors

---

[7] https://www.thesun.co.uk/news/3046889/baby-jessica-mcclure-opens-up-about-1987-rescue.

responded to an unusual Humane Society appeal. They contributed $50,000 which paid for a mid-Pacific rescue for Forgea, a rat-catcher dog which had been mistakenly abandoned on a tanker. (The dog, once rescued, was taken to Hawaii.) We're not saying any of these cases is intrinsically 'better' or more deserving than the other. But there's clearly no rational basis for the differentiation.

Assessing Value?

Clearly, when we are made aware of a specific identifiable victim and we connect emotionally it drives giving. But why? Professor Small says that a significant body of psychological research suggests 'people pay greater attention and have stronger emotional reactions to vivid rather than pallid information.'

So, part of the answer seems to be the emotional *intensity* of the cases above. You might almost say 'the drama makes the difference.' The way our brains respond to this vivid information is interesting: our minds respond to proportions, rather than absolute values. Professor Small maintains 'This is why we gasp when we see a 50%-off sale, regardless of whether the original price is $5 or $500.' She goes on, 'Similarly, saving 10 lives out of a group of 100 is a high proportion and thus evokes a greater emotional response than saving 10 lives out of one million. An identifiable victim is the extreme, in this sense. When a victim has been identified, she becomes her own frame of reference—there was only one Baby Jessica to save—and thus receives the greatest level of sympathy.'

We seem to struggle to organise our emotional response sensibly. We are unable to compare scales of magnitude in terms of disaster. 2,973 people died in the immediate impact of 9/11. This is a tiny number when compared with the scale of slaughter in the Rwandan genocide or perhaps 800,000. Yet one event seemed to attract less attention. You could of course argue that even the Rwanda slaughter was dwarfed by the 35 million who have died of AIDS. Small's research seems to reinforce our earlier conclusion about how un empathetic and unengaged System 2 can be: 'Thinking about problems analytically can easily suppress sympathy for smaller-scale disasters without, our research suggests, producing much of an increase in caring for larger-scale disasters.'

Empathy in Action: How Close Are You?

Consider these scenarios:

Scenario 1: A trolley is running down a train track, out of control. Five workers are making repairs on the tracks and if you do nothing they will be killed by the trolley. There is a lever nearby which, if you pulled it, would divert the train away from the five workers, but the trolley would then kill one worker standing on the other track.

Question: Would you pull the lever and kill one person, instead of killing five? Most people would say yes, since killing one person is better than killing five.

Scenario 2: Same as first scenario with five workers on the train track.

Question: This time, instead of a lever to pull there is a large man standing next to the tracks. If you push him in front of the train, he would be killed, but the other workers will be saved.

Would you push the guy and kill one person instead of killing five?

Most people say: 'No, I would not push the guy, even though it is still killing one vs. five.'

There are several philosophical and psychological perspectives on this riddle, but neuroimaging provides a fresh perspective on how we come to those decisions.

In *Scenario 1*, pulling a lever, there is no direct contact between the subject and the people involved, the brain sees a maths problem and only the brain parts involved in problem-solving are activated. In *Scenario 2*, involving physical contact, brain parts involved in emotions are activated.

In today's world, much of what we do does not involve others directly. The knock-on effect is we run the risk of feeling nothing as we make decisions affecting others who are distant or different. Think of drone 'pilots' using screens to aim at targets many thousands of miles away. The output can look very much like the kind of thing you see in a computer game. Also consider that the cost of one quality-of-life improving guide dog for a person in UK is the same as the cost of life-saving drugs for perhaps 20 people in sub-Saharan Africa.

A Range of Emotions

Human beings experience and express a wide variety of emotions, and psychologists have tried to group them. The most popular classification is Paul Ekman's seven basic emotions: Happiness, Surprise, Sadness, Anger, Fear, Disgust, and Contempt.[8] The important points are:

- This is only an overarching basic framework, and a longer list of nuanced emotions can be included under each basic one. For example, under *happiness* we can list a spectrum of possibilities including feeling cheerful, content, satisfied, grateful, excited, thrilled, terrific, glad, loved, calm, etc.
- Most of the basic emotions are negative: sadness, anger, fear, disgust, and contempt. Surprise is neutral, and happiness the only positive one. From an evolutionary point of view, some researchers believe, negative emotions have a stronger survival value than positive ones. Feeling fear when faced with a dangerous beast, or anger against an enemy, or disgust on seeing strange-

---

[8] For more on Paul Eckman see https://en.wikipedia.org/wiki/Paul_Ekman.

looking food, may help us avoid danger. Going through life with fewer positive emotions might not be a very cheerful way to live, but it isn't a serious survival threat.

- Surprise, while usually neutral, is a special emotion and highlights the fact that we get used to our environment and what does not change. So we can slip into a state of *habituation*. Under habituation, the usual stimuli do not attract our attention, and we need a surprise to engage. This is one of the reasons that it works so well in advertising.[9]

- In addition to the *type* of emotion, *intensity* is another important dimension. We might experience any of Ekman's emotions at low or high intensity. We are more likely to move from *feeling* to *doing* when we experience an emotion at high intensity. Research has established that the key factor in ensuring videos go viral on YouTube was the use of high arousal emotions.[10]

Feeling Your Way to the Answer

Let's be clear, emotions do not always distort decisions—we need them to make sound decisions.

When we approach an issue, our position and action depend on how close we are, physically and metaphorically, to the people involved. If we are distant, we approach the issue through System 2, and apply logic using data and numbers. However, if we are close to the issue or people involved, System 1 dominates, and our emotions initiate our reaction and action.

In fundraising it is important that the supporter feels close to the recipient of the donation. That's why many individuals prefer to donate in their locality, where they are physically or socially close to those they are supporting; or to their church, where they feel spiritually close.

---

[9] For more on this see a range of examples quoted by Patrick Fagan in *#Hooked*, Pearson, 2017, Chapter 6.

[10] Nelson-Field, K., Riebe, E., & Newstead, K. (2013). 'The emotions that drive viral video.' *Australasian Marketing Journal, 21*(4), 205-211.

Physically pushing the fat man onto the tracks makes us feel *responsible* for the act of killing one person. This is not true when we pull the lever, even though we are still killing a person. The two options are logically similar, but psychologically very different. When you communicate with a supporter, you want them to feel that they are psychologically responsible for the desired result of their donation or campaign action.

Make it Real

Creating empathy is harder when raising funds for causes where the context, people or culture may be unfamiliar. It may be hard to generate empathy for a campaign action on behalf of sufferers of an illness that is not well known or widely understood. In these cases, it may be useful to create the feeling of closeness in creative indirect ways. Some examples of where Bernard Ross and his company, =mc have helped with this:

- *Scottish Opera* had high net worth supporters walk up several flights of stairs to the cheaper seats, where most had never been, to help them understand the need to make access easier for older patrons or those with disabilities.
- *Oxford Museum of Modern Art* sent corporate prospects a nail with a direct mail appeal asking for help to secure the kind of exciting and challenging art to be hung on the gallery walls.
- *The Asthma Society* used a straw, and asked people to try and breathe through it to help people without breathing difficulties to understand how hard it is to cope with asthma.
- The *British Film Institute* gave a supporter a piece of crumbling nitrate film with a clip from their favourite movie to show the impact of decay and the need for conservation.

Context: Get Up Close and Personal

Let's consider how people actually define identifiable victims in a little more detail. It helps with the connection if the victim is 'one of us' in some way. There are two key triggers that help create this sense of affinity. These are:

- **In-group vs. out-group:** It can help to make supporters feel that they, and the recipients of their help, belong to the same group. This may be easy in cases where both belong to the same ethnic group, geographic region, or religion. These group connections can be very strong and relatively easy to establish. But they can also be antithetical to your philosophy or programme—you might want men specifically to understand the impact of sexism or male violence on women. If a donor and a recipient are clearly not in the same group, it may be more useful, to find a common ground related to more general values and human feelings—for example, 'As a parent,' 'As people living in the rich developed world,' etc. Sometimes a value is universal for a specific group 'Only a woman can understand what it is like to ...'

- **Close vs. distant:** If supporters do not feel closely involved with the recipients of their support, they may view the issue in a cold, logical, System 2 way and perhaps do the maths before deciding whether to help or not. If you want supporters to act with passion, you need to make them feel close to the recipients of their help, if not physically, then metaphorically. For example, 'Right now, in Somalia, another family just like yours is sitting down to eat a very different meal.' The increasing use of virtual reality in fundraising and campaigning may help to promote this. The ultimate distancing is to de-humanise others, which happens often in times of economic distress, giving a chance to extremists to spread their us vs. them propaganda.

	In-Group	Out-Group
Close	Family	Friends
Distant	Relatives	Strangers

As discussed in **Chapter 4** many non-progressive causes use *lack of affinity* to their advantage. We can see this in the growth of anti-refugee sentiment in Europe, fuelled by some politicians and media using associated offensive language like 'swarms of immigrants,' and 'hordes of refugees.' (Readers may also remember the furore in 2018 when Donald Trump was reported as branding Haiti, El Salvador and unspecified African nations as 'sh**hole countries').

Fundraising and Fairness

Meredith Niles, the Executive Director of Fundraising and Engagement at Marie Curie in the UK, and a leading proponent of neuroscience in the UK, has some interesting comments on *in group vs. out group*. 'One thing that I think is often frustrating to fundraisers is that they sometimes believe their cause is "more deserving" than another cause based on some sort of objective calculation, and they are annoyed that people will often choose to give more to causes that are (physically, psychically) closer to them. And instead of engaging with this challenge, they just shout louder about how deserving they are. There's some evolutionary psychology behind this and how foolish it is for fundraisers, and other social campaigners to ignore it. There is a lot of evidence that in-group preference is hard-wired and universal (Paul Bloom, for example, shows babies from a very early age prefer to look at faces that look like their parents and strongly prefer their own language—which they clearly can't even speak yet—to others).[11] Evolutionary psychologists posit this in-group loyalty bias is possibly because there were strong incentives to avoid contact with "out groups" that might harbour different diseases for which your tribe had no immunity, because of competition for resources, because of the need to reciprocate favours to fellow tribe members, etc. Whatever the explanation, in-group preferences are effectively hard-wired, so it's worth recognising them. There is a lot of discussion within moral psychology (Bloom, Haidt, Pinker, etc.) about how this in-group preference plays out in terms of altruism: it's why to most people Singer's drowning chid (right in front of you) intuitively demands your attention whereas it is a 'nice but not necessary' to save the starving child (far away) in Africa. *I think one of the most important jobs that fundraisers have is to figure out how to frame their cause so that it bridges that mental distance for supporters.'*

---

[11] Paul Bloom: *The Moral Life of Babies* www.nytimes.com/2010/05/09/magazine/09babies-t.html.

The Power of Perception

Note though, there can be a conflict between what respondents *say* is happening to them emotionally and what is *really* happening. Nice examples of this distinction are outlined in several intriguing neuroscience experiments explored in David Eagleman's book *The Brain: The Story of You.*[12] The fact that these are *neuroscience* experiments is important. The insights are the result of observing *actual* brain activation. Simply asking direct questions to the participants and recording their answers might well have met with denial about the response. (Keep that in mind when reading the studies below.) The implication is that real decision-making often happens at the subconscious level, and people don't really know what's impacting on their decisions.

Eagleman describes one study that is a variation of an *in-group vs. out-group* experiment. Participants saw an image of a hand on a computer screen. The disembodied hand was touched with degrees of firmness either by a cotton swab or a needle. When the hand was 'stabbed' with the needle, the scientists were able to see the viewers' pain area in the brain activated. This established the response base line.

Next, the same experiment was repeated with the same group. But this time the hands appeared on the screen with one of six labels attached: Christian, Jew, Muslim, Atheist, Hindu, or Scientologist. The hands were then stabbed with a needle in exactly the way they were in the first pass. Among the participants were members of each of these clusters and none.

What is interesting is that this time the participants' brains showed a larger and more empathetic response—as measured by the brain activity—when it they saw someone from their *in-group* in pain. And they showed less of a response when the hand was identified as belonging to a member of an *out-group*. All it took was a label on the hand, for a few seconds.

This *might* suggest that religion is divisive. But in fact, even the atheists showed a larger response to pain when they saw the hand

---

[12] Pantheon Books, London, 2015.

labelled atheist. So, the results are more about which group we perceive someone in trouble belongs to, religious or not.

The conclusion is that we empathise much more with a person we perceive to be in our in-group. And the further implication is if you want someone to empathise with another's situation, you need to know to what in-group—by gender, culture, age, sexuality, etc.—they consider themselves to belong. And finally, you need to find something they have in common with whoever you are trying to help. Advocacy or awareness campaigns can then help expand the active in-group segment and pave the way for further engagement, support, and donations.

Whether for fundraising or campaigning, try to find a circle to which the supporter *and* the beneficiary belong. It must be a 'felt' and important circle. It is easy to say we all belong to humanity, or to the universe. Nice sentiment, and one that many people would agree with intellectually. But the reality is the smaller the in-circle, the stronger the empathy. The circle, however, does not have to be a religious, ethnic, or political group. It very well could be a relationship, a value, or a belief.

Stand up Against Empathy!

On identifiable vs. statistical victim, and empathy, Paul Bloom makes an interesting case in his book *Against Empathy.*

Bloom's main point is that empathy is a poor guide to morality. While he acknowledges that when we empathise with others, we become more willing to help them, it has its downside in that it is biased to those who are attractive, or like us, and is insensitive to numeric facts. Empathy can steer us in the wrong direction and make us help one, instead of one hundred. Empathy can also have negative consequences for the empathising person, possibly leading to what's called 'empathetic distress.' Bloom advocates instead compassion, which is a more rational and distant concern for others, yet still kind and loving, based on moral principles, instead of the emotions triggered by putting ourselves in someone else's shoes. http://bostonreview.net/forum/paul-bloom-against-empathy.

But Don't Manipulate Emotions Unethically

Consumers find it hard to make an objective decision when they suffer from choice overload, and especially when they are under pressure, such as pain. There is some troubling evidence that companies consciously use incentives to confuse their consumers, as there will then be a tendency for those consumers to opt for the status quo and make a poor choice.

The Australian Competition and Consumer Protection Commission brought a case against Reckitt Benckiser, makers of Neurofen, the ibuprofen-based pain relief. The company falsely claimed that they had different types of this generic drug for back pain, period pain, migraine pain, and tension headache. In fact, the active ingredients of all of these formulations were exactly the same, as was clear in very small print on the back of the box. But they were packaged and advertised differently, and had varying price points related to consumer perceptions about how 'hard' the different pains were to tackle. (Migraine relief was the most expensive.) This was a company working to confuse consumers in order to increase profits. And it worked in sales terms. Thankfully, Australia's Federal Court were not impressed and in December 2016, Reckitt Benckiser were fined AUS$6 million for misleading conduct.

Women Working Together:
the Red Cross-Red Crescent Tiffany Circle

The Tiffany Circle is a programme exclusively engaging higher-net-worth women in a philanthropic endeavour connected to the Red Cross and Red Crescents' work. There is a strong emphasis on the unique role that wealthy women can play in making a difference in the world.

It originated in the US, but has now been exported to a number of countries especially in Europe. The basic in-group is successful, high-achieving women. Bernard's company, =mc, worked with this group to identity how their sense of identify allowed them to make a distinctive philanthropic difference.

This universal category of in-group can, in our experience, be replicated almost everywhere. For example, =mc has also worked with a local authority in Rotherham in the UK to create a group of women concerned to help safeguard local heritage.[13]

Monetising Customer Emotions

Emotions are big business. When organisations connect consciously and systematically with customers' or supporters' emotions, the payoffs can be enormous. The exact scale of this payoff has now been qualified, thanks to research published in a *Harvard Business Review*.

---

[13] On the other hand, in our experience diasporic fundraising—for example raising money from immigrants in one country to support a project or programme in the country they originated—is more problematic. Many fundraisers suggest it just does not work. Interestingly, what seems to happen is that the immigrants try to identify more with their adopted country, supporting domestic causes. We saw this effect with a campaign we advised on for African Develoment Solutions (ADESO), an Africa-based INGO. They wanted to fundraise from the US Somali community to tackle poverty and drought in Somalia. Despite the fact there was an identifiable audience that it was possible to contact online, and there was a clear need in Somalia, the results were disappointing.

Consider these anonymised examples it mentions:[14]

- *After a bank created a credit card aimed at Millennials designed to inspire emotional connection, the use among the target segment increased by 70%. And new account growth rose by 40%.*
- *A leading household cleaner manufacturer launched products and some linked messaging building on emotional connection. The result was that market share losses were turned into 10%+ growth in less than 12 months.*
- *When a nationwide clothing retailer reshaped its merchandising and customer experience towards its most emotionally connected customer segments, there was a x3 growth in sales.*

For charities, we can see the power of emotional connection in the runners who take part in the UK *Race for Life*.[15] In this sports-based charity fundraising event participants often pin messages to their running gear such as 'In honour of my mother' or 'In memory of my beloved sister' and weep with pleasure *and* pain *and* pride as they cross the finish line. Likewise, the extraordinary public response to the story of Stephen Sutton and his bucket list which included raising over £4 million for Teenage Cancer Trust before he died.[16] Or the power of the short films that populate the UK's Comic Relief Telethon, many of which drive mass donations up to totals of £500 thousand or more after a single showing. While each of these activities might appear to be more obviously emotional than credit cards, cleaning products, or even clothing, they too are high performing in their category.

In both for-profit and not-for-profit cases, you could argue that the fundamental underlying offering—a credit card, a charity race

---

[14] This chapter draws on insights and examples from *The New Science of Customer Emotions* by Scott Magids, Alan Zorfas, Daniel Leemon, HBR November 2015 https://hbr.org/2015/11/the-new-science-of-customer-emotions.

[15] *Race for Life* is essentially a UK version of *Race for the Cure*. You can find out more about it here. http://raceforlife.cancerresearchuk.org/index.html.

[16] To find out more follow this link: https://www.teenagecancertrust.org/get-help/young-peoples-stories/stephen-sutton.

—are *rationally* similar. What marks out the success of these apparently 'me too' offerings is their ability to connect strongly and emotionally with their target market. And, of course the emotional connection then allows them to key into the System 1 decision process.

There is an enormous opportunity to create and monetise additional value. Charities and campaigns *should* pursue these emotional connections in a disciplined, scientific way. But our research suggests that for most, building these connections is more guesswork than science. There's a lot of opinion out there, but a lot of that opinion is not really based on a rigorous understanding of what really works and whether any specific efforts will produce a desired result.

The authors of the *Harvard Business Review* article are clear that the emotional connection need not be a random process. 'Our research across hundreds of brands in dozens of categories shows that it's possible to rigorously measure and strategically target the feelings that drive customers' behaviour.' They call these targeting elements *emotional motivators*. The Harvard team goes further claiming 'they [the motivators] provide a better gauge of customers' future value to a firm than any other metric, including brand awareness and customer satisfaction, and can be an important new source of growth and profitability.' We believe that the same logic can be applied to charities marketing social causes or public agencies trying to create strong identification with changes in, say, health.

Many of the most sophisticated commercial companies are already making emotional connection an integral part of their marketing and communications strategy. To ensure this is systematic they tap into every element of the customer journey—from product design, to website engagement, to retail outlet experience, to warranty fulfilment.

The Harvard team have identified a number of these *emotional motivators* which can help drive supporter or consumer behaviour. Below are the ten that they believe significantly affect emotional value across all the commercial categories they have studied. We've adapted them for charities and social organisations and think they are essentially the same.

Name Your Emotion

An interesting experiment in France explored different options to persuade customers to put money in a charity box. The boxes were placed in 13 stores on different days. All were close to the cash register. They were tested with three different slogan options:

- No slogan just a message asking for donations
- The slogan DONATING=HELPING
- The slogan DONATING=LOVING

With everything else the same, the average donations were:

€54 for no slogan

€62 for the 'helping' slogan

€1.04 for the 'loving' slogan

Simple emotional prompts can be powerful drivers of behaviour.

Defining Emotional Motivators

The Harvard research grew from an awareness that companies knew customers' emotions were important but couldn't establish a consistent way 'to define them, connect with them, and link them to results.' The research team finally created a rather daunting list of more than 300 motivators that fit their definition: '*emotional connection*' with a brand is when it aligns with a customers' motivations and helps them fulfil profound, perhaps even unconscious, desires.' On the following pages is a list of ten of the most important and relevant of these they identified. *Column 1* outlines the basic emotional motivator. *Column 2* explores more how the motivator finds expression in an individual, and how brands or causes can connect to them. And finally, *Column 3* shows how charities can and should use them to make the connection.

Note that one important part of this research is the reality that customers and supporters may not be completely clear what their motivators actually are. Or they may confuse one with the other. For example, someone might say or believe that they are supporting a contemporary art exhibition to stand out from the crowd when, in fact, the real motivator is to feel a sense of belonging to an elite. Likewise, an environmental campaigner keen to take part in a risky publicity mission might claim their motivation is purely to do with a noble desire to save the environment. But as many campaigning organisations know, adventure seekers are sometimes keen to put on dangerous stunts with limited campaigning value that suggest their motivation is more likely a justifiable sense of thrill.

How to Use Emotions to Connect to Supporters

I am inspired by a desire to:	Brands including not for profits can use this motivator by helping supporters to:	Charity approaches that can help deliver this:
1. Stand out from the crowd	Project a unique social identity; be seen as special, different or even just distinctive.[17]	Become a major donor and have a building/project named after me; pay for a signed 'brick' in a building project.
2. Have confidence in the future	Perceive the future as better than the past; have a positive mental picture of what is to come; seek to help to create this positive future.	Support charity, run future leader/artist programmes to develop potential in young people. Support a consciously 'visionary' cause like http://www.peaceoneday.org.

[17] You can stand out from the crowd by being Distinctive, and not necessarily Different. The System 2 way of standing out from the crowd relies on providing facts and details about how a product or organisation works differently from others, in order to persuade the audience to buy that product or support that organisation. System 1 standing out relies on being distinctive, by owning and communicating consistently, and in using a number of iconic assets in a refreshing way. These include the brand colour, logo, tagline, celebrities, certain images, etc. Nike shoes or sports attires probably aren't really different from or better than other brands? So why buy Nike? Because its swoosh stands out, its advertising is emotional, and it brings to mind the feeling we can Just Do It.

For more on Distinctiveness vs. Differentiation see *How brands grow—what marketers don't know* by Byron Sharp, OUP, 2010.

I am inspired by a desire to:	Brands including not for profits can use this motivator by helping supporters to:	Charity approaches that can help deliver this:
3. Enjoy a sense of well-being	Feel that life measures up to expectations and that balance has been achieved; seek a stress-free state without conflicts or threats.	Take part in a 'give-up' better health campaign such as Dryathlon —where you agree to give up alcohol for a month. Support a cause that helps promote well-being, a mental health or a faith project.
4. Feel a sense of freedom	Act independently, without obligations or restrictions, and in accordance with your desires and values, or enable others to do so.	Support a cause such as Amnesty or a LBGTQ campaign to secure equal rights for others. Or provide bursaries for emerging talented students to pursue their dream to attend a high-level institution.
5. Feel a sense of thrill	Experience visceral, overwhelming pleasure and excitement; participate in exciting, fun events.	Take part in a trek to Machu Picchu, or do something scary like skydive. Run a marathon or take part in a challenging social action such as a Greenpeace demo at an oil terminal.
6. Feel a sense of belonging	Have an affiliation with people they relate to or aspire to be like; feel part of a group; work to join a more desirable group.	Join a movement-type organisation —e.g. Amnesty—to feel part of something bigger. Join volunteer programmes like those at the UK's Wildlife Trust or the Red Cross/Red Crescent
7. Contribute to humanity, or humanity's future. Or feel part of the universe/planet.	Sustain the belief that the environment is sacred; take action to improve their surroundings; defend other parts of the Earth or wildlife.	WWF builds this sense strongly. with references to the need to defend the earth and *all* of its inhabitants. Equally the UK Woodland Trust offers a chance to safeguard ancient woodland.
8. Be the person I want to be	Fulfil a desire for ongoing self-improvement and self-actualisation; live up or to develop into their ideal self-image.	This can range from 'no make-up selfie' to 'drop a dress size'-type promotions. Or the encouragement might be to be a 'proud Scot,' a 'concerned citizen,' a 'committed feminist,' etc.

I am inspired by a desire to:	Brands including not for profits can use this motivator by helping supporters to:	Charity approaches that can help deliver this:
9. Feel secure	Believe that what they have today should be there tomorrow; want to pursue goals and dreams without worry.	Many supporters invest in medical research programmes as a kind of insurance against the possibility they will develop a similar illness. Likewise supporting a foodbank or money advice service might underpin civic security.
10. Succeed in life	Feel that they lead meaningful lives; find worth that goes beyond financial or socioeconomic measures.	Supporting an artistic cause—a theatre or museum—might fit in here, seeing culture as an essential part of life. Try volunteering as a guide in a local natural or heritage attraction to improve social skills and the local amenity.

Why Do Emotional Connections Matter?

Emotional connections matter for three main reasons:

1. Supporters may be aware of you and your brand—even respect and trust it. But emotional connections go further than that, they help supporters forgive your failings and defend you in a 'blood is thicker than water' way.[18]
2. They key into System 1, permitting you to extend your support in a non-rational way. This is rather like the life-long support a person might give a football or baseball club despite their consistently terrible results.
3. They allow you to call on supporters in times of challenge. It was interesting during the 2016 attacks on UK charities by the right-

---

[18] For example, when a high-profile children's UK charity was itself involved in scandal that involved their failure to safeguard a child. Donations went *up* when they wrote to supporters admitting their failing, and asking for help to do better.

wing populist *Daily Mail* newspaper that Oxfam reported an *increase* in giving from core supporters—despite the criticism.[19]

See below for a fourth, and perhaps, surprising reason, the potential to monetise emotions.

How to Key Into Your Supporters' Motivations

Keying into your supporters' motivations is a relatively straightforward, if challenging, three step process:

Step 1: Review any research you have to identify the specific emotions at work for your supporters. Do people feel '*Angry* about homelessness' or '*Sorry* for the homeless'? Do they join your campaign in order to meet new friends who share a set of social values, or stand up for a principle even if it means they might damage their existing social relationships? Then do more research to add detail to your understanding of those emotions. Make sure you test them out as best you can. Remember *you are not the target market*, so don't assume that you know what motivates supporters. Young people may be motivated to take part in your volunteer scheme from a sense of social give back—*or* in order to have some fun away from their parents.

Step 2: Establish who are your 'best' supporters and focus on them. This could be your biggest donors, your longest serving members, or those who share your messages most on social media. (Be clear on the metric you need to establish 'best.') You should then check out which of the motivators above resonates most with this group. The premise here is that it is more important to get your top supporters to commit more strongly, than to spend a lot of time appealing to

---

[19] The *Daily Mail* newspaper launched a damaging series of attacks on charity fundraising methods, focusing on several which they claimed were improperly pressuring donors. For background see here http://www.civilsociety.co.uk/fundraising/news/content/20008/daily_mail_launches_personal_attacks_on_heads_of_fundraising.

those who simply feel averagely about you. Less is more in this case. Sometimes charities are obsessed with *awareness*, especially unprompted awareness. But awareness may not drive *engagement*.[20]

Step 3: Build these key emotional connections in the supporter journey. Use emotional connection language when you are communicating with your supporters: 'defend', 'protect', 'fight back' rather than 'empower.' A good commercial example we had recently was when one of us had to cancel a holiday because of illness and put in a claim to the insurance company to recover the costs. Bernard reports his experience: 'Every time I spoke to the company they mentioned in various ways how sorry they were about the holiday "loss," how "disappointed" I must be, and how much they'd like to "fix things for me." This was in complete contrast to previous insurance claim experiences where the focus was on the money and the scope and mechanics of cost recovery. I'm now a fan of that emotionally intelligent company.'

Make Your Proposition Feel Worth It: Monetising Emotions

We have seen how emotional connections add value, profitability, to products as the connections become more intense. Interestingly this is as true for bland, commoditised products as it is for intense social offerings, according to the Harvard research team.

The table on the next page shows the baseline of 'satisfied but not emotionally connected customers' at 100%. Building out from this baseline, the data is compelling. Customers who are *not* emotionally connected deliver 18% less in profitability. Satisfied, but not fully

---

[20] Jeff Brooks, the CEO of one of the top US DM agencies, and respected marketing guru said in a blog: 'Two-step fundraising is a colossal waste of money. You basically double your cost and get nothing in return. The truth is, if you have limited resources, there's almost no way you can justify spending them on awareness campaigns. For the awareness campaign to be worthwhile, it would have to improve fundraising by 67%. If you've been in fundraising for more than a couple of years, you know how unlikely that is. The reality is that most awareness campaigns make no measurable difference for fundraising campaigns.'

emotionally connected' customers, are worth an additional 13%. But 'fully emotionally connected' customers are worth, on average, a significant 52% more than baseline customers who are *only* 'satisfied.'[21] This marked difference explains why so many companies are working hard to create emotional connections in their products and brands. It also explains why so many of them want to use the power of Corporate Social Responsibility (CSR) or Customer Relationship Management (CRM) with charities to drive emotional value. See, for example, the UNICEF/Pampers case study below.

For charities and NGOs, the implication is you need to focus even more on creating emotional engagement for your supporters, whether they are donors, members or campaigners. This emotional engagement, the evidence tells us, will drive income or more action.

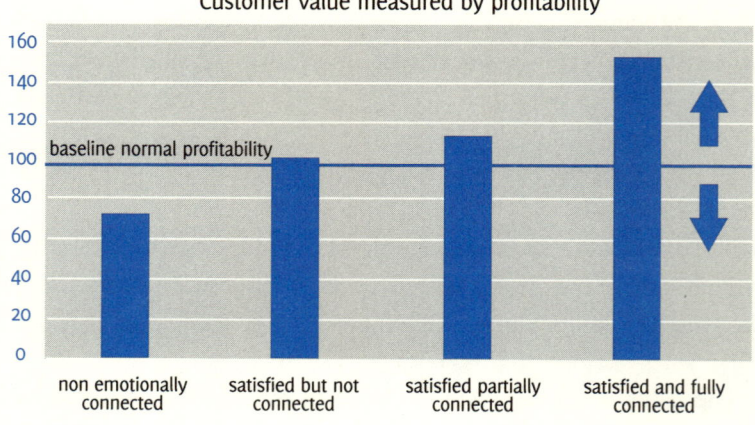

Customer value measured by profitability

You might imagine that emotional connection will be more obvious in certain product categories such as food, cosmetics or jewellery. To test this the researchers explored nine different categories including some that seem at first to have limited emotional connection potential such as credit card swipes. When emotional connections were used in all the categories, even the seemingly 'unemotional'

---

[21] This chart is adapted from one in HBR, mentioned earlier, *The New Science of Customer Emotions* Nov 2015 by Scott Magids, Alan Zorfas, and Daniel Leemon.

ones, there was an increase from +27% to +103% in spending compared to the 'normative' result.

- Household cleaner purchases +103%
- Consumer banking products +35%
- Hotel room stays +41%
- Online retailer purchases +52%
- Fast-food visits +27%
- Credit card swipes +60%
- Casino gaming spending +23%
- Tablet app purchases +82%

Happy Birthday to You: UNICEF-Pampers

The UNICEF-Pampers campaign, featured a number of advertisements that showed the connection between mothers and babies all over the world. They all belong to the same circle, in-group, of mothers and babies, regardless of race, religion, or colour.

One version used a universally popular event and its melody to stress the universality of the emotion we all feel: the Happy Birthday song.

This advertisement shows mothers from different parts of the world carrying their young babies while Happy Birthday plays in the background. The Happy Birthday theme is universal, and so is a parent's desire to celebrate their babies' birthdays. Pampers and UNICEF together provide vaccines for mothers and new-borns against tetanus, which takes the lives of many babies in developing countries. The communication is subtle and not directly about the Pampers product or UNICEF. But there is a strong emotional connection.[22]

---

[22] You can see the advertisement here https://www.youtube.com/watch?v=IWa14kluJnggoo.gl/Xre48h. The text is in Dutch. But even if you don't speak the language, you'll get the message!

Paper Power and Digital Delusions

In recent years there has been a significant 'rush to digital' in fundraising and campaigning. It is a common belief among many agencies that the digital online experience, or better still immersive virtual reality, beats old school paper every time. 'Common sense' that enemy of real science, says that must surely be true. The digital experience, they claim, *must* be richer with photos, videos, sounds, interactivity, etc. In fact, a recent research study, using fMRI brain scans, showed some very different results.[23]

The study used the same messaging, delivered in a variety of media to a common audience. First, and perhaps most important, the researchers found our brains process paper and digital marketing very differently and in different parts of the brain. There were three key conclusions about messages conveyed through tangible materials like paper letters, printed photos etc. versus digital experiences on or offline:

- **Tangibles leave a deeper footprint in the brain:** Printed photos, paper messages, and assorted enclosures create what the researchers call 'a deeper footprint.' Note: this isn't just because these stimulate sight and touch. Subjects were pre-tested with random physical materials, so the results were adjusted to account for this. These materials generate more activity in the area of the brain associated with the integration of visual and spatial information. This suggests physical material is more 'real' to the brain.
- **Physical material involves more emotional processing:** When a person is presented with an advert with physical elements—like

---

[23] Millward Brown, the market research and advertising company, worked with the Centre for Experimental Consumer Psychology at Bangor University, Wales. They studied how the brain processes physical marketing materials, such as direct mail, compared to digital advertising materials presented on a screen. *Using Neuroscience to Understand the Role of Direct Mail* http://www.millwardbrown.com/docs/default-source/insight-documents/case-studies/millwardbrown_casestudy_neuroscience.pdf.

those used in a typical response pack[24]—the researchers discovered more processing takes place in the area of the brain that deals with emotionally powerful stimuli and memory. This suggests that tangible materials generate more emotionally vivid memories[25]. Linked to this is the phenomenon in which physical/motor activity generates increased activity in the area of the brain associated with spatial and emotional processing.

- **'Touchables' produced more varied brain responses:** The parts of the brain associated with emotional engagement were activated more by physical adverts than online material. These areas included the area most associated with a person's internal emotional response to outside stimuli, suggesting greater 'internalisation' of the adverts. In the study context, this suggested that participants were relating the stimulus to their own thoughts and feelings. This effect is sometimes called *embodied cognition*, where we learn about something through our bodies.

If you are looking for a classic example of the power of tangibles, try this famous direct mail from the UK charity Help the Aged, now Age UK, and subsequently adapted and used by other charities worldwide. Recipients were sent a pack that included a number of photos of individuals affected by cataracts. They were also sent a small square of cloudy plastic. The Direct Mail (DM) letter asked the recipient to look at the photos through the plastic to help them to understand what it was like to have a cataract. The pack was so successful variations of it are used to this day.[26]

---

[24] A charity response pack will often involve, for example, sets of photos with case studies, a badge or sticker to use, or even materials for an engaging activity like bee-friendly seeds to plant.

[25] A study by Nils Jostmann showed when people hold a heavier weighted clipboard, they considered the issue presented to them to be more important (literally weightier) http://journals.sagepub.com/doi/abs/10.1111/j.1467-9280.2009.02426.x.

[26] To find out more about this case study visit the Showcase of Fundraising and Innovation (SOFII) website. http://sofii.org/case-study/help-the-aged-...little-piece-of-plastic-direct-mail-acquisition-pack.

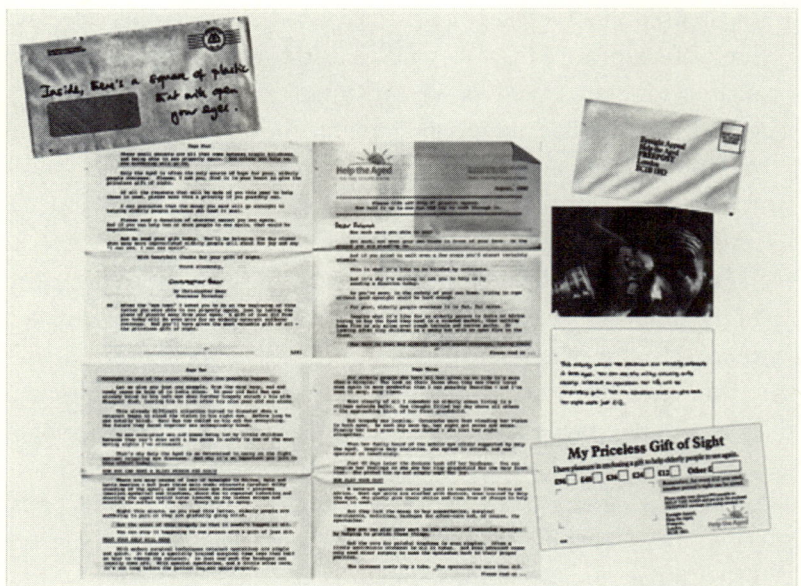

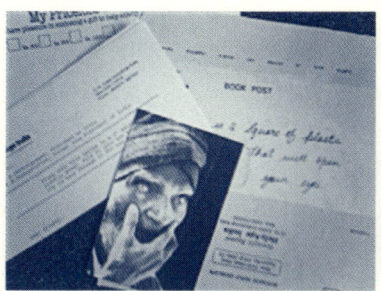
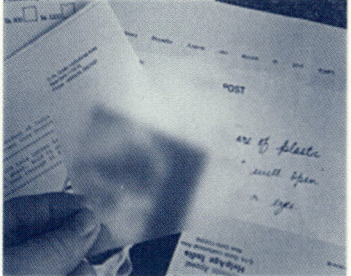

The frosted plastic demonstrating the effect of cataracts

To be clear, the Millward Brown-Bangor University study does not suggest that digital is not useful or powerful. Digital adverts or VR experiences do different things better. Online engagement can obviously be targeted more directly—based on past user interests or searches or even real-time choices. But the learning in this study shows the importance of thinking about how emotionally engaging a package might be through the kinesthetic quality of the materials included and even the different kinds of materials included—samples, photos, case studies etc. Consider too the interesting impact of the *sequence* in which a package is unpacked and explored, something Apple does well. Unboxing your new Apple product is a real pleasure. The British Red Cross has a great 'banker'—high performing—DM package that includes a letter from the fundraising director, a 'lift letter' from a famous supporter, a badge, a pen, a coaster and even a teabag so you can enjoy a hot drink while reading about their important work and how you can help. Unboxing it is an experience.[27]

Learning from Emotions

There are several key messages in this chapter. Number one is that you engage supporters or potential supporters best with emotions. To do this:

- Be aware people are most likely to help those they perceive are similar to themselves—identifiable victims—e.g. in terms of nationality, culture social category etc.
- Tell emotional stories about an *identifiable victim*,[28] don't share *data* about an abstract statistical group of victims.
- Do not mix facts and data with your emotional story, if you do you may actually reduce supporters' empathy and sympathy.

---

[27] To see tangible vs. digital in action in a commercial setting, have a look at this fun video https://www.feelmore50.com/emma-le-trfle. There's a wonderful punchline in the final shot. According to research undertaken by System 1 Agency, an advertising agency very informed by behavioural science, with a focus on driving emotional salience in advertising, this advert had the highest 'emotion into action' score for 2014. As you will see, it was literally about the conflict between digital and paper.

[28] Note, we are not suggesting that every person for whom you want to garner support or show solidarity is strictly a victim. (In the same way, many prefer the word 'survivor' for those impacted on by rape or torture.) We are using it simply to reinforce the importance of the *identifiable victim* approach.

- The looser the connection and the greater the psychological difference or distance, the weaker the identifiable victim effect.
- Make the supporter feel there is something she or he has in common with the 'victim' on a very deep level—create empathy.
- Using emotion is not only about a richer experience, it is actually more *quantifiably* valuable. Make sure you maximise that added value.
- Communicate emotions in subtle ways, so the recipient does not feel they are being manipulated.
- Use all the senses: a piece of music can stir sadness, a well-shot picture makes you feel you could almost reach out and touch the child, the tactile quality of a paper leaflet means you feel that the product itself will be good quality.

- Execution matters: pay close attention to your choice of words, metaphors, images, colours, and sound, including music.
- Design your supporter experience and journey in ways that maximise the number and intensity of emotional touchpoints.
- It's generally easier to secure a change in behaviour change when an existing habit or life pattern is disrupted. This might include a major life event like having a baby, a key birthday, getting married, or even buying a house. Often these involve high emotions.
- You need to decide how you want your proposition or idea to be perceived, and what is the best channel: in person, written, online. A good choice will make the decision process easy.

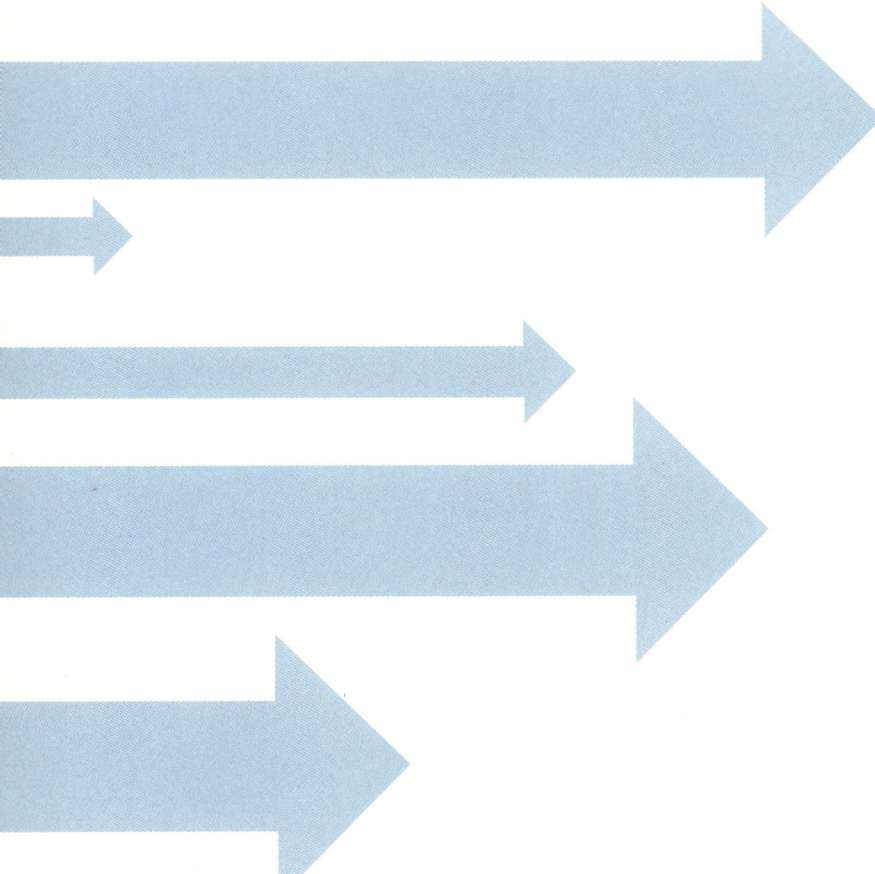

Chapter 9

Make Just Enough Information Available

Summary

The availability heuristic describes our tendency to make judgements based on the ease of access to information, rather than the quality or validity of that information. For example, we assess the probability of events by how quickly and easily other examples of the same thing come to mind. In a similar way, we often make decisions based on what we already know rather than examining all the alternatives. Most of the time we exploit this heuristic without even realising it.

The upside is that this gives our brains a shortcut to an answer. By and large, these assessments are accurate. ('It's icy underfoot, I should be careful.') But there are downsides, as with any shortcut, and sometimes we make decisions about situations or people, including ourselves, based on a false assessment.

Some events are easier to recall than others. They are not necessarily more common but they stand out in our minds. One example is media headlines related to injury or death—whether from car crashes, terrorist attacks or murders. As a result, we tend to worry more about these events and take more precautions against them. In fact, you are more likely to die from crossing the road, developing Type 2 diabetes or even choking on food than to die in a violent or dramatic setting.

You are also far more likely to believe something is commonplace if you can find just one example of it, and far less likely to believe in something you have never seen or heard of before. When this one example comes from someone we trust, it combines with the *social proof* heuristic to become very powerful. So, if a close friend tells you of a bad experience at a restaurant with a vivid tale of bad food it is almost impossible to shift that opinion.

Perhaps more worryingly you may form inaccurate or inappropriate judgements about other people, or even yourself, based on the inadequate information available to you. Central to this is the idea of What You See Is All There Is (WYSIATI).

Over time these judgements may take the form of codified prejudices against others or self-limiting beliefs about ourselves. These *mental models* may then impact directly on our real-life performance. Tackling these kinds of unhelpful mental models is becoming increasingly important in the worlds of economic and social development.

Availability is the Answer

Is the letter 'K' more likely to appear as the first letter in a word or as the third letter? For most people, the answer is 'K' appears more as the first letter than the third letter. Why? Because it is much easier to recall words that start with a K (Kite, Kaleidoscope, Kangaroo) than words where K is the third letter (Sorry, we can't think of any right now.) You can even check the dictionary under the letter K to find words that start with K. But the dictionary doesn't have a section for words where K, or any other letter, is the third letter.

Let's try another example. Are there more words ending in 'ing' or with 'n' as the letter before last? Most people give the entirely illogical answer of 'ing,' which is a *subset* of words ending with 'n' as the letter before last. Again, there are more words ending with 'ing' which come easily to mind than words where 'n' is the letter before last.

These questions, from Sutherland's *Irrationality*[1] and Kahneman's *Thinking, Fast and Slow*, are an illustration of the errors caused by

---

[1] Stuart Sutherland, Irrationality: *The Enemy Within*, 2013.

the availability heuristic: we think that events or info that come easily to mind are more common (are *more available*) than those that are harder to bring to mind (*less available*).

There are many studies that show people overestimate the prevalence of events that are highlighted by the media *versus* those that are not. For example, people estimate that more members of the public die of murder than of suicide, because murders are vividly reported in the media, while suicides generally are not. Other quandaries might include: what is more likely, dying by shark attack or jellyfish sting? Which professional group has the highest incidence of sexual scandals? What is the most likely thing that is going to cause our death?

To answer these questions properly, we really need System 2 to get involved, to collect data and analyse it, or at least search for existing information that addresses these topics. But that is too much work. Our faster, lazier System 1 takes the lead and immediately thinks of incidents of these phenomena. Shark attacks get shock coverage but not the less dramatic deaths from jellyfish stings. The media is full of news of politicians and celebrities' sexual scandals, but not accountants or fundraisers or international development staff (all too boring to be involved in such things?). Car accidents and cancer are often mentioned in the news, but not heart attacks.

Belief	Reality
Accidents cause more deaths than strokes	Strokes cause almost twice as many deaths as all accidents combined
Death by disease is as likely as death by accident	Death by disease is 18 times more likely than death by accident
Death by accident is 300 times more likely than death by diabetes.	Death by diabetes is 4 times more likely than death by accident.

The availability heuristic applies not only to facts, statistics, and probabilities, but also to ideas and opinions. The more available opinions, usually driven by the media and, increasingly, social media, are often more believed than less available ones. The objective truth is not the key issue we consider.

Let Me Tell You One More Time

> → *A reliable way to make people believe in falsehoods is frequent repetition, because familiarity is not easily distinguished from truth.*
>
> Kahneman: *Thinking, Fast and Slow*

Availability comes in various forms, the most common of which are:

- **Dramatic events:** These are events that receive the heavy and extended media exposure that makes you think such a thing is common and likely to occur. They include some natural disasters—such as a tsunami or earthquake, a plane crash, a coup d'état, etc. In today's world, both mass and social media should be taken into account. The two often work in sync, though it can be hard to know which one triggered the other: mass media reports that a certain topic has become very popular on social media, while social media quotes news and articles from the mass media.
- **Unusual phenomena:** These are the strange events that you come across in the media or through friends and acquaintances: family murders, strange encounters with animals, surprises in sports—for example, a low seeded tennis player beating a high seeded champion. Paradoxically, dramatic and unusual events enjoy high publicity because they are very rare, but the weight of reporting makes them feel like they are frequent and likely to occur again.
- **Personal experiences:** These are events that happen to us personally, or to one of our family members, friends, or acquaintances. For example, because our important business or holiday flight was delayed we judge that that particular airline is always late. A negative experience with a salesperson in one shop con-

vinces us that the company's customer service is very poor. A visit to a beautiful city on a cold, wet day leaves us thinking it is overrated. In all these experiences, no amount of data or statistics would assure us otherwise.[2] Have a look at TripAdvisor for a place you love to see evidence of this experience.

The extreme variability between the facts of a situation and our mainstream and social media-driven perception of its reality is best captured by the 'deaths-per-news-story,' which measures the number of people who have to die from a given disease or condition before the media devotes a story to the case. For example, one analysis found that it took 8,571 smoking related deaths to have one story on smoking reported on the BBC, compared to 0.33 deaths from mad-cow disease, CJD.

Of course, it is not just the media to blame. Two personal factors play a big role in this:

- **Personal relevance:** What we do is more available to us than what others do. In several studies couples were asked about their own and their partner's percentage contribution to household chores, such as 'taking rubbish out.' The amounts claimed by either person usually added up to much more than 100%. The couples were not necessarily lying. They were simply more aware of their own work than that of their partner. It was more *available* to them. While people are influenced by what the media presents to them, they are more likely to *notice* what's relevant to them. For example, pet owners are more likely to notice stories about animals. People are more likely to donate to health-related organisations dealing with diseases from which family or close friends have

---

[2] According to Jared Diamond, scientist and author of *The World Until Yesterday*, we tend to overestimate the risk of events we have no control over (e.g. airplane crashes, terrorist attacks), and underestimate the risk of those events for which we do have control (e.g. slipping in the shower, car crashes, smoking). It is wiser to be careful in the shower, or to take fewer showers, than to worry about an airplane crash or a hurricane.

suffered (e.g. heart disease, cancer), than to donate to organisations dealing with globally more important diseases, that afflict many more people (malaria, diarrhoea).

- **Social reinforcement:** We increasingly see the pernicious impact of social media allowing the sharing of unprogressive or downright repressive ideas. It is perhaps understandable that racists should share information on Twitter/Facebook, etc. that confirms their prejudices. What is more worrying are some of the channels that allow young people—especially girls and young woman—to share eating disorder 'hints' and pictures of self-harm. And of course, governments are not immune from this. The Saudi Government has a number of Facebook and twitter links that allow citizens to report other citizens for un-Islamic behaviour.[3] Examples of such behaviour range from 'wearing nail polish' to 'practicing black magic.' These sites reinforce bizarre and internal—does black magic exist?—frames of reference.

Implications for Campaigning

The multi-sided availability heuristic has many implications for campaigners.

- **Supporter understanding:** Campaigners must get closer to their current and potential supporters—what is on their supporters' minds, and what is important for them? Instead of asking 'How can I convince them that X (the cause or issue) is important, and they should support it?' the question becomes 'Given that it is issue Y that is important to them, how can I relate my message to it?'[4]

---

[3] The article explains how some of these sites are being slightly reformed. But only slightly. https://www.csmonitor.com/World/Middle-East/2013/0523/With-youth-pounding-at-kingdom-s-gates-Saudi-Arabia-begins-religious-police-reform.

[4] 'When there are only a few facts available, they may occasionally help us change our minds.' 'Ah, given that new information, I may need to reappraise my position.' By contrast, an oversupply of facts gives our confirmation bias a free rein to work its

- **Bring perception closer to reality:** People do not give to objectively assessed priority causes. They support, or donate, based on what they *perceive* to be important issues. And what they perceive to be important issues is partly influenced by what the media or their social circle focuses on. So, it definitely helps if the issue you are raising money and concern for is 'available' in people's minds. You need to make sure your 'issue' is top of mind for those you seek to influence, and for those who influence them.

- **Emergencies:** Giving to perceived emergencies, natural disasters (earthquakes, hurricanes) or man-made (wars), are a special case of issues people donate to. They differ from ongoing issues in that they are dramatic, unexpected events, which receive heavy media coverage, usually including images and personal stories making them emotionally loaded. As Kahneman says '*People tend to assess the relative importance of issues by the ease with which they are retrieved from memory—and this is largely determined by the extent of coverage in the media.*'

Emergencies and Fundraising

Not all disasters receive equal media attention. And the coverage is often a function of the drama of the event rather than its magnitude. A sudden catastrophe that kills hundreds in seconds will generate more coverage than an ongoing famine that kills thousands every day. It is important for fundraisers and others involved in social change to check not only the media coverage, but their target audiences' awareness of such coverage.

Anecdotal evidence suggests that during emergencies donors donate to organisations they are familiar with, to organisations that are 'available'

---

magic. Don't like these facts? Well, not to worry, if you pick the data-points slightly differently, we can make the truth a little more to your liking. From The West Wing:

Josh: '*Did you know that 69 per cent of Americans oppose [cannabis] legalisation? Only 23 per cent support it.*'

Dr Griffith: '*The number gets a lot higher if you ask people under 30.*'

Josh: '*Well, that's a shock. Did you know that the number gets even higher if you limit the polling sample to Bob Marley and the Wailers?*'

to their mind. For example, following the 2004 tsunami, there was a strong correlation between the amounts raised by an organisation and the agency's spontaneous awareness in France (Correlation coefficient 0.83).

Donations to Organisations in France After the 2004 Tsunami

Organisation	Donations	Spontaneous Awareness
French Red Cross	115,778,000	46
UNICEF	57,482,301	20
Secours catholique	36,472,698	24
Fondation de France	20,682,986	4
Secours populaire français	14,508,053	24
Action contre la faim	14,357,002	9
Médecins Sans Frontières (MSF)	13,168,879	21
Médecins du monde	11,486,787	14
Handicap International	10,062,959	12
Comité catholique contre la faim et pour le dévelopement	2,832,389	4

In a similar contemporary example, Bernard was involved in developing a strategy for MSF/DWB during the 2015 Ebola outbreak. We estimate that MSF raised almost US$400M extra in funds globally despite the facts that:

- MSF was not running a direct major campaign on Ebola anywhere in the world, although it was working on the issue on the ground.
- Although other agencies, for example, the Red Cross, did much of the work, MSF was the top of mind organisation, as the name ('Medécins', 'Doctors') is naturally associated in people's minds with diseases and epidemics.

Meredith Niles has an interesting view on the issue of why emergencies have such an impact. Her hypothesis is that brand awareness matters exponentially more for charities that engage in disaster relief than it does for other types of charity because there is so much more 'event-driven' giving.

She explained in a comment to us: 'When an earthquake/tsunami/flood/famine, etc. happens, especially if it is in a part of the world that people living in the developed world have some concern for, there will follow media reports that will be widespread, emotional and intense. These will cause people to be moved, without a specific charity having asked them to donate. Their donation will therefore go to whatever charity they can think of first. We can't know which natural disasters will happen when, but we can, reasonably reliably, count on there being a steady stream of them. And, of course, climate change may trigger even more. These will, when they happen, generate lots of intense, emotional media coverage that will in turn trigger donations. If your charity doesn't spring to mind, you'll be left out. There aren't really similar parallels for other issues: media coverage is less assured, less emotive, less intense, and most giving is not "event-driven" but rather follows an ask, so spontaneous awareness is less of an issue. Therefore, there might be a stronger incentive for international aid charities vs. other types of charities to invest in pure brand advertising.' We think she's probably right.

Life's a Lottery

Lotteries are a good example of us making poor decisions. The harsh reality is your chance of winning the Powerball jackpot in the US is around 1 in 292,000,000. In the UK, it's a more hopeful 1 in 14,000,000. When the odds are so low it makes you wonder—'why do as many as 2/3 of the population buy tickets for lotteries?'

Robert Williams, a professor of health sciences and gambling studies at the University of Lethbridge in Alberta, thinks he knows the three key behavioural phenomena which underpin this pretty irrational behaviour. He shared them when interviewed by *Business Insider* magazine. The section below is based on this article.

1. We Can't Get Our Heads Around Big Numbers
Professor Williams says we can manage numbers at a modest level- the difference between a village of 10 people, versus one of 100 or even 1,000. But once the figures get much greater, we find it hard to deal with them. Huge numbers were never relevant throughout most of human history, Williams says, so our brains haven't really evolved to think of them.

The implication? Odds of 1 in 292 million don't sound all that different to the unmathematical ear from odds of, say, 1 in 100,000.[5] But they are.

2. We Believe in The 'Close Thing' Effect

The 'close thing' effect is when you got three of six or seven numbers 'right,' so you believe you *almost* won. The implication is maybe if you tried again you might get a bit closer. (This is also called the positive expectation bias.) A simple grasp of maths confirms even with your three numbers you were not remotely close to winning. The 'near miss' is a complete fantasy.[6]

But because we think we were 'close' it seems to encourage us to try again. Even though when trying again our odds of success are set right back to the previous most impossible level.[7]

3. The Lottery Keys Into Our 'Availability Bias'

The 'availability bias' varies on how strong our memories are of a similar event. When we try to figure out our odds of scooping the dream prize, we remember most strongly and clearly the stories of lottery winners in the media.

---

[5] A change in the US Powerball lottery meant that the chances of winning recently went from 1 in 175 million (when you had to select six numbers between 1 and 59) to 1 in 292 million has little impact on people's willingness to participate in the lottery.

[6] How *do* you work out the odds of getting three out of six numbers? You might think you should divide the chances by two since you got half the numbers. In the US lottery, the implication would be your odds then reduced from 1 in 292 million to 1 in 146 million. That's not massive progress. The news gets worse. The chances of getting half of the numbers right are around 1 in 600. Worst still, for guessing 3 out of 6 numbers, the maximum you might win is $7.

[7] Imagine you're playing a game of 'Heads or Tails' with a friend. As you flip a coin repeatedly each time you guess if it'll land heads or tails. You know you have a 50-50 chance of calling it right each time. But if you've flipped the coin ten times already, and it's turned up heads every time, surely, you might think, the next throw must be more likely to be tails. The answer is 'no.' The chances of tails or heads on the next spin are still 50-50. And they are 50-50 every time. The gambler's fallacy occurs when we place too much weight on past events and confuse our memory with how the world actually works, believing that they will have an effect on future outcomes.

We don't hear about the very many millions of people who *didn't* win.[8] The only stories we have available are of those who did win.

How is this relevant for people trying to encourage engagement in social causes? Partly it's because so many of the social issues we need to try and address are huge and almost impossible to 'win' at; the number for people in poverty globally, the number still dying of HIV, the number denied human rights, etc. These numbers, if made explicit, could lead to alienation, as supporters realise the impossibility of success, or at least suffer an abrupt System 2 intervention. Maybe we can learn from lotteries and focus on:

- Sharing manageable numbers: a person, a village, a small community
- Explaining how close success is
- Reporting on a series of singular individual successes

Even if these tactics aren't about reality.

Create a Reaction

Marmite is a UK savoury spread. The product's marketing slogan *Love it or hate it* has become a descriptor of anything that polarises opinions strongly. While most brands try to appeal to the largest number of people possible, Marmite's strategy is to have some people hate it, as long as there is a sizeable group of consumers who love it. This fits in with the idea that the worst emotion is not hatred, but indifference. Notice too that the company actively promotes the idea that some people actively dislike the product. What they're doing here is using information that might appear not to be in their interest, but at the same time playing into the confirmation bias of supporters, and their sense of being an in-group. Some campaign groups, like for example People for the Ethical Treatment of Animals (PETA), do something similar, by

---

[8] http://uk.businessinsider.com/psychological-reasons-why-we-buy-lottery-tickets-2016-1?r=US&IR=T.

appealing to their supporters' existing point of view rather than trying to convince neutral people. The advert below is simply designed to reinforce the view of committed animal rights activists.

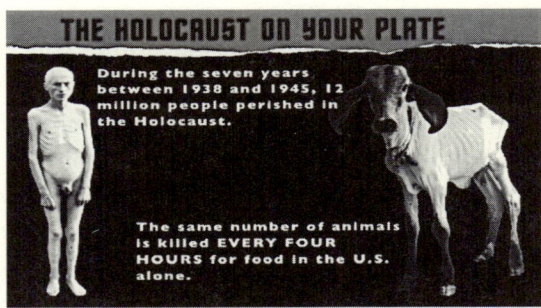

The message for fundraisers and campaigners is clear: it is better to be the loved number one organisation for some supporters, and maybe lose others, than to be a merely 'acceptable' alternative for a bigger cluster of supporters.

You can also attract people's attention and interest with a deliberate mistake. A great example comes from Egypt where MacDonald's ran a cause related marketing campaign about education, asking customers for donations. As part of the campaign boxes were printed with a deliberate spelling mistake. The result? A huge growth in social media traffic as people initially mocked MacDonald's for the apparent boo-boo. This mockery soon, however, turned to admiration as people realised the mistake was deliberate, and designed to encourage people to share images of the 'mistake' and the campaign on twitter, Instagram, Facebook etc.[9]

---

[9] https://thinkmarketingmagazine.com/mcdonalds-egypt-just-created-one-best-viral-campaigns-2017.

Branding and Availability

> *The Law of Least Effort: If there are several ways of achieving the same goal, people will eventually gravitate to the least demanding course of action.*

In our workshops on decision-making we show participants two images from a brain scan; one with heavy neural activity and the other with a much lower level of brain activity. We then ask participants to tell us which of the two images is the result of the subject seeing their usual (strong for them) brand, and which is the result of their seeing a non-usual (weaker for them) brand.

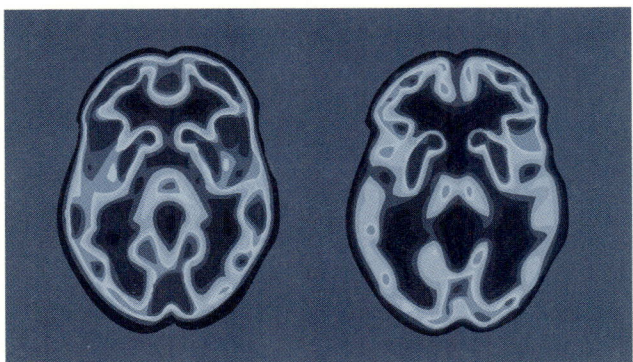

Invariably, nearly all participants say that the image of heavy brain activity, on the left, is the one that follows exposure to the subject's usual brand. They assume wrongly. One of the benefits of being someone's strong usual brand, whether it is a washing powder or a charity, is that it makes the purchase-donation-endorsement decision easy. It is a no-brainer (pun intended).

In behavioural economics terms, branding can be seen as a subcategory of the *availability* heuristic. A strong brand makes the organisation more available in the supporter's mind compared to others. The availability of the brand is driven by several factors, such as awareness, salience, and familiarity.

There are several ways of measuring awareness. One is prompted awareness where you give respondents a list of organisations and ask whether or not they have heard of each of them. This is a very blunt measure and often results in high, and sometimes over-claimed, scores. Researchers sometimes insert the name of a fictional organisation to help adjust the figures closer to reality. For example, maybe 20% of respondents will say they are aware of an organisation called Kemto, which does not exist. Researchers can then use the 20% figure to adjust claimed awareness for other organisations.

A more reliable metric is *spontaneous awareness*. You simply ask respondents, for example, 'What humanitarian organisations are you aware of?' The responses to this question cannot involve over-claiming, and will reflect the brands' genuine presence in people's minds. However, simple awareness doesn't drive action. (We can both name several brands of cigarette, but neither of us smokes.)

The Recognition Heuristic

The *recognition* heuristic is a subset of the availability heuristic, and considered by some to be the simplest of the heuristics. It implies that 'If one of two objects is recognised and the other is not, then infer that the recognised object has the higher value.' For example, when subjects are given names of foreign cities they are not familiar with and asked to indicate their population ranking, in general they assume that the city whose name they recognise more easily has a higher population. This leads, slightly bizarrely, to the suggestion that knowing less about a topic can be more helpful than knowing more. In a simple test, students from the University of Chicago in the US, and the University of Munich in Germany, were asked which of two American cities— San Diego or San Antonio—had the higher population. Sixty two percent of the American students came up with the right answer and 100% of the Germans. The explanation for this unexpected result is that many of the German students had to resort to the recognition heuristic because they had little knowledge of US cities. They recognised San Diego but not San Antonio. The American students, however, knew of both cities. They did not know enough to know which had a higher population, but enough to prevent them from using the recognition heuristic. Many similar tests have confirmed this phenomenon in different contexts. (Those who selected the stocks of the companies they recognised did better than those who knew more companies, foreigners estimated which football club would win the domestic league title because they only recognised the best clubs, etc.)

In many cases the relationship between knowledge and decision-making takes a shape similar to an inverted U ($\cap$). With additional knowledge, the accuracy of responses increases up to a point, and the starts declining as more knowledge is acquired.

The recognition effect might have an evolutionary basis. No animal died from eating familiar food. Going for what you know, and avoiding what you don't, is often a winning strategy. Our human brain evolved over millions of years and under very different circumstances. For most of our history we lived in relatively small communities where the familiar faces of extended family and friends were trusted. Unfamiliar strangers were, more often than not, distrusted enemies. In those early societies, judgment errors could be fatal, and encouraged us to adopt conservative attitudes. In today's world, most daily decisions have no life or death consequences, but our risk aversion still lingers. If you're thinking about rebranding make sure you leave enough of the existing brand to ensure people don't feel the switch is risky.

Recognition, Social Attitudes and Risks

The *recognition* heuristic also has implications for social attitudes. These in turn can affect political policy, fair or unfair legislation, or personal behaviour or attitudes towards individuals or groups. The heuristic that was useful in helping our ancestors avoid dangerous situations that appeared similar to previous ones could also make us exaggerate danger from contemporary 'moral panics'—refugees, terrorists, or even benefits-seeking teenage mothers. Certain groups of people may be perceived as undesirables, scroungers, or even criminals based on unconscious stereotyping.

Some threats seem more important than others. How important depends on the level of *emotion* the risk engenders, its *familiarity*, and what is called *salience*—the extent to which anything is *noticeable*. Salience can distort our perception quite markedly.

You Are in the Jury for Mr. Sanders. What Is the Guidance from Judge Salience?

People give greater importance to some information, even if it doesn't have real relevance—just because it is there and makes an impact. This is an aspect of salience.

Imagine you are in the jury and being asked to consider the case of Mr. Sanders. You know from the police evidence that he ran through a red light while driving. He then collided with a rubbish lorry. He was arrested and accused of drink driving. He is on trial. Here is what happened in experiments run by US researchers, Reyes, Thompson, and Bower, in 1980.

Two separate 'juries', composed of ordinary citizens, were asked to assess Mr. Sanders' guilt or innocence in a mock trial. Each group was given the same evidence, with one variation: the description of his behaviour in a restaurant *before* the accident:

- **Version 1:** 'On his way out of the door, Sanders staggered against a serving table, knocking a bowl to the floor.'
- **Version 2:** 'On his way out of the door, Sanders staggered against a serving table, knocking a bowl of guacamole to the floor and splattering dip on the white shag carpet.'

The two juries reached different verdicts. Those who heard the additional information about the guacamole were more likely to believe that Mr. Sanders was guilty. But should they have allowed what was an irrelevant detail to impact on their assessment of guilt? Clearly not, since it was unconnected to the accused's possible intoxication through drink or drugs.

In decision science terms, the information about the guacamole made the incident more 'salient'—it stood out against other pieces of information. Even though both juries were actively thinking about whether Mr. Sanders was drunk/on drugs and attempting to weigh the evidence objectively, their automatic System 1 told them that this piece of information was decisive. It made the possibility he was guilty more 'real.' Adding more, even if slightly irrelevant, details to a story, can often make it feel more real.

Powerful emotions often cause individuals to empathise with the negative impact of an outcome, out of all proportion to the realistic probability it will happen. A risk that appears highly stressful—such as the possibility of being involved in a terrorist incident, will be seen as more serious than a less familiar but more likely risk, such as the chance of contracting skin cancer from sunbathing.

It is not surprising, then, that the public is often quite wrong in its opinion about what the key facts are, and builds a false conclusion based on inappropriate emotionally laden data. If you're looking for a real-world example consider the impact of Johnny Cochrane, OJ Simpson's defence lawyer, saying 'if the glove don't fit you must acquit.'[10]

It Doesn't Need To Be True to Have An Impact

Most years IPSOS Mori, the international polling firm, publishes a list of statistical misconceptions based on interviews with a representative example of the UK public. They illustrate just how wrong people can be on a number key social policy issues. (You may like to think about how accurate your own views are.) Among the top ten misperceptions in a recent version of this poll are:

- **Teenage pregnancy**: On average, we think teenage pregnancy is 25 times higher than official estimates. We, the general public,

---

[10] http://www.telegraph.co.uk/news/worldnews/northamerica/usa/9530838/OJ-Simpson-murder-trial-glove-was-tampered-with-by-defence-lawyer-Johnnie-Cochran-claims-prosecutor.html.

believe that 15% of girls under 16 get pregnant each year, when official figures suggest it is around 0.6%.

- **Benefit fraud**: People estimate that 34 times more benefit money is claimed fraudulently than official estimates. The public think £24 out of every £100 spent on benefits is claimed fraudulently, compared with official estimates of £0.70 per £100.
- **Foreign aid**: 26% of people think foreign aid is one of the top items of Government expenditure, when it makes up under 2% (£7.9bn.) More people select this as a top item than pensions, which cost ten times as much, £74bn (2011/12 figures).
- **Immigration**: The public think that 31% of the population are immigrants, when the official figures are 13%. Even estimates that attempt to account for illegal immigration suggest a figure closer to 15%.

The *recognition* heuristic means that such inaccurate data has significant importance for the great 'folk devils' of UK public opinion.[11]

Watch Out for Terrorist Bees: Or Don't Worry, Be Happy

Death from terrorist acts is statistically a tiny risk. However, for many British people it remains a major concern. Partly this is because we are exhorted on trains and planes to be aware of packages or anyone acting suspiciously. But since 2001 fewer British citizens have been killed by terrorism than by bee stings.[12]

Part of the reason this risk has been so over-exaggerated is that, when they happen random, violent attacks are hugely emotionally charged. They have special salience because we have no control over them. Remember the scenes after the 2015 Charlie Hebdo bombing or subsequent attacks in Nice, Brussels, London, etc. As familiar cities for many Europeans and North Americans, these places are salient—they stand out. When such events happen in Mogadishu or Lahore, where they happen more frequently, they attract less interest.

---

[11] We owe much of the insight and content here to http://nataliecargill.com/the-availability-heuristic-and-public-policy-priorities.

[12] http://www.telegraph.co.uk/news/uknews/terrorism-in-the-uk/9359763/Bee-stings-killed-as-many-in-UK-as-terrorists-says-watchdog.html.

The Negative Social Consequences of Misjudgments

These misjudgements don't simply exist in our minds. Undue response due to the 'availability' of a risk drives disproportionate, and sometimes simply wrong, legislation. Let's continue with the terrorism, immigration, and state benefits examples.

- **Terrorism Overreaction:** Since 2000, the UK parliament has passed six separate terrorism-related Acts. These have variously allowed the state to indefinitely detain foreign nationals without charge, to commit suspects to pre-charge detention in terrorism cases, and to stop and search citizens without suspicion.
- **Immigrant Influx:** The UK has agreed to allow just 5,000 Syrian refuges into the UK over five years. This is in response to the greatest refugee crisis affecting Europe in the last 100 years— and despite the fact that Germany has admitted over 1 million asylum seekers. (Population of Germany 80 million, population of UK 65 million.)
- **Bedroom Scroungers:** Since 2013, people living in social housing in the UK with a spare bedroom have had their benefit payments reduced by 14% or 25% respectively. This rule has been applied even when a person's disability has meant they could not move to a different house. 64% of all claimants found themselves in this situation.

The implications here are important for anyone campaigning on public policy issues. We need to make sure:

- Accurate information is available to the public and to those who make legislation. Or we run the risk of having poorly judged legislation. (Our lawmakers aren't immune.)
- Any information is put in context. Should we put energy into collecting taxes or reducing scrounging as a way to support social programmes?
- Inaccurate data that seems to unfairly vilify individuals or groups is challenged. If we don't it can lead to discrimination.

More generally, each organisation should compare the real facts and data related to the cause it is championing, to the public's perception, and take action accordingly. False news, as we know, is a real phenomenon that can cause significant challenges.

Challenging Mental Models

As we have seen, the availability heuristic creates mental models that may stay with us. Some hold us back. When these models are 'out of sync' with the real world, they can significantly limit the amount and form of information anyone making a decision uses. This may then cause them to 'fill in' details of a situation with unhelpful assumptions. Some can enable positive thought and action. When the mental models people use are suitable and appropriate, they can help improve their status and attitude.

The World Bank is a relatively late 'convert' to the world of decision architecture. But their *World Development Report 2015* shows how they have been trying to make use of a number of heuristics to drive positive, long-term outcomes. (See also the example in **Chapter 1** on helping poor people make good choices on securing credit.)

A 2011 World Bank study in Ethiopia found disadvantaged people, especially in rural settings, reporting a sense of *low agency*—feelings of disempowerment in their lives. In interviews they would typically say, 'We have neither a dream nor an imagination,' 'We live only for today.'[13] These interviews suggested respondents had mental models which reinforced the view that they could not change their future. And that belief limited their ability to take advantage of opportunities which did exist.

A team of researchers developed an experiment designed to discover whether they could change that mental model. They made a series of four short video documentaries based in a specific area in

---

[13] See *Learning with Others: A Field Experiment on the Formation of Aspirations in Rural Ethiopia*, 2013 Bernard, Dercon, and Taffesse 2011.

Ethiopia. The videos were designed to have an inspirational tone. They showed 'typical people' from the area succeeding in changing their lives through their own action. The researchers then visited other villages locally and invited a random group of villagers to watch some videos including the inspirational ones. The individuals featured in the documentaries described how they had improved their status and economic situation. The embedded messages suggested success derived from setting achievable goals, making considered choices, and setting out and following a plan of action.

A follow-up survey six months later found that the individuals exposed to the embedded messages in the videos had increased their life aspirations and had put in place small but tangible changes. For example, viewers had higher total savings and had invested more resources in their children's education compared to a control group.[14]

How Mental Models Work and How We Use Them

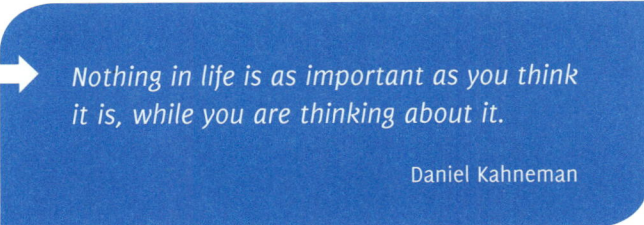

> Nothing in life is as important as you think it is, while you are thinking about it.
>
> Daniel Kahneman

At any given point, there is a huge quantity of data we could take in through our senses—sights, sounds, smells, touch. But we humans have relatively limited powers of observation and capacity for processing observed data. Our mental models affect where we direct our attention. They offer us default assumptions about the people we interact with and the action to take in situations we face. As a result, we may ignore information that challenges our assumptions,

---

[14] *The Future in Mind: Aspirations and Forward-Looking Behaviour in Rural Ethiopia,* Bernard and others, 2014 https://www.csae.ox.ac.uk/workingpapers/pdfs/csae-wps-2014-16.pdf.

and automatically fill in missing information based on what our mental models suggest is likely to be true.

The models represent a kind of System 1 thinking. Although both perception and autopilot thinking involve the construction of meaning, people are mostly unaware of 'constructing' anything. They imagine they are responding in an objective, System 2, way, to the stimulus or the situation.

We can see this in our cultural interactions. Since we are social animals, our mental models often incorporate the taken-for-granted beliefs and routines of the culture in which we were raised and the behaviour that is seen as appropriate in different settings. Take flowers, for instance. In a Western culture roses generally signal romance, and sunflowers signal happiness. If you turned up at a colleague's work retirement party with a bunch of twelve roses as a leaving gift, colleagues—including the recipient—might be puzzled, whereas the same number of sunflowers would be acceptable. This is us responding to a cultural norm or shared signal.

In other cultures, the norms are different and about different things. Signals about status or identity can, for example, affect an individuals' performance significantly. This is so even when this is entirely subjective and there is no actual difference at all.

In an experiment in India, high-caste and low-caste boys from villages were randomly assigned to groups. The participants were given the same series of maze puzzles to complete. When their caste was not revealed to each other, the performance of the high and low-caste boys in the groups was the same. However, revealing the caste of participants in mixed groups *before* the task reduced the performance of the low caste boys. (Interestingly when caste was revealed in segregated groups the performance of both low *and* high-caste boys was reduced. But the performance between groups was statistically indistinguishable.) Caste is a kind of mental model.

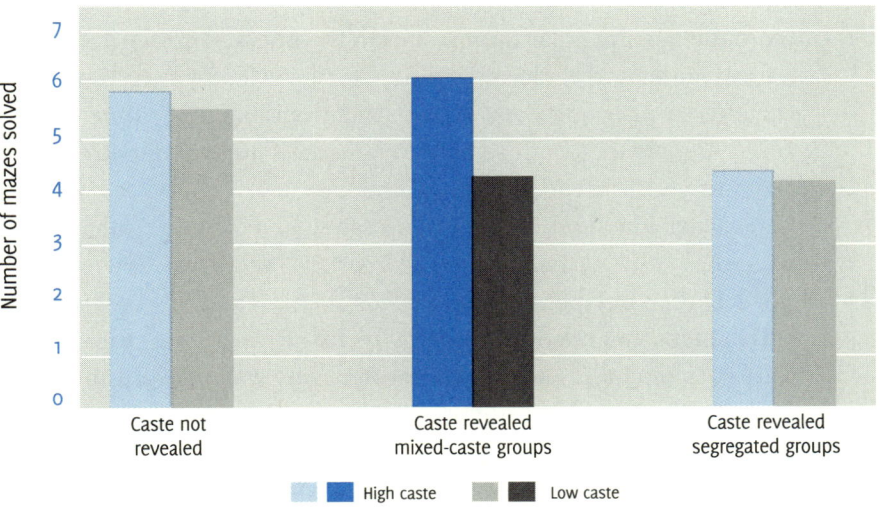

Number of mazes solved

High caste   Low caste

Don't Confuse Me: Make Choosing Easy

To make choosing appropriately easier the key rule generally is 'less is more': simply reduce the number of available options. Although people *say* they like choice, they are confused by too much of it. In a study conducted by Boatwright and Nunes[15] a reduction in the number of options for specific products in a supermarket markedly increased sales.[16] An online grocery store reduced the choice in a set of products by an average of 54% and sales increased in that set by 11%. Not only that, 75% of customers visiting the website spent more as a result of the reduced choice. (This parallels and reinforces the implications of the jam case study in **Chapter 5**.)

To help people make easier decisions—even if they're not necessarily the ideal ones—we suggest the following:

- **Be Selective in Promotion**: If reducing available options isn't appealing or practical, instead promote a small sub-set of options that is likely to appeal to the average or new consumer. e.g. pro-

---

[15] Boatright and Nunes: Reducing Assortment: An Attribute-Based Approach. http://journals.ama.org/doi/abs/10.1509/jmkg.65.3.50.18330.

[16] *Journal of Marketing*, Vol. 65, July 2001, pp. 50-63.

mote the most popular option chosen by others. Or offer people a small number of choices at a time. The www.lendwithcare.org[17] site offers you a choice of three social entrepreneurs at a time you could support with your social investment. If none of the three is right for you, you can click to another set.

- **Offer Decision Support Tools**: You can help people to figure out what they want by asking specific questions that close down options. Online interactive decision aids such as the UK's USwitch, which helps you choose an energy or mobile provider, or Levi's Curve ID for clothes, do this rather well.[18] By walking consumers through a series of questions about typical behaviour they feel less overwhelmed by the number of choices. Identifying the most suitable option for you becomes easier. The Lend with Care site, mentioned earlier, allows you to narrow down your options by applying filters that identify gender, country, and area of activity for your investment focus—for example, Peruvian women in agriculture, Indian men making consumer goods for sale.

- **Implement Default Settings**: Defaults help people find the simplest, easiest route to a decision. Defaults may also imply that a specific option is the most popular, giving us the social reassurance to choose it. In various airline booking systems, such as EasyJet once you have booked a flight, the site offers you the opportunity to select a hotel, rent a car, pay a carbon tax, invest in cancellation insurance etc. You have to 'untick' these options which are there by default to progress. Lyft, the taxi company, will allow you to round up the fare and donate the difference to charity.

It is also much easier for the consumer to have a default setting: normally, for example, 'your current energy plan' as a benchmark

---

[17] Lend with Care brings together entrepreneurs in developing countries with people with individual social investors keen to help them. Run by Care, one of the world's leading aid and development organisations, the scheme offers investment help to small scale local entrepreneurs in developing nations.

[18] http://www.uswitch.com; http://www.levi.com/US/en_US/category/women/clothing.

when evaluating options. They can then compare these to the default. This is much more straightforward than comparing each option relative to every other option. (Some travel sites like Expedia allow you to compare up to 4 options, choosing your own benchmark.)

Don't Confuse Me: Don't Ask Me to Think About Duration or Probability

As we saw earlier in **Chapter 4** people find it hard to think long term. This means they are often unable or unwilling to process the value of a modest short-term investment. But they also find it hard to think about duration. For example, providing a condom—a very cheap short-term cost—could have a massive impact on the future life chances of an individual in sub-Saharan Africa. (Unprotected sex could lead to a long-term impact such as an unwanted pregnancy or an unwelcome sexually transmitted infection.) A small regular investment in a pension fund started very early could build to a significant sum over say 50 years.

But we find it hard to think against these longer time lines. We have a bias against longer duration and find it hard to manage probability too. *The Economist* recently explored this in the unlikely context of why people are so reluctant to pay for premium features in dating apps. Their argument is that many users of dating apps don't pay for premium features such as early notifications or filters for sexual preferences. The magazine suggests users may think that while the costs of these features are small, they are seen as concrete and immediate. On the other hand, the payoffs of such features, while they could be significant—meeting your perfect life partner—are uncertain and possibly distant. *The Economist* quotes Spencer Greenberg of ClearerThinking.org on why this bias exists.[19]

'People tend not to think in probabilistic terms. Humans don't necessarily do a good job of evaluating uncertain outcomes; we are

---

[19] ClearerThinking.org is a consultancy that trains people to improve the quality of their decision-making, including recognising and avoiding decision biases.

much better at assessing the value of a new TV than a raffle which gives us some small probability of receiving a new TV." His conclusion is that paid features on dating apps are hard to value correctly, because they require us to think not just about probabilities but about marginal probabilities. We find it hard to work out how will paying for the app affect the probability of meeting a suitable partner, relative to the probability of meeting such a partner through free alternatives? His assessment is that a 'duration bias' exists. 'Humans are not very good at taking into account how long we will receive a benefit for when deciding the value of that benefit.' This is especially relevant for dating. 'You may end up dating that person for years, or even be with that person for the rest of your life,' says Greenberg. 'But we humans don't necessarily take into account the duration of a benefit when we're considering how valuable it is.'[20]

Keeping it Simple and Real

First launched in 2006, the P&G Pampers and UNICEF campaign is perhaps the most famous Cause Related Marketing programme of the last 20 years. In 2008 two different adverts were aired in April and November. Both involved the basic premise that for every pack of disposable nappies sold, a child was vaccinated against tetanus. But had a slightly different voice-over message at the end.

The first said 'One pack of Pampers equals one life-saving vaccine.' This was enormously successful, raising income for UNICEF and boosting Pampers sales. It has been credited with helping to provide 150 million vaccines.

The second advert was identical, apart from the strapline. 'Together we can help eliminate newborn tetanus.' It was much less successful. Why? The slogan was more abstract, didn't include the possibility of direct personal impact, and avoided the key emotional phrase *life-saving*.

---

[20] *The Economist*: https://www.1843magazine.com/ideas/the-daily/why-are-we-reluctant-to-pay-for-love.

We need to provide information in the right—simple and succinct —format. There are three keys to effective messaging in this format:

1. **Reassurance:** Supporters can be sceptical and need to know that your proposition will deliver impact. Reassure them by being specific about what the money will do: 'equals' is a powerful promise.
2. **Tangibility:** The more concrete the proposition the better. Buying a nappy that will in some general way help fight tetanus globally is not really tangible. Paying for a vaccine will save one specific child's life.
3. **Emotion:** Rather like the word 'home-baked' or 'artisan' adds 'cake'; the strong adjective 'life-saving' adds the emotional content to the more prosaic noun 'vaccine.' It gives a clue to what the exciting outcome is saved.

Research demonstrates supporters can give two to three times more when an intangible need is replaced with a specific impact. The effect is even stronger when a specific beneficiary has been identified. In a field experiment, two groups of supporters were asked to contribute to a Habitat for Humanity home. The group told about a specific family that would live in the house gave 25% more than the group told one of four 'possible' families would have the house.[21]

Here is an advert from Volkswagen illustrating the importance of simplicity. Note how the highlighted words contain the key message.

DSG is our clever gearbox which has two separate clutches. With the 7-speed Direct Shift Gearbox, each change can be practically seamless, which helps save a lot of energy. So not only do you get smooth acceleration, but you also use less fuel.

Another example of Volkswagen efficiency

And in 2017 a Cancer Research UK in Scotland campaign took a similar, simple approach to get its message across.[22]

On simplifying and benchmarking large numbers, the Oxfam annual Inequality report, released around the January Davos meetings, provides good examples. Here's one facto id from their 2018 report.

It takes just four days for a CEO from one of the top five global fashion brands to earn what a Bangladeshi garment worker will earn in her lifetime. In the US, it takes slightly over one working day for a CEO to earn what an ordinary worker makes in a year.

For more examples, see the report summary https://www.oxfam.org/en/pressroom/pressreleases/2018-01-22/richest-1-percent-bagged-82-percent-wealth-created-last-year.

---

[22] https://twitter.com/CRUKScotland/status/909696760922206208.

Learning from Making Just Enough Information Available

- For anyone campaigning, it is important to know your audience and to know how much each segment knows about your organisation, or your cause, and to tailor your messages accordingly.
- Fundraisers should not assume that giving supporters more information automatically increases donations. And equally for campaigners, giving people more information about your campaign will not necessarily increase the likelihood of their commitment nor its strength.
- Use familiar iconic elements, including descriptors like 'an area the size of Wales,' or 'the weight of 10 elephants,' or 'the same cost as the entire defence budget' to engage people. (Note these are relatively meaningless to System 2. But System 1 loves them.)
- A self-reinforcing process is one in which a collective belief gains more and more plausibility through its increasing repetition in public discourse; or repeat something long enough and it will become true. Remember; The Trump election, 'Hilary the Criminal,' The Brexit '£350 million a week for the NHS' claims.
- When your website, brand, or product is referenced repeatedly by others, people are more likely to think highly of it. The more social buzz you generate, the better. Make sure you are mentioned by others.
- Avoid confusing people. You can do that by offering them too many choices, or asking them to consider data levels that are too big for them to get their heads around. Or even by asking them to think too long-term. Make choices simple and immediate with a defined direct pay off.
- The same message applies to the language or images used. Make them simple, direct and relevant. Cut away any extraneous material or ideas so that it's clear what the decision to be made is.
- Offer attractive defaults where you can ethically. And where you can't, offer easy-to-use decision-making tools that allow the person to feel they have made the choice—even if you have nudged them in a particular direction.

Chapter 10

Keep It Normal and Personal

Summary

For behaviour change to take place, two complementary heuristics need to be in place—*normalisation* and *personalisation*. In one sense these are opposites. *Normalisation* involves making the behaviour you want appear to be part of a common and acceptable experience or activity. It is about ensuring that the individual whose behaviour we want to change feels her/his specific concerns and interests are being recognised and addressed.

Normalisation—mentioned in **Chapters 3** and **6**—plays directly into our background as a social animal and to the evolutionary imperative to be part of one or more tribes. Of course, 'normal' is a loaded word. In one sense it is positive and something that everyone seeks. After a disaster or tragedy, survivors often express the view that they 'just want to get back to normal.' Equally, after disruption, the transport authorities seek to assure everyone that 'normal service will be resumed as soon as possible.' (Even if the normal service was not very good.) And people always want to feel their culture, physicality, sexuality or beliefs are accepted as 'normal.'

Our desire to be like others has a neurological underpinning. The existence of mirror neurons, for example, helps explain some aspects of how empathy works—an essential component in philanthropy. We can build on this neurological phenomenon to create positive social change for people who are not part of our *in-group*.

Unfortunately, there's a danger that certain kinds of negative behaviour—such as 'everyday sexism' or 'casual racism'—start to be seen as 'normal.' It then becomes very difficult to challenge, and individuals who do not match this normative mindset, can feel judged or excluded. They are not conforming to the stereotype or 'ideal.' Despite its negative potential, normalising is, in general, a helpful part of our decision architecture toolkit.

Normalising is not the same as generalising. It is essential that any communication designed to affect our behaviour also appears personalised, making people feel as though they are important as individuals. Personalisation supports our sense of identity. When combined with normalisation we have a powerful tool to build momentum for change.

Personalisation can be delivered in a number of ways. Data mining and powerful CRM can ensure we learn to understand individuals and their motivations based on their patterns of behaviour. At the other end of the spectrum the simplest personal addition to a communication—a signature, a handwritten greeting—can make a massive difference to people feeling recognised.

'I'll Have What She's Having'. Matching

We're sure you've seen the very funny scene in the film *When Harry Met Sally*.[1] The two key actors, Harry (Billy Crystal) and Sally (Meg Ryan), are having a meal in the famous Katz's Delicatessen in New York. 'Sally' offers to demonstrate how easy it is for a woman to fake an orgasm. As she does so she attracts the attention of many of the other diners in the restaurant. One older lady in particular at the next

---

[1] Interestingly the film itself was promoted using a form of marketing called platform release which relies strongly on social proof. In this technique the film was released in a small number of cities to selected crowds. They then used word of mouth to generate interest and publicity for a wider release. The film eventually became an almost $100 million success.

table notices the orgasm and assumes it is connected to the sandwich Sally is eating. When asked by the waitress what she wants to eat the lady diner says 'I'll have what she's having.' (Other diners, and perhaps many of the movie goers, clearly have the same thought.)

This is a great example of matching—the desire to copy others in social situations—as a driver of human behaviour. And matching is an aspect of normalisation.[2] Dutch behavioural researcher Hermans[3] thinks this unconscious desire to match explains many common social dining quirks, such as why we tend to eat more in the presence of others, and why drinking partners often sip their drinks simultaneously, especially when each is focused on what the other is saying.

This can work even when the interaction is virtual. The next time you watch a film or TV show with friends who have glasses in their hands, notice how often they raise them to drink in sync with the actors on the screen. This type of behavioural 'orchestration' usually happens below the level of conscious awareness. And of course, many skilled influencers proactively use the body-language-matching technique to build rapport with others.

The key learning is that when people don't know what to do, they follow each other. In doing so, they adopt different 'copy' strategies depending on the context. So they might copy:

- *The majority*, especially when in public—see earlier examples of choosing restaurants with queues outside when unsure where to eat.
- A *successful individual* in a work or sports setting, to 'model' their success. Hence also bestseller books like *The Seven Habits of Highly Effective People*.

---

[2] Many evolutionary psychologists suggest that the instinct to fit in (and to reciprocate gift-giving and punish selfish behaviour) is hard-wired, because we needed the group to survive. One of the most interesting manifestations of the fact that we are always matching is that over time, couples start to look like each other (and sometimes even their dogs). Prolonged time together subconsciously matching each other's facial expressions can lead the muscles of the face to develop in similar ways.

[3] Herman: *The Possible Antecedents and Consequences of Matching of Food Intake: Examining The Role of Trait Self-Esteem and Interpersonal Closeness*, https://www.ncbi.nlm.nih.gov/pmc/articles/PMC4686593/.

- *Socially skilled individuals*—people who seem to be successful in fitting into a range of situations—parties, dinners, receptions etc. Think the Fonz and his 'be cool' strategy.
- *Family or friends* when group cohesion is important—at a funeral or a hen party—when we have to adopt unusual or uncomfortable behaviour.
- *Someone who acts with a sense of authority* or has some symbols of status like a briefcase, uniform or badge.[4]

Copying is often a 'safe bet.' Others may know what they are doing, so if you do what they are doing it's more likely to be the right thing to do. As social influencers we can build on this desire for others to copy by offering contexts or models providing the appropriate stimulus.

There's a direct connection here to certain aspects of philanthropy as individuals seek to gain status by demonstrating behaviour that others admire or respect. Dean Karlan and Margaret McConnell of Harvard University, ran a 2014 research study *Hey Look at Me: The Effect of Giving Circles on Giving.* (2014). The study was designed to establish which had the greatest impact on increased giving in a group: 'improving your public social image' or 'the ability to influence others.'

They ran the experiment with Yale University alumni who had the opportunity to join one of three giving circle levels. Fundraisers phoned over 4000 alumni asking for donations at one of the three levels. Essentially the study proved that while a desire to influence others was a driver of increased gifts the potential to be named and publically recognised was a greater driver. This drove both *more gifts* and *higher levels*.

This is important in constructing fundraising campaigns. It explains why public recognition, from names published on online

---

[4] A famous 1950s experiment by Lefkovitz, Blake and Moulton showed, when crossing against the red light, pedestrians were more likely to follow a smartly dressed businessman than exactly the same person dressed in scruffy shorts. *The Connected Leader: Creating Agile Organizations for People Performance,* Emmanuel Gobillot, Kogan Page.

platforms to sophisticated recognition boards, is important.[5] There are a number of other studies that confirm this broad conclusion. Karlan and McConnell quote Ariely, Bracha and Meier (2009) '[who] present evidence that individuals exert more effort in generating gifts for charity when their work is publicly observable. In addition, Lacetera and Macis (2010) show that individuals are more likely to donate blood when they receive publicly announced awards.'

The Dark Side of Normal

Let's explore the dark side of normal, or more formally the challenge of normalising negative social traits or social attitudes.[6]

The 'Is Steve a librarian or a farmer?' exercise[7] in **Section One** illustrates a common bias we may have that assumes certain stereotypical characteristics apply to people in specific jobs. You can see how this kind of thinking can too easily move from a misjudgement about employment into stereotyping in terms of gender, sexuality, culture, race, etc. It also demonstrates, yet again, System 1's lazy, unquestioning acceptance of the information supplied. Just a minute in rational, System 2 thinking and it would be completely obvious

---

[5] For a more detailed version of this study see. https://www.povertyactionlab. org/sites/default/files/publications/336_187%20hey%20look%20at%20me%20 May2013.pdf. The research team also quotes other studies showing broader relevance.

[6] http://www.bbc.com/future/story/20170314-how-do-we-determine-when-a-behaviour-is-normal. Jessica Brown 20 March 2017.

[7] In case you've forgotten the case here it is again.

Description: *Steve lives in the US and is very shy and withdrawn. He's invariably helpful but with little interest in people or in the world of reality. A meek and tidy soul, he has a need for order and structure, and a passion for detail.*

Question to answer quickly: *is Steve more likely to be a librarian or a farmer?*

Where we have introduced this question in workshops, two-thirds of participants guess that Steve is a librarian. As it happens, male farmers in the United States outnumber male librarians by a ratio of about 20 to 1. So statistically he is more likely to be a farmer. Had we included this framing or information, participants might have concluded that Steve is probably a farmer. But because most people focus only on the information in the description, they come to a wrong conclusion.

there are many more farmers in the US than there are librarians—
and therefore Steve is much more likely to be a farmer.

We have a recent example of this troubling side of normalisation.
Jessica Brown,[8] a BBC producer, noted in an excellent online article
that during the 2016 presidential campaign Donald Trump made a
number of troubling statements revealing his misogynist and racist
attitudes. This didn't seem to affect his electability, as Brown points
out, even when Hilary Clinton, the Democratic candidate, openly
challenged Trump's behaviour and attitudes on a number of occasions.
Clinton recognised the wider danger when she said: 'My campaign is
not going to let Donald Trump try to normalise himself.'

Despite her best efforts during the campaign, there were clear
signs among parts of the US electorate—'Just locker room talk'—that
Trump's attitudes and behaviours were indeed being normalised.
Teju Cole, the respected writer and journalist described this, in an
insightful essay for the *New York Times Magazine*. 'All around were
the unmistakable signs of normalization in progress. So many were
falling into line without being pushed. It was happening at tremendous speed, like a contagion.'[9] (Quoted by Jessica Brown in online
BBC article—see [6] below.)

The worrying conclusion is that as Trump and his behaviour
become more familiar, he becomes more acceptable, even to those who
initially disapproved of his actions. And that makes it more difficult
for those of us involved in social change to counter these attitudes and
the behaviour that they encourage. (See below for more on this.)

What's Normal Anyway?

Academics who have studied the normalisation process have come
to some intriguing conclusions about how we form ideas about what

---

[8] A number of the examples quoted here are from Brown's excellent article, available
here: http://www.bbc.com/future/story/20170314-how-do-we-determine-when-a-
behaviour-is-normal.

[9] https://www.nytimes.com/2016/11/11/magazine/a-time-for-refusal.html.

is normal. Two leading academics Adam Bear and Joshua Knobe of Yale University, again quoted by Jessica Brown, claim people tend to blur what is 'desirable' and what is 'average' into a 'single undifferentiated judgment of normality.'[10] They argue that, as Trump "continues to do things that once would have been regarded as outlandish," these actions are not only being seen as more typical—but also more normal.

In a paper in the journal *Cognition*,[11] Bear and Knobe explain how they ran a series of experiments that explored how people decide whether something is normal or not. They found that 'when people think about what is normal, they combine their sense of what is typical with their sense of what is ideal.' Normal, in other words, 'turns out to be a blend of statistical and moral notions.'

They illustrate this finding with a simple example based on two questions. 'Ask yourself, "What is the *average* number of hours of TV that people watch in a day?" Then ask yourself a question that might seem very similar: "What is the *normal* number of hours of TV for a person to watch in a day?"'

They put these questions to individuals taking part in an experiment. For many participants the answers to the two questions were different. Most participants said the 'average' time to watch TV daily was about four hours. But they were clear that the 'normal' number was about three hours. When pushed, participants had a third perception, which was that the 'ideal' number was about 2.5 hours. These distinctions, the two researchers argue, have an interesting implication: 'people's conception of what is normal deviates from the average in the direction of what they think *ought* to be so.' So we seem to be able to carry in our heads three distinct but linked standards.

This distinction links to the criticism of Thaler about nudges and paternalism discussed earlier in **Chapter Three**—who should judge what's the *right* behaviour that we should seek to encourage? And when looking to normalise a behaviour which of these three percep-

---

[10] https://www.nytimes.com/2017/01/28/opinion/sunday/the-normalization-trap.html.
[11] http://www.sciencedirect.com/science/article/pii/S0010027716302645.

tual models should we focus on? This is a big challenge for campaigners or educators working on other cultures. We can see the challenges gender equality campaigners face, for example, over Female Genital Mutilation (FGM). See below[12] for BBC interviews with Kenyan Masai women *in favour* of FGM. Many other less extreme examples exist across cultures, genders and faiths.

Research in recent years has found that many behaviours and attitudes can be normalised over a period of time. They can even be almost unnoticed until you compare views over time. The banning of smoking in restaurants and bars—controversial when it was introduced—is now almost universally accepted in UK. For young people, drug taking, still controversial in wider society, is now accepted as a leisure activity which happens to be illegal. Our language reflects this particular change with the use of the phrase 'recreational drug use'[13] now in general parlance. 'The new generation of drug user' say three eminent researchers in *Illegal Leisure*, 'can no longer be seen as mad or bad or from some weird subcultural world—they are ordinary and everywhere.'

Katy Waldman makes some interesting distinctions about cultural assumptions in a *Slate* article about normalisation. She says: 'In conversations about social justice, normalization often exists in opposition to intolerance or bigotry. A law or cultural product may *pathologize* (portray as sick), *demonize* (portray as evil), or *exoticize* (portray as alien). You can fight these othering impulses by harnessing empathy and imagination to recast difference as commonality. For instance, we can normalize trans-people by deploying gender-neutral pronouns and we can normalize those with disabilities by making sure our workplaces provide wheelchair ramps and accessible bathrooms.' Again we can see the importance of language as a nudge and empathy

---

[12] https://www.pri.org/stories/2014-07-02/why-do-these-women-kenya-support-female-genital-mutilation.

[13] *Illegal Leisure: The Normalization of Adolescent Recreational Drug Use*, Howard J. Parker, Judith Aldridge, Fiona Measham. In this study, three academics share the results and implications of their detailed, five-year study into young people and drug-taking. They argue that drugs—from cannabis, to LSD, amphetamines and ecstasy—have become broadly socially acceptable.

as a way to build understanding. But there is dark-side potential too. Shifts in our collective perception of 'normal' can move incrementally, often helped along by changes to language. Notice how some media sources have replaced the term 'extreme-right' with 'alt right.' This can be seen as a way of helping to normalise and make acceptable what are actually extreme, and offensive, political views.

It's not just views or opinions, of course that are impacted. The 'alt right,' have invented the interesting term 'alternative facts.' The phrase seems to us to be an oxymoron. But you can hear about alternative facts on social media, in specialised websites and even from US presidential communication professionals. By and large these 'alternative facts' are simply easily spottable lies. But what explains the growth in this phenomenon and its power to impress? A team of Harvard Business Review (HBR) researchers set out to test how the context in which people process information affects their willingness to actively verify ideas or claims.

They conducted a linked series of eight experiments, see below for details. These experiments established that people fact-check much less often when they evaluate statements in a collective setting. In a version of the *bystander effect* (see **Chapter 6**). People seem to assume that someone else in the group must be checking the data. Interestingly, the result is broadly the same whether people are physically together or if they are simply in an online group—for example on Facebook or other social media settings. Having others present, actually or virtually, seems to reduce participants' individual vigilance. The result of mass participation is much lower levels of fact-checking.[14] This reluctance to fact check can drive opinions and from there, behaviour.

For those involved in the social justice agenda it makes it more important to tackle 'fake news' and 'alternative facts' whenever they appear. And, of course, to be vigilant about your own ability to study and interrogate information or news.

---

[14] *Being in a Group Makes Us Less Likely to Fact-Check* by Rachel Meng, Youjung Jun, and Gita V. Johar, HBR Review AUGUST 01, 2017 https://hbr.org/2017/08/research-being-in-a-group-makes-us-less-likely-to-fact-check.

Normalisation for Good

Normalisation can also, thank goodness, change attitudes and behaviours for good. And the very good news is there has been significant effort, and progress, in a number of areas. We could mention perhaps sexism and gender stereotyping, environmental awareness and the treatment of people with disabilities.

Normalisation can be super simple. In 2007 Kathy Taylor, Mayor of Tulsa, Oklahoma decided that the city's printers were to be set to two-sided printing by default. The result, even then, was a saving of $41,400 a year. And a lot of trees.[15]

Learning Disabilities: Tackling Stereotyping Through Normalisation

A good example of the potential to normalise positively relates to society's views of people with learning disabilities.

According to Jessica Brown, quoted above, major steps towards normalisation for people with learning disabilities began in Denmark. In 1959 the Government passed a law guaranteeing people with learning disabilities should have living conditions as close as possible to others in society. From that spark came a number of progressive practices worldwide. For example, over the 70s and 80s residential institutions in many parts of the world were closed. The 'new normal' for people with learning disabilities was to be living and, if possible, working in the community.

Institutional changes, however, don't by themselves bring about positive normalisation. A necessary complementary change is in language that helps reframe or nudge social attitudes. Brown points out that terms like 'spastic' or 'retarded,' once regarded as acceptable descriptors, have become unacceptable. Even social organisations that used these terms have abandoned them. In 1994 the UK's Spastics Society changed its name to Scope as part of a process to positively promote attitudinal change.[16] And in the U.S. the law promotes the use of the phrase 'intellectual disability' over 'mental retardation.'

---

[15] http://nudges.org/category/blog-posts/page/52/.

[16] https://everydaysexism.com "The Everyday Sexism Project exists to catalogue instances of sexism experienced on a day to day basis. They might be serious or minor,

There's been a wider impact too. Instead of identifying people with their disability such as 'the disabled,' 'the blind,' 'the mentally ill,' language and attitudes now reflect the idea that people with disabilities are first of all people. So, the preference is now 'people with disabilities,' 'people who are blind,' and 'people living with mental illnesses.'

Normalisation and Marketing of Real Beauty

Women and their Bodies have historically been a challenging area for normalisation. There have been numerous campaigns run by NGOs to try and tackle sexism, over-sexualisation of young women, inappropriate normalisation and body shaming. A notable example is the Every Day Sexism Project[17] which seeks to identify the unconscious biases that pervade a great deal of society.

With all this concern in the social change community it's interesting that one of the best known and most influential campaigns in recent years came from a commercial company. And more than that a company primarily concerned with the prosaic business of selling soap and other cleansing/beauty products. The 'Dove' brand, now used on a range of products by Unilever, was originally focussed on a fairly straightforward bar of soap when it was launched in 1957. For almost 40 years the company used a range of conventional marketing strategies—claims it was better than other soaps at moisturising, that it was based on science, that it was used by film stars, etc. (For

---

outrageously offensive or so niggling and normalised that you don't even feel able to protest. Say as much or as little as you like, use your real name or a pseudonym—it's up to you. By sharing your story you're showing the world that sexism does exist, it is faced by women everyday and it is a valid problem to discuss." See also the Gender Ads Project.

[17] https://everydaysexism.com, "The Everyday Sexism Project exists to catalogue instances of sexism experienced on a day to day basis. They might be serious or minor, outrageously offensive or so niggling and normalised that you don't even feel able to protest. Say as much or as little as you like, use your real name or a pseudonym, it's up to you. By sharing your story you're showing the world that sexism does exist, it is faced by women everyday and it is a valid problem to discuss."

an interesting history of the brand see www.slideshare.net/laurafa-lotico/dove-brand-evolution.) But by the early 2000s, however, senior marketers in Unilever were concerned the brand looked old fashioned and was losing ground to newer formats for cleansing products, like gels and liquid soap.

In 2004, they decided to re-launch the brand, associating the product with 'real women,' in improve sales? This was not simply a nice idea, but was designed to key into some research they had commissioned which established that as few as 2% of women worldwide 'liked or loved' their body.

The marketers saw an opportunity to associate Dove with the idea of real or natural beauty. Of course, that's a proposition that many other companies could also claim. (For example, Body Shop could attest not just that it promoted some idea of natural beauty *but* that it used organic ingredients, *and* had some version of fair trade-none of which Dove could really claim. So in theory Body Shop should, if System 2 was dominant in our decision making, have had a massive advantage.) So how did Dove succeed in claiming this space?

In *Decoded*, Phil Barden shares some interesting thoughts on what he sees as some of the key signifiers used that made a difference in the Dove campaign:

- The images tended to be of *groups* of woman, not individuals.
- The women were of different ethnicities, ages, shapes, and sizes.
- They were smiling and making eye contact with the audience in a confident way.
- They were shown in 'pyjama-party' type social gatherings having fun.
- The advert settings signal there was no sexual or 'attractiveness' competition.

See the image example below. The goal with these images, according to Barden, was to normalise how woman felt through relief about not having to aspire to some artificial and unachievable ideal shape or size.[18] So normal became 'what you are.'

The campaign attracted a lot of attention. It has also consistently been reported as being enormously successful in marketing and sales terms—though Unilever, a notoriously secretive company, has not released any data over the almost decade and a half it has been running.

In fairness to Unilever there was a direct philanthropic payoff from the campaign. In 2004 Dove created a fund to support a range of related social initiatives. They worked in partnership with organisations like the Girl Scouts, Boys & Girls Clubs of America and Girls Inc. The funds supported programmes and activities around gender, including promoting discussions about online bullying and photography projects allowing girls to capture the beauty in the world around them.

Dove. Real Beauty Campaign

---

[18] The campaign was based on a major piece of research. In the early 2000s, Unilever's PR agency, Edelman, interviewed more than 3,000 women across 10 countries. The aim was to learn about women's priorities, concerns and interests. One of the key findings was that only 2 percent of the women interviewed considered themselves beautiful. Dove executives saw an opportunity. They decided to do two things: to move beyond the simple bar of soap; and to introduce other linked products like shampoo and body wash. They would then link this to beginning a conversation allowing ordinary women to define beauty. Their argument was pragmatic: a campaign that tapped into what women were thinking and feeling about what was normal could help Dove become more relevant, sell more, and, of course, become more profitable.

There is some interesting learning here for anyone trying to build a movement for social change:

- First, the importance of a research based approach: identifying what matters to the audience and to address this.
- Second, to build, where possible, on an existing trusted brand—which Dove was—and reframe it.
- Third, stick to simple but easily understandable messages helping to identify the approach you want as normal or, if necessary, the new normal.

Going Green

Another sector in which positive normalisation of attitudes and behaviour has made progress is in awareness of the green agenda. Ruth Rettie, Chris Barnham and Kevin Burchel, researchers at Kingston Business School, wrote an influential paper in 2011 entitled *Social Normalisation and Consumer Behaviour: Using Marketing to Make Green Normal*. This paper reviewed the research on campaigns and initiatives and looked at what the evidence suggested on how to progress environmental awareness and action. They had two complementary recommendations: to position eco-friendliness as mainstream or normal, rather than niche; and positioning unsustainable behaviours as non-mainstream or abnormal, and so unacceptable.

The paper probably picked up on and amplified a zeitgeist. Consider the scale of increased environmental effort going on. More people are recycling than ever. More adverts encourage us to recycle and show it as a normal part of life. Green behaviours have become more normative and talked-about. So in 2015–16, 43.9% of household waste in the UK was recycled, composted or reused. This compares to less than 1% in 1983–84, according to the UK Office for National Statistics.

As Brown says in her comment on this result: 'Being described as "normal" can influence our behaviour without us even realising. We welcome normal, we protect it, and we fall into its trappings.'

Make it Personal

As indicated in the summary, personalisation is a *complementary* heuristic to normalisation. It's not the opposite. By personalising experiences in different ways you can achieve a number of things. You can:

- Help promote empathy or understanding of another's' situation.
- Emphasise the importance of personal agency—you can do something.
- Make individuals feel special and important—reinforcing the connection to your cause.

All of these are helpful in our mission to deliver social change.

Who Am I?

Personal is not a simple unitary concept. We tend to think of ourselves as having one or more particular social identities. This is often connected to links with demographic groups like mothers, cultural identity groups like Jewish, geographical community, local citizen or even shared experiences like 'cancer survivors.' When we're reminded about that identity, or have it reinforced in a communication we feel more inclined to act in ways that feel consistent with it. This is important in fundraising as well as more generally.

Kessler and Milkman[19] showed that when donors were reminded of their 'identity' as previous donors, they were more likely to give again. (These studies were part of a major set of field trials with the American Red Cross.) Specifically, they saw higher donation rates when the charity reminded prospective donors of their previous support by listing the date of their last donation on the current appeal. Interestingly they also observed even higher contributions when a donation request primed a potential donor's identity as part

---

[19] *Identity in Charitable Giving:* Judd B Kessler and Katherine L Milkman, The Wharton School, University of Pennsylvania, https://site.stanford.edu/sites/default/files/kesslermilkman_identityincharitablegiving.pdf.

of a city community—'as a proud Chicagoan'—even though the appeal was clearly labelled as looking for funds towards a national programme. Again, this reinforces the importance of giving individuals a sense of personal recognition and agency that feels normal.

Paul Bloom in *Against Empathy*, mentioned earlier, makes an important distinction between Empathy and Compassion. *Empathy* is emotional and involves putting oneself in someone else's shoes (I could have been a victim of a similar earthquake). Empathy encourages help, but has a spotlight effect which can drive one to support one victim, instead of a million. *Compassion* is a more rational approach based on what's morally right, and priority, without necessarily putting oneself in someone else's shoes (I don't have to imagine myself dying of diarrhoea caused by open-air defecation to think that something needs to be done about diarrhoea related child deaths).

Empathy and Mirror Neurons

One of the challenges we face in promoting social change is that the individuals or groups we are seeking help or support *for* are often completely unlike the group we are seeking support *from*. (So older white male supporters in a developed nation might be asked to help young women's empowerment in a developing nation.) Success in this context requires empathy—the ability to understand the situation and feelings of another. Empathy is often seen as an aspect of emotional intelligence. So if you are highly emotionally intelligent you might well be able to understand the situation of another person who is completely different from you—younger, older, a different sexuality, gender etc.

From a decision science point of view this ability to have empathy is important. It can help us to behave sympathetically or even philanthropically towards another group or individual, for example, to appreciate the challenges brought about by mental health issues, drug use, domestic violence etc. As decision scientists and campaigners we need to be able to promote empathy or stimulate it. The good news is that there is evidence that there is a neurological and not just psychological base to this ability to empathise.

In the 1980s Italian neuropsychologist Giacomo Ritzzollati and his team conducted a series of experiments which have proved enormously influential in understanding this neurological basis. They placed electrodes in the brains of macaque monkeys while studying the neural activity when the monkeys picked up food. In the process they discovered something unexpected. The same neurons that fired when the monkey picked up the food also fired when they simply saw a human researcher do the same thing. This, and a number of subsequent studies, led to establishing the existence of what are called mirror neurons. Essentially these neurons drive a process that means when we see someone doing something we experience it at some level ourselves.

The implication is that we can experience empathy in many situations. If we see someone fall, we may feel a similar anxiety and even say out loud 'ouch.' Or if we see someone eat a banana we may be able to bring to mind the taste and feeling of banana. (And possibly want one too.)

Many charities are using this neurological phenomenon to promote engagement in their campaigns. At its simplest you see adverts with photos of individuals seeking help, looking out at you from a magazine or leaflet with first person testimony. ('I need your help.') You can, to some extent, recreate alien or unusual experiences and promote empathy in this way. But let's not forget that even something as 'old school' as a book can promote empathy. Reading *I Know Why the Caged Bird Sings* you can feel enormous empathy for the young Maya Angelou as she survives and grows through the most horrific experiences as a young black girl in the Deep South. Few of us will have had similar experiences. That's a tribute to the quality of her writing.[20]

---

[20] On the subject of empathy and literature, it is probably apocryphal but nonetheless widely reported that Abraham Lincoln remarked on meeting Harriet Beecher Stowe 'So you're the woman who wrote that little book that started this great war.' (*Uncle Tom's Cabin* was the best-selling novel of the century, and the second best-selling book behind the Bible.) A more contemporary example might involve the way the UK TV film *Cathy Come Home* led to the setting up of Shelter, the homelessness campaign.

There are interesting developments in the social use of immersive experiences to promote empathy. Clearly technology can help bring an experience into the mind of a supporter, most often using an adaptation of the Virtual Reality (VR) glasses used in gaming. Agencies like Amnesty, United Nations High Commissioner for Refugees (UNHCR), Greenpeace and others use this approach to bring home to viewers the reality of life in refugee camps or to see the impact of environmental degradation. A prospective supporter may be stopped in the street and asked to put on VR glasses and headphones and taken into one of these 'worlds.'[21] The payoff, of course, is that having had this powerful shared experience the supporter may then be asked for a donation.

While these experiments are interesting and offer exciting potential there's mixed feedback about their effectiveness at the moment —for example the experience focuses on the visual and auditory senses—and so lacks 'tactile' elements. This can make the experience feel unreal and even alienating. And there is still a need for talent in the telling of the story. VR is still developing, both as a technology and our ability to use it[22].

You don't need to use sophisticated technology to create immersive experiences that generate empathy in an individual. You can do it in a practical real world 'simulation.' Below are examples of exer-

---

[21] If you're keen to see an online example of this kind of work, have a look at https://with.in/watch/clouds-over-sidra/, in which a 12 year old girl, Sidra, guides you through her temporary home the Zaatari refugee camp in Jordan, which houses 130,000 Syrians who fled the violence and civil war in their country. Tragically, children like Sidra make up half the camp's population. In the 8-minute film she leads you through her daily life: eating, sleeping, learning and playing in the vast desert city of tents.

[22] In fairness some of these campaigns have been extremely effective. Another noteworthy VR campaign was premiered at an evening gala at the Metropolitan Museum of Art in December 2015. Prominent men and women were treated to a lavish dinner and then headsets were brought out. The party of 400, each in their own VR headset, watched a video produced by the NY-based agency charity: water. They raise funds to ensure poor people around the world have access to clean water. The video showed a young girl Salem's challenges collecting water for her family. In that night alone, donors at the event committed $2.4 million, much more than the planners had anticipated. The charity also reported that, shortly after the video's premiere, a donor came to the office planning to give $60,000, watched the video and was so moved by it that he upped his donation to $400,000 on the spot.

cises designed to create empathy. This kind of direct immersive experience borrows from the world of theatre. Often the experiences use actors and directors.

The Crossroads Foundation, a Hong Kong-based INGO, hosts a regular event at the World Economic Forum in Davos. Here they use an immersive simulation to help political and business leaders experience what it's actually like to be a refugee, challenging the at-a-distance normalisation of this experience and seeking to promote empathy. Over several hours this programme recreates some of the struggles and choices refugees face to survive. As part of the exercise senior business and governmental people are 'processed' like refugees: forced to hand over personal documents; having their valuables removed; shown threatening behaviour by men with guns; and subjected to aggressive questioning on their status, their plans, etc.

The experience was co-developed with refugees, internally displaced persons and aid workers to create as realistic a scenario as possible. As well as empathy, the project targets issues that the Foundation believes need to be addressed by global leaders: the impacts of ethnic conflict, weak legal infrastructure, corruption, and discrimination.

By encouraging these leaders to understand and empathise with refugees they hope to encourage them to take action to improve the situation of refuges in their own countries and internationally.

Former UN Secretary General Ban Ki-moon taking part in the Refugee Simulation Project.

A project called Dialogue in the Dark http://www.dialogue-in-the-dark.com does something similar to create empathy for individuals with sight impairment. As a sighted paying participant you join a group and are led on a personalised journey through a specially built cityscape with full size shops, roads with traffic, a park, a boat ride and even a supermarket—all completely in the dark. Your guide asks you to tackle some everyday tasks without the benefit of sight. For example, you do shopping for vegetables or are asked to order and eat coffee and snacks in a café. Over the 1.5 hours of the tour you experience realistic sounds, smells, wind and textures. There are unexpected steps and slopes to catch you unawares, and motor car horns blaring on the street to make you extra anxious. Dialogue in the Dark both educates sighted people about what it is like to be blind or visually impaired, and provides employment for a number of sight impaired guides. These guides can enjoy feeling more empowered as they help people who find they are suddenly significantly less competent in the dark. The Dialogue in the Dark project is so successful that it is currently available in 21 countries in permanent and touring variations.

Having experienced Dialogue in the Dark, in Mexico, Bernard can attest to how challenging it is to navigate a world when a key sense you use without thinking is suddenly taken away.

Combining Normalising and Personalising for Fundraising

The UK's Behavioural Insights Team (BIT) worked with the Corporate Social Responsibility team of Deutsche Bank in London as part of a fundraising campaign in support of two charities—Help a Capital Child and Meningitis Research UK. Their aim was to improve the uptake of an existing employee support scheme run by the bank. The existing scheme asked employees to donate a day of their salary to a designated charity on one specific day of the year. (Obviously with some of the bank employees being very high earners this could be a significant source of funds for the two causes.[23] But the secret of success was uptake.)

The bank only matches individual involvement for the designated day. Experimenters were keen to test different approaches—based around *normalisation* and *personalisation*—that would drive the highest levels of take up. The goal was to test which approaches would have the biggest impact. On the morning of 'giving day,' all 8,000 employees were randomly allocated to receive one of two emails from the CEO:

- A standard one addressed to 'Dear Colleague'.
- A personalised one to them by name (e.g. 'Dear David').

In addition, some employees, depending on which specific office location they worked in, were greeted by volunteers who were themselves giving up the day's wages. These 'normalising' volunteers adopted two different tactics:

- Some handed individual flyers to colleagues as they arrived for work.
- Some gave out small tins of sweets as well as the flyers.

In the control group—those receiving the 'Colleague' email—around 5% of employees gave a day of their salary. When they were also given sweets as they entered the building this more than doubled to

---

[23] The scheme has already been made tax effective through gift aid. And each donation was to be matched £ for £ by the bank. The implication was that a £1 donation from a donor who was a UK top rate tax payer could be worth almost £3.00 to a charity.

11%. Interestingly, the sweets were almost as effective as receiving a more personalised email from the CEO ('Dear Diane'), where 12% gave a day of their salary to charity.

But by far the most effective intervention was the combination of giving people both a personalised email from the CEO *and* some sweets by a volunteer as they entered the building. The impact here was that the engagement level tripled compared to the control group. Those agreeing to take part and donate the day's wages went up to 17%.

Overall, bank staff gave more than £500,000 to charity on a single day. In itself that's an impressive result. But the implication is that if the staff had received what proved to be the most effective approach—a personalised CEO email and sweets—they would have contributed more than £1 million. Sometimes the simplest things have a massive impact.

Deutche Bank Personalization and Normalisation Donation Experiment Summary

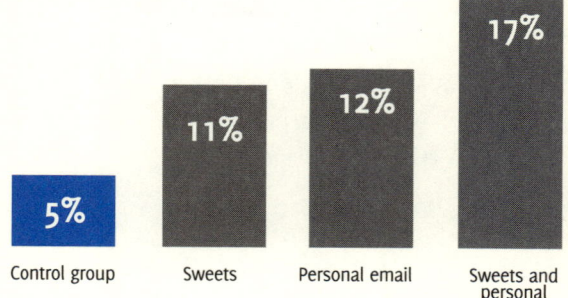

Personalisation can take many odd forms. Greenpeace in Argentina tested a number of options for donation requests on the phone. They were seeking a one-off gift from existing donors in honour of various special days in the supporter's life. Among the options tested were: Mothers' Day, Fathers' Day, Argentina's national day, the prospect's own birthday. The day connection that drew the highest donation? To make a gift in honour of the birthday of the donor's pet. People like their personalisation the way they like it.

You can deliver a personalised message just by the tone and language in a communication. If you're a fundraiser, you have heard of the red/blue circle test. This asks you to look at one of your supporter communications and circle every time you mention your self or your organisation in red. And every time you mention the supporter in blue. Your 'blue' score should exceed your 'red' score. You should be talking about *them*.

Facebook and Amazon, as we know, target our preferences by making personalised suggestions to us—people we might want to be friends with, or purchases we might want to consider. This is all done by sophisticated algorithms rather than teams of emotionally intelligent elves. These algorithms can provide extraordinary results.

Personal Pregnancy Prediction

Every time you go shopping, online or in real life, you are sharing with the retailer some very personal details about your lifestyle and consumption patterns. As part of the process of data mining many of those retailers are using that information to figure out not just what what you'd like now, but what you might want or need in the future.

Almost every major retailer, from grocery chains to investment banks and the Post Office, now has a 'predictive analytics' department. Their job is not just to understand your shopping habits but also to seek monetisable insights from your personal habits or attitudes. The purpose is very simple—to market more efficiently to you.

Some companies are significantly ahead of others in this field. One example that received significant publicity, was when US supermarket chain Target data-mined its way into a customer's womb.

In an insightful *New York Times* article, reporter Charles Duhigg explored how Target identifies potential new parents by some very early purchase behaviours. Once the purchase metrics suggest a possible pregnancy, the CRM system kicks in and promotes more of the stuff prospective parents might feel they need to buy online. Target statistician Andrew Pole explained in an interview, how the company gains these 'pregnancy' clues. Target assigns every customer a unique identifier, linked to their credit card. This identifier creates a rolling data record of the customer's purchase history. They also link to this record any other social or demographic information collected: age, sex, etc. (It may even combine data about the customer bought from external sources.) Pole and his team of data diviners established, in parallel, key purchase patterns associated with women who had signed up to baby registries. They were then able to combine the two data sets. And work out who might be pregnant.

The level of detail Pole and his team went into is described in the *New York Times* article. 'Lotions, for example. Lots of people buy lotion, but one of Pole's colleagues noticed that women on the baby registry were buying larger quantities of unscented lotion around the beginning of their second trimester. Another analyst noted that sometime in the first 20 weeks, pregnant women loaded up on supplements like calcium, magnesium and zinc. Many shoppers purchase soap and cotton balls, but when someone suddenly starts buying lots of scent-free soap and extra-big bags of cotton balls, in addition to hand sanitizers and washcloths, it signals they could be getting close to their delivery date.'

The result was 25 signature product purchases—the key predictors of pregnancy, even if the customer had not formally signed up to the baby registry. The Target team was able to assign each shopper a 'pregnancy prediction' score. Even more creepily they could even estimate someone's due date to within a small window. This allowed Target to send baby-related promotions with serious levels of granularity—even timed to very specific stages of a pregnancy.[24]

Duhigg shares an anecdote that describes just how insightful the data mining and profiling is: 'An angry man went into a Target outside of Minneapolis, demanding to talk to a manager. 'My daughter got this in the mail!' he said. 'She's still in high school, and you're sending her coupons for baby clothes and cribs? Are you trying to encourage her to get pregnant?'

---

[24] A follow up article in Forbes magazine by Kashmir Hill describes this example: https://www.forbes.com/sites/kashmirhill/2012/02/16/how-target-figured-out-a-teen-girl-was-pregnant-before-her-father-did/#45cb90d56668 "One Target employee I spoke to provided a hypothetical example. Take a fictional Target shopper named Jenny Ward, who is 23, lives in Atlanta and in March bought cocoa-butter lotion, a purse large enough to double as a diaper bag, zinc and magnesium supplements and a bright blue rug. There's, say, an 87 percent chance that she's pregnant and that her delivery date is sometime in late August. And a good chance the baby is a boy."

The manager didn't have any idea what the man was talking about. He looked at the mailer. Sure enough, it was addressed to the man's daughter and contained advertisements for maternity clothing, nursery furniture and pictures of smiling infants. The manager apologized and then called a few days later to apologize again.

On the phone, though, the father was somewhat abashed. 'I had a talk with my daughter,' he said. 'It turns out there's been some activities in my house I haven't been completely aware of. She's due in August. I owe you an apology.'

Personalised, sure, but maybe a little creepy? If only many health education agencies could command this level of data insight and use it for good.

'It's All About Me'

We like information that is personalised to us. Both Facebook and Google make use of our searches and personal data to create adverts that are targeted for us.

But it's even simpler than that. We like our own names especially —for example, we notice our names at a party in the midst of all the other noise. This isn't just an adult phenomenon, children as young as six months old pay attention to their own name, even if they probably don't consciously recognise it's their name.

This desire for personalisation has been taken to extremes by Coca-Cola who developed a fantastically successful marketing campaign by putting first names on bottles and cans. In fact, Omar was so keen on this he has a bottle he keeps on his desk now.

According to Coca-Cola, reported by Patrick Fagan, this campaign has been one of the most successful in the company's history. And this from a company that has a significant track record of successful marketing. The campaign attracted almost a billion Twitter impressions and 250 thousand #shareaCoke hashtag tweets. 150 million personalised bottles were sold. According to Coca-Cola the campaign has been credited with turning around 10 year sales decline in the USA. It also increased UK sales by 4.93% in 2016 when the cola market grew only 2.75%.

'But Maybe It's Not All About You'

Personalisation needn't necessarily be about providing detailed connection to the person targeted. It sometimes just needs to be about being more personal overall. It can even work by sharing more about yourself.

Randy Garner, a Professor of Behavioural Sciences at Sam Houston State University wanted to test something very simple: 'What are the most effective ways to persuade people to comply with a relatively complicated and demanding task?' In Prof Gardeners' case the task was to persuade students to fill in a 152-question, 8-page questionnaire to help his research. He tested three personalisation options with varying degrees of success. Part of the background was that he knew all the students slightly, but not well. The tested options were:

- **Test A:** Recipients were simply given an envelope with the questionnaire enclosed and with a printed note asking them to return it when completed.
- **Test B:** Others were given the same envelope and + questionnaire, but with a handwritten Post-It message saying 'Please take a few minutes to complete this for us'.
- **Test C:** The last group were asked to fill in the exact same questionnaire, and with the same 'Please take ...' Post-It message. However, this one was also signed 'Thank you! RG'.

What was the effect of that simple level of 'requester' personalisation? Almost 75 % of respondents complied with the request in **Test C**, compared with 40% for **Test B**, and 10% for **Test A**. More than that the quality and detail in the answers in **C** was also better. The learning? Make clear your communication is personal. Use something that draws attention to the personalisation. (In a follow-up set of experiments the impact of a visual disruption became clear.)[25] And finally, make a clear and concrete request.

---

[25] For information on the follow up experiments see https://hbr.org/2015/05/the-surprising-persuasiveness-of-a-sticky-note.

Learning from Making it Normal and Personal

The implications and learning from this chapter are simple:

- In your campaigns or fundraising appeals, make sure you reinforce previous behaviour, where appropriate, and confirm your supporter's idea of themselves individually as an important member of a special group.
- Make sure you are making any call to action ask feel more relevant and personal and you'll help them feel more connected.
- Emphasise your supporters' or potential supporters' connection to a certain neighbourhood, gender or sexuality, a specific alumni group, or any other dominant factor that links them to your cause.
- Avoid using general assertions of need and make sure you do not confuse people with numbers they cannot understand.
- Build *empathy* by creating personal settings—real or virtual—that enable individuals to share the experience of others.
- Combine the *personalisation* with *normalisation* and *nudging* to make people feel … that what you want them to do is a common and socially acceptable behaviour.
- Include messages or information personal to the recipient that shows you have paid attention to them and are concerned about them, and their interests.[26]

---

[26] *Mary Steffel is an assistant professor of marketing, Northeastern University; Elanor Williams is an assistant professor, Indiana University, Bloomington, and Ruth Pogacar is a PhD student in marketing, University of Cincinnati. This article was originally published on* The Conversation.

Part 3

**Designing Decisions:
Creating Choice
Architecture**

Be Systematic—Avoid Assumptions

Throughout the book we've shared a number of principles from decision science illustrating some of the biases and quirks, codified as heuristics, that inform the way we make choices and commitments.

We've illustrated many of these principles with examples from the commercial world. Partly this is because our assessment is that business may be as much as 10 years ahead of not-for-profit organisations in implementing the findings from research in this field.[1] This book is designed to help speed up the process by which NfPs can adapt and incorporate these powerful ideas. By using them successfully and systematically, we can make a massive difference to the way we improve the world by helping groups and individuals to make positive choices.

---

[1] There is some good news. Not-for-profits and public authorities are off the starting block. We have included examples of good or excellent 'social' applications from health, social justice and, of course, from fundraising, where the connections to marketing are perhaps strongest.

In this final section, we summarise the fundamental principles underlying the three disciplines we've drawn on—evolutionary psychology, neuroscience, and behavioural economics. We also share a simple 10 point checklist we've developed to help you incorporate key ideas into your work. We want to stress that to succeed in introducing effective decision science in your work you should avoid slavishly copying any one of the good ideas in chapters 1–10. Or, just as bad, simply comparing one technique against another.[2] Instead you need to create systematic decision architectures—that is, *sequences* of action and thinking for your subject. And then you need to test them rigourously.

Failure to adopt this rigorous approach may mean you experience the unintended consequences of poorly thought through social initiatives. For example, you may well have heard of the childcare nurseries introducing fines for parents who were late to collect their children. The intention was to stop the parents turning up late. And someone, explicitly or implicitly, thought—'let's use the *avoid loss heuristic* and impose a fine' to encourage parents to turn up on time. What happened, however, was that parents began to see a fine of, say, £20 as a reasonable price for flexibility and an extra hour or so of childcare.[3] Trying to *normalise* certain behaviour, 'turn up on time,' by the crude use of the *avoid loss* heuristic, in this case didn't work. The loss wasn't great enough, and 'turn up late' seemed OK.

In another unhappy example, the Petrified Forest National Park in Arizona[4] also inadvertently nudged visitors in the wrong direction. Park Rangers put up signs explaining that 'many visitors' removed petrified wood, which was damaging to the park's ecosystem. Un-

---

[2] Indeed, this is what fundraisers are doing when they run simple A vs. B testing. They keep on trying out variations of text, pictures, and gift amounts in the hope of hitting on an effective way to increase contribution, retention, or some other factor. This *can* work, just as you might hit a bull's eye in a game of 'darts in the dark.' But it's not very systematic.

[3] For a wider ranging set of examples of this challenge see *A Fine Is A Price*, Uri Gneezy and Also Rustichini http://rady.ucsd.edu/faculty/directory/gneezy/pub/docs/fine.pdf.

[4] For more on this see https://theswedishnudgingnetwork.com/2014/12/18/nudging-can-backfire.

fortunately, this new sign seemed to encourage removal more than the previous one warning visitors not to take it.

The new sign inadvertently signaled a bad *social norm*, and visitors found it more acceptable to break the 'no removal' rule *because they were told many others did*.

A final example comes from the great Swedish website: theswedishnudgingnetwork.com. First, you need to know that in Sweden there is a state alcohol monopoly. Only a store called Systembolaget is allowed to sell alcohol. Their mission: 'To minimize alcohol-related problems by selling alcohol in a responsible way, without profit motive.' Over Christmas they had a campaign to promote this very noble mission on the plastic bags given with purchases. The message says, in translation:

The fact that we're the only place that sells beer, wine and liquor may be a bit awkward for you. But these are the good things you contributed to this year:

- 2,000 saved lives
- 20,000 fewer violent crimes
- 11 million less sick days

We're slightly worried the message that arrives is 'drinking drives social good.' And we're not completely sure that's what they meant.

There are also, of course, nice Scandinavian examples of decision architecture. In Stockholm, there have been a number of interesting linked initiatives to improve driving behaviour including:

- Changing the measurement unit. In Denmark, presenting fuel economy as krona per kilometre rather than euros or pounds per litre or gallon, to encourage sensible driving.
- Giving feedback. Roadside machines giving drivers immediate feedback—a flashing 'slow down'/smiley emoji—about their speed, resulting in a 10-15 percent speed reduction.
- Offering reinforcing rewards. In the city, average speeds dropped from 32 to 25 km per hour when drivers staying within the speed limit were entered into a lottery.

The mistakes made by the Petrified Forest, children's nursery and even Systembolaget are to do with trying to apply one technique in isolation. To succeed consistently in the application of decision science you need not just a grasp of specific heuristics but also an understanding of the basic principles behind decision architecture. Decision architecture is technically the *sequence and type of heuristics used to encourage a target audience to adopt a specific behaviour*. Using such a sequence and selection effectively will help you—whether you're an advocacy specialist, social campaigner or fundraiser—to come up with your own hypothesis on how to change behaviour in a testable and systematic way.

A Push Me Pull You

Examples of poor decision architecture exist in every aspect of design including 'ordinary' architecture. Thaler recounts a couple of very practical examples in a famous article. '[There is a] failure of architecture to accommodate basics, even in the simplest area of psychology. Life is full of products that suffer from such defects. Isn't it obvious that the largest buttons on a television remote control should be the power, channel, and volume controls? Yet how many remotes have the volume control the same size as the input control button (which if pressed accidentally can cause the picture to disappear)?'

He also relates the story of how students in a classroom he used constantly tried to *pull* at a door that needed to be *pushed*. The problem was the door had large ornate handles—a signal worldwide of a door that needs to be pulled. The students constantly fell for the 'pull-me' cue.

Securing Higher Tips: The Systematic Application of Decision Architecture

In a study published in the *Journal of Applied Psychology*,[5] we can clearly see the impact of a thought through sequence of actions designed to drive a specific outcome—a decision architecture—at work. A research team studied the impact on levels of tips to waiters when mints were offered to diners at the end of a meal. There were two complementary studies, each with a related conclusion. The first showed that customers who were given after dinner mints[6] tipped more than those who were not. The second showed that the value of the tips varied with the number of sweets given *and* how they were given.

A control group of diners were not given any mints. Of the three other groups studied:

- **Group 1. Mints + Bill:** The waiter supplied the gift of the mints without mentioning them with the bill
- **Group 2. Mints + Mention Them + Present Bill:** The waiter presented the mints as an 'extra gift,' and mentioned this to the diners. The bill was then brought separately
- **Group 3. Mint 1 + Mention Them + Bill + Mint 2:** The waiter brought the bill, with a mint. After a pause, he offered the diners a second mint making it clear he was favouring them.

In each case the level of service provided during the meal, the food quality, and even the total number of mints was exactly the same. But the 'architecture' of the sequence made a massive difference. Giving a low-cost mint plus variable behaviour increased the level of tips over the control group by:

Group 1: 3%　　　　**Group 2: 14%**　　　　**Group 3: 21%**

---

[5] http://onlinelibrary.wiley.com/doi/10.1111/j.1559-1816.2002.tb00216.x/abstract.

[6] If you want to know more about the Science of Tipping then this might be of interest http://www.bbc.com/capital/story/20171122-the-psychology-that-motivates-tipping.

This study demonstrates the direct measurable impact—*the desired behaviour*—that a small series of systematically applied influence steps can have.[7]

Decision Science and Dinner

Restaurants generally are great for decision architecture. In many, both high-end and fast-food, a great deal of thought and planning goes into the music, the furnishings, the décor,[8] the room temperature, the crockery and the skills of the servers. What you may not have noticed is quite how much planning goes into what might look like a simple menu. If you are keen to know more we suggest you look at a wonderful infographic developed by Aaron Allen and Associates, the world's most famous restaurant consultants. It shares 14 principles to guide designs. http://aaronallen.com/blog/the-psychology-of-menu-design. For example here's just one of their powerful pieces of advice.

---

[7] To be even more successful, earlier in the meal the waiter might also have followed Robert Cialdini's advice to waiters:

- **Be Likeable:** Approach the diners and build rapport; perhaps ask what the occasion was, or check who was fond of meat, fish or vegetarian, etc. This could also extend to being attentive towards all the guests, and maybe saying 'great choice' to a dish selection.
- **Emphasise Authority:** Check what wine variety or type the party like and then suggest wine X and perhaps an alternative choice Y, even, 'Y is just as good, but a better value than X.' This also primes and anchors a 'reasonable' price for wine.
- **Suggest Scarcity:** Mention that some of the special dishes often sell out by 19.30. And to secure the specials it would be good to order early. Maybe offer to go and check the situation in the kitchen.

In this way, additional techniques can be combined in sequence to deliver an efficient decision architecture. And increase tips.

[8] You may not have noticed that many US-based fast-food chains share the same colour scheme for interior decor. Wendy's, McDonald's, Pizza Hut, Carl's Jr., and Burger King all play with the same red/yellow colour palette. This, as you can probably guess, is not chance. Research from the University of Rochester showed red and yellow make you want to eat more. Red causes you to eat faster. And a number of research projects have shown that 'yellow' stimulates your appetite. This does so by encouraging telling the brain to generate serotonin, the 'happiness hormone.' So the experience feels subjectively good.

> ## THE GOLDEN TRIANGLE
> When we look at a menu, **our eyes typically move to the middle first** before traveling to the top right corner and then, finally, to the top left. This has been dubbed the 'Golden Triangle' by menu engineers, and these three areas are where you'll find the dishes with the highest profit margins.

We believe that many social agencies could apply the learning from the Aaron Allen menu 14 principles to their printed communications from annual reports to appeals.

Thinking More About Goals

In the waiter example part of the reason for success is that the waiter is clear on his or her goal: increased tips. The architecture of 'mints + bill' is shaped by that. But it's also important to think about what the goal or motivation is of the individual or group you're trying to influence.

Their goal could be: As a campaigner, communicator or fundraiser you have goals too. But you need to not just focus on the outcome you want.

It's vital to begin by considering what the goal or motivation is of the individual or group you're trying to influence. If you understand what they want, and can show or suggest how they can achieve it, you're much more likely to get what you want.

When you think about their goal it is likely to fall into one of two big clusters:

* *Psychological:* To deliver a perceived enhancement to status or mental wellbeing.

- *Physical:* To improve a perceived practical, health or economic payoff.

Let's spend a little more time on goals. Everyone has them—desires, ambitions, needs. If the proposition we offer and the way we offer it helps, or appears to help, deliver those goals, then the consumer is likely to follow our course of action and to achieve the result we want.

Not-for-profit organisations, possibly due to the fact they usually work for 'noble' causes, often make the mistake of only focussing on *their* own goals, and how *they* operate e.g. 'We help bring support to people in need.' 'We deliver medicine to the sick.' Rather than focussing on the goals of the supporter: 'I want to feel I made a difference to poor people.' 'I want to improve the health chances of women.' (It is tempting to think of the old analogy of a power drill company *selling* strength and speed and the consumer *wanting* a neat round hole.) Supporters want to feel agency—a sense of *their* ability to do or achieve something. Your proposition should involve that.

Homo sapiens are a goal-seeking species. Even the most hipster or digitally native of modern humans operates using what is basically a 200,000-year-old brain. From an evolutionary perspective, therefore, apparently irrational behaviour—such as extreme risk aversion—makes very good sense.

At one level, everyone's most fundamental goal is survival. This involves two complementary dynamics, *promotion* and *prevention*. *Promotion* is seeking food, sex, company, etc. It means you need to go out looking for, and getting, dinner. *Prevention* is avoiding risks and dangers. It is avoiding becoming dinner.

Both of these then branch out into more specific drives. Promotion becomes adventure, excitement, exploration, etc. Prevention becomes security, care, trust, etc. Make sure when designing your very clever decision architecture to identify and, as fully as possible, meet the goal or goals of the target audience. (And be aware, see the *Milkshake Mystery* mentioned earlier in **Section One**, that these goals may not be obvious even to the audience.)

What's in It for Me?

The goals connection probably isn't considered a System 2 one. Once you have received a communication from your brain—in a microsecond and without being aware of it—you compare the offer with how closely it matches your goals. If there's a good match, then a 'go' decision is taken. If the match is not clear or awkward then the 'no' or 'think about it,' System 2, button is pressed. Timing and desire are key. If your goal at that moment of receiving a 'buy-a-chocolate bar' signal is to receive an 'energy boost,' then a particular kind of chocolate bar has preference. (Let's say a Mars Bar.) But if the incoming signal is that of a 'luxurious indulgence' chocolate bar—like a Bounty Bar—there will be a negative response. In a social sector setting, if I want to get a sense of belonging by donating to 'people like me,' but the fundraising images are of people I cannot relate to, I may decline to help. If there is a mismatch I may, at best, look for data that leads me to a more rational System 2 decision.

Your task as a change agent, fundraiser or a campaigner, is to help make as easy as possible a decision that involves a fast and implicit cost/benefit analysis against a goal. The *cost* can be the money paid to buy a product, the level of donation needed, or the time or effort required to engage with the campaign. The *benefit* is the emotional reward or practical payoff that we get. Job one is to make sure you target the right goals as explicitly as you can.

Systematic Shopping

We can find examples of decision architecture at work in every part of our lives as consumers. For example, when you enter a supermarket you may have noticed some large-scale decision architecture at work:

- *Vegetables and fruit are usually the first items you encounter.* This is to encourage you to choose some of these early in your shopping. Sadly, this is not because supermarkets care about our health. Research has shown that if we buy these healthy items early we feel more inclined to buy *unhealthy* items—pizza, chocolate, etc.—later as we already have healthy food in our basket. We've done our 'good deed.'

- *Your senses are subtly engaged.* Fresh produce—fruit, vegetables, flowers—provide lots of colour which helps to put you in a good mood. And the happier you are the more you are likely to spend. Your sense of smell is also engaged. Newly baked bread or roasting chickens are designed to reinforce how fresh and ready everything is. The smell may, in a Pavlovian way, make you feel hungry. Even your hearing is engaged. Slow rhythm music tends to make you move more slowly. You spend more time in the store. And spend more.

- *The geography is designed to get you to wander.* Stores often have hot or cold air, depending on the season, at the entrance to welcome us in to shop. They tend to be more brightly lit towards the back to steer us further in. (In some stores, the floor slopes gently towards the back too.) These cues are all part of the same process to make coming in and wandering around physically attractive to our subconscious. Stores like to place essential items at the back and far away from each other so you have to look for them. And while searching for your essentials you come across a few things you do not actually need, but decide you want to buy along the way. A common retail 'trick' is keeping eggs in strange places so you end up on an egg hunt.

- *Premium items, costing more, are carefully positioned.* We are more likely to select an item positioned at an easy-to-see-and-reach height, which is why more expensive brands will be there. Manufacturers may pay a promotional premium to have their product located there. All of this planning is shaped by a planogram, 'a diagram or model that indicates the placement of retail products on shelves in order to maximise sales.' Essentially a decision architecture plan.

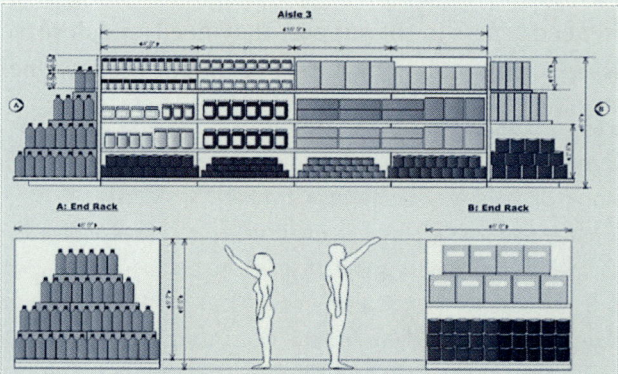

Example of a planogram

Why Socially Concerned Decision Science Matters

We're all aware of elegant buildings designed by clever architects that just don't work in real life. Or the path made by people to cut off a corner, when the planner wants you to go the long way around. We need to make sure *our* design for social change is real world friendly.

We're delighted if you've designed your latest project using some of the ideas and frameworks in the book. Many of these are based on commercial examples. As we said at the start the not for profit world may be 10 years behind in adopting these powerful techniques. As socially-concerned behavioural economists, we need to be willing to learn from the strangest places—from the way supermarket layouts engage us to the ease with which we can order a multi-topping pizza online.[9]

We need to make it easier for us to do good. And we need to make is easier for those we are meant to help to access systems supposed to support them.

The negative effects of making processes difficult don't simply create inconvenience. You may have seen the multi-award winning film *I, Daniel Blake* by socially committed filmmaker Ken Loach. The film, based on real-life case studies, explores how the poor decision architecture of the social welfare system in UK—from hard-to-fill-in forms and rule bound officials—leads to tragedy. Sadly, that's not just happening in fiction. A lack of understanding denies many people in need access to the support they need, and deserve.

Decision science and behavioural economics can, we believe, be part of the solution.

---

[9] https://www.fastcompany.com/3030124/the-hidden-psychology-of-ordering-food-online.

> *It doesn't matter how beautiful your theory*
> *is. If it disagrees with experiment, it's wrong.*
> *In that simple statement is the key to science.*
>
> Richard Feynman, Nobel Prize-winning Physicist

A Fast Summary

A *traditional economist* starts with a theoretical model based on the assumption that people are rational individuals who conduct cost/benefit analysis, calculate utility, and then make a decision. The *behavioural economist* observes what people do, formulates a hypothesis about their *likely* reaction in certain contexts, and finally, and this is essential, *tests* the hypothesis. A key part of the architecture approach is to try out your idea, modify it in the light of harsh reality, and *only then* roll it out or scale it up.

We have to recognise that when we design our decision architecture:

- We are dealing with people, and people are different and may respond differently at different times to different stimuli.
- We need to accept that the behaviour people claim they will do or the beliefs and values people claim to have are not always accurate.[10]
- We are dealing with a number of variables, and a number of heuristics. When these are combined this creates complexity and possibly conflict.

---

[10] Again, we are indebted to Meredith Niles for a great example. She told us about the book. *Everybody Lies* which has a number of great examples on this subject. For instance, if you look at Facebook profiles where you can signal to your friends what your interests are, very few men select 'Taylor Swift' as one of their musical preferences. But if you look at Spotify streams, the gender split on actual listens to Taylor Swift is much more balanced. Google searches are also far more revelatory about what we actually care about because when we are searching, we are highly motivated to find exactly what we are looking for, as opposed to trying to impress anyone.

- We are often blind to our own biases. It is essential, therefore, to test any specific hypothesis about what will deliver the desired behaviour in the target audience.
- Finally, we need to recognise that people and cultures are different and so, while a general principle might apply, it could need changing to meet a specific context or culture.

A *traditional economist* says, "Let's assume ..." A *behavioural economists retorts* "Let's test ..."

After your brilliant bit of behavioural design, you must complete the feedback loop and check if your architecture achieved the desired result. If not, go back and change one element—seeking to improve the architecture until it's right and it delivers the behaviour you want.

10 Principles to Help You Think Like a Socially Good Decision Scientist

1. Start with the target donor, supporter, or beneficiary's goals. Adapt your message to make it relevant to *their* goals and needs. If the goal is apparently functional or rational, identify the deeper emotional goal behind it.

2. Appeal first to System 1. Depending on the context, System 2 might be best, but be careful about mixing them. If in doubt, stick to System 1. Keep in mind that System 2 will be slower and may lead to a less engaged result.

3. Design a decision architecture. Use heuristics around the ten chapters in Section 2. Use them selectively and in a suitable sequence. Test the sequence to see if it works. And if it does not, adjust.

4. Frame your message carefully. The context—time, social setting, and culture—may be more important than the message itself. Consider alternative framings (e.g. positive vs. negative, changing the unit of measurement, redefining the issue, etc.).

5. Limit choices and focus attention. Offer supporters a choice because this gives them a feeling of being in control. But remember more choices are not always better and may lead to confusion. Make the choice seem like a normal one.

6. Tell simple emotional stories. Ideally use ones that relate to acceptable archetypes and involve overcoming the odds. These are powerful. Remember that the supporter is the hero, and the organisation the mentor.

7. Make what you are doing, or asking the audience to do, appear 'normal' and something others do. Use peer reference to support your message. If appropriate, mention respected figures that the audience can look up to.

8. Assume nothing. Test to establish the objective truth, and pay attention to seemingly irrelevant factors. Avoid using your own biases to confirm ideas you like or prefer. Take nothing on trust.

9. Innovate. A given approach might work initially, but if you keep repeating it, after a while it will cease to stimulate your audience, due to the *habituation effect*. Monitor for *wear-out*, and consider when to balance familiarity and freshness.

10. Make sure you are behaving ethically. Ensure that what you are persuading your audience to do is for the greater good, that you are not limiting their choices unfairly, and that you are accountable for the outcome.

Recommended Reading

While Kahneman and Thaler are the undoubted leaders in this field a number of others have contributed to expanding the understanding of the science. If you only have four books you can buy we would recommend the volumes below by Kahneman, Thaler, Ariely and Barden. We'd like to acknowledge our debt to them and encourage you to read their books too.

Ariely, Dan. *Predictably Irrational: The Hidden Forces That Shape Our Decisions* Harper Collins, 2009.

Barden, Phil. *Decoded: The Science behind Why We Buy* Wiley, 2013.

Brafman, Ori and Brafman, Rom, *SWAY. The Irresistible Pull of Irrational Behavior.* Virgin Books, New York, 2008.

Cialdini, Robert, *Influence: The Psychology of Persuasion,* Harper Business, 2006.

Eagleman, David. *Incognito: The Secret Lives of the Brain,* Canongate, 2011.

Fagan, Patrick. *Hooked: Why Cute Sells, and Other Marketing Magic That We Just Can't Resist,* Pearson, 2016.

Dobelli, Rolf. *The Art of Thinking Clearly*, Harper Paperbacks; Reprint edition, 2014.

Halpern, David. *Inside the Nudge Unit: How Small Changes Can Make a Big Difference*, WH Allen, 2015.

Kahneman, Daniel. *Thinking, Fast and Slow*, MacMillan, 2011.

Kenrick, Douglas T. and Griskevicius, Vladas. *The Rational Animal-How Evolution Made Us Smarter Than We Think*, Basic Books, 2013.

Kurzweil, Ray. *How to Create a Mind: The Secret of Human Thought Revealed*, Penguin Books, USA, 2013.

Martin, Steve; Goldstein, Noah and Cialdini, Robert. *The Small Big: Small Changes That Spark Big Influence*, Grand Central Publishing, 2014.

Russo, J. Edward, and Schoemaker, J.H. *Decision Traps: The Ten Barriers to Brilliant Decision-Making and How to Overcome Them*, Fireside, 1990.

Swaab, Dick. *We Are Our Brains: From the Womb to Alzheimer's*, Allen Lane, an imprint of Penguin Books, England, 2014.

Sutherland, Stuart. *Irrationality: The Enemy Within*, Pinter & Martin Ltd; 21st anniversary edition, 2013.

Thaler, Richard H. and Sunstein, Cass R. *Nudge: Improving Decisions About Health, Wealth, and Happiness*, Penguin, 2012.

Thaler, Richard H. *Misbehaving: The Making of Behavioural Economics*, W. W. Norton & Company (12 May 2015).

World Bank Group. *Mind, Society, and Behavior*, World Development Reports, 2015–7.

ONLINE RESOURCES

www.bhub.org houses the Behavioural Evidence Hub. This is an online resource that brings together promising innovative solutions from around the world into a single tool. It offers evidence-based initiatives that offer deep insight into a range of social, economic and cultural challenges—from staying in college and increasing savings rates to improving medication use and healthy lifestyles. The site also features solutions and implementation guidelines for practitioners interested in using the insights and innovations in their own work.

www.managenentcentre.co.uk. The Management Centre =mc is a leading consultancy working to deliver social justice by working alongside INGOs and local CSOs through fundraising, management development and management consultancy. Bernard Ross, one of the directors, is the co-author of this book, and has written widely on psychology and influence. Our main office is in London UK, but we have partners working globally. Get in touch if you want to know more about our work on decision science.

www.worldbank.org/en/programs/embed is the website of the World Bank team dedicated to exploring how behavioural insights impact on development issues. It's run by the Mind, Behaviour, and Development Unit (eMBeD), the World Bank's behavioural sciences team. They work with project teams, governments, and other partners to diagnose, design, and evaluate behaviourally informed interventions. By collaborating with a worldwide network of scientists and practitioners they contribute to the global effort to eliminate poverty and increase equity.

www.behaviouralinsights.co.uk. The Behavioural Insights Team (BIT) is a social purpose company jointly owned by the UK Government; Nesta (the innovation charity); and the employees.

BIT started life inside 10 Downing Street in the UK as the world's first government institution dedicated to the application of behavioural sciences. The team aims to make public services more cost-effective and easier for citizens to use, improve outcomes by introducing a more realistic model of human behaviour to policy, and enabling people to make 'better choices for themselves.'

www.nudges.org. The Nudge blog is the online companion to Richard Thaler and Cass Sunstein's book mentioned above *Nudge: Improving Decisions About Health, Wealth, and Happiness.*

Here you'll find much more about nudging, choice architecture, libertarian paternalism, and many other terms you won't read about in standard economics books. It's full of nice little examples of projects that have worked and some that are still just ideas.

Decision-Making Glossary

This glossary is designed to help you identify most of the key terms in behavioural economics and decision science.

Anchoring: A stimulus—a number or a suggestion—that produces a change in the likely result or decision in an individual. Anchoring occurs when people's estimate of an unknown (Gandhi's age at his death, percentage of African countries in U.N. membership) is influenced by a number, or fact, they are given earlier (Was Gandhi 35 or 114, or the last digits of your social security number). People are influenced by a figure they are exposed to, regardless of whether that figure is relevant to the subject (e.g. Gandhi's age) or completely unrelated (e.g. social security or phone number).

When people have no clue about the value of a given measure (e.g. how many people die of hunger, how much it costs to save a life, how much people donate, etc.) any figure given to them can act as a helpful anchor.

Association: The tendency of the brain to link subconsciously two disparate elements: for example, a person and a brand, or a sound and a feeling. Commercial brands always seek positive associations that would influence consumers to buy their brand. For example, a soft drink brand might advertise its brand in the context of happy people partying on the beach. Subconsciously, every time the customer sees the brand, happiness images will be activated. Sometimes association works through more links. A beauty care brand might advertise using an attractive celebrity, driving brand associations with the celebrity and the product. Consistency helps enforce these associations.

Auto-Pilot: The part of our brain which controls unconscious activity—from changing gears in a car to performing some mental calculations and labelling or disliking individuals. Since our brain is about 2% of our body weight but consumes more than 20% of its energy, we search for ways to save mental energy. Once we master a skill such as riding a bike, driving a car or writing a fundraising appeal, our brain shifts it from pilot to auto-pilot. The advantage of doing so is that we save mental energy, which may now be directed to other more challenging tasks. The disadvantage is that we might fall into a mental trap of 'This is how we've always done it.' It is advisable, but not easy, to step back from time to time and ask 'Should I switch back to pilot on this matter?'

Automatic System/Automatic Thinking: Thaler and Sunstein's term for natural 'human' thinking, which is often irrational, instinctive and unhelpful for the people thinking in such a way, as opposed to Reflective or 'System Two' (Kahneman-Tversky) thinking:
Automatic (System 1) thinking = 'Human', instinctive, emotional, subjective, irrational, heuristic.
Reflective (System 2) thinking = 'Econ', logical, rational, objective, unemotional.

Automatic Thinking: see Auto-Pilot.

Availability: It's one of the primary heuristics or 'nudges' identified by Kahneman and Tversky, and is featured in Nudge theory by Thaler and Sunstein. 'Availability' refers (rather misleadingly) to the **perceived popularity or rarity of something**, which is significant in people's (heuristic, unreliable) assessment of its credibility, level of threat/opportunity, social acceptance, etc. An alternative broad name for this heuristic or nudge is 'visibility' or 'commonness.'

According to Kahneman, 'People tend to assess the relative importance of issues by the ease with which they are retrieved from memory—and this is largely determined by the extent of coverage in the media.' So, next time you wonder why people don't seem to care about an important fact or issue, think of availability.

Behavioural Economics: The body of psychological thinking and decision-making that looks into how people actually make decisions, including their systematic errors and biases, not how they should make those decisions. Its method is based on observation and testing, not assumptions and models. Behavioural economics was popularized by Daniel Kahneman's book *Thinking, Fast and Slow,* the psychologist who won the Nobel Prize in economics in 2002, and by others, notably Dan Ariely, author of *Predictably Irrational*, and Richard Thaler and Cass Sunstein, authors of *Nudge.*

In fact, the titles of these three books provide a rough outline of behavioural economics: a) We have two ways of thinking, fast and slow (System 1 and System 2) b) Our errors are predictable because they are systematic and therefore can be studied and addressed, and c) We don't have to persuade people to

behave in a certain way using rewards and penalties. We can nudge their behaviour to good use by making small changes to seemingly irrelevant factors.

Being Watched: This is an aspect of social behaviour. As social beings we behave in a socially correct way when we feel, rightly or wrongly, that we are being observed by others, because we want to ensure we continue to belong to our social groups and be respected and valued by them. The risk of group punishment or ostracism is a high one for a social being.

Bias: This term features often in Nudge theory, for example in 'Status quo bias'. Bias means weighting or leaning to a particular view or behaviour. Other words which equate to bias are spin, inclination, and preference. When thinking has a bias or is biased towards something then it is not balanced or truly objective or neutral. A bias is different from an error. An error might be a random event. A bias is a regular and predictable type of behaviour, and therefore can be analyzed, addressed, and put to good or bad use. The common existence of bias in people's thinking is a central aspect of Nudge theory.

Bounded Rationality: The term used by Herbert A. Simon in the context of decision-making. It implies that when human beings make a decision, they act in a rational way, but their rationality is not absolute. It is limited, or bounded, by the mind's cognitive limitations and the time available to make a decision. Simon used a scissors analogy, where one blade represents cognitive limitations and the other blade represents the structure of the environment. The mind deals with its cognitive limitations by identifying clues in the regularity of the environment. This idea evolved later on and behavioural economists started identifying the mental short-cuts (Heuristics) we use to make decisions, given our bounded rationality.

Buridan's Ass: Named after a 14th century French philosopher, Jean Buridan, this paradox refers to a hypothetical situation in which an ass finds itself exactly half way between a pile of hay and a pail of water (two piles of hay in some versions.) Since, theoretically, the ass should go towards the closest source it will die of hunger and thirst since it cannot find any rational reason to choose one source over the other. The idea was expressed in slightly different ways earlier on by Aristotle and El Ghazzali. The idea is that sometimes the options provided to us seem to have the same value that we cannot decide which one to take, even though deciding on either is a better option than indecision. Buridan's ass was popularized in the media including The Big Bang Theory, as there are obviously many situations in real life where we feel placed in between equally attractive options.

In fundraising, we need to make sure that we don't place our donors in a Buridan's ass situation. We can do so by nudging them using many of the available tools such as default options or social reference.

Bystander Effect (The Genovese Syndrome): The tendency for individuals to not get involved in a situation when others are present, and, conversely, to intervene when there is no one else around. There is an inverse relationship between the number of people around and the likelihood of intervention. The common explanations for this strange socio-psychological effect

is a combination of ambiguity (Why aren't others intervening, they probably know something I don't?) and diffusion of responsibility (Why should I intervene, there are others around?).

Choice Architecture: Thaler and Sunstein use this term to refer to the (large but not all-embracing) heuristic area of Stimulus Response Compatibility, and this usage is not fully consistent with their term 'choice architect', which refers to the role of a person/leader/authority who uses the (all-embracing) entire range of heuristics in designing choices for people. So this term has two meanings: namely Stimulus Response Compatibility, or more broadly a system or structure of choices designed for people, in the course of applying Nudge theory.

Choice Design: A central idea and expression of Nudge theory, referring to the principle and methodology of developing and offering situations or interventions for people, from which people are free to select whichever option they prefer, including the option to make no decision at all. Choice design is typically done by a 'choice architect,' but may also refer to choices which exist through accident or circumstance, or from cynical purposes like lots of marketing and advertising, and processes (increasingly online) or contractual 'smallprint' designed to fool consumers.

Clean Language: Not a Thaler-Sunstein term, but a methodology that is very relevant to Thaler-Sunstein and Nudge ideas —specifically that the way communications are worded can dramatically affect the way that meanings and moods are perceived.

Commitment Devices: Any mechanism for engagement which encourages an individual to agree consciously or unconsciously to a given action: liking on Facebook, signing a pledge form, etc. Future commitment is a way to drive long-term commitment, despite current reluctance to do so. In a famous example, employees were reluctant to make a deduction from their current salary to a social security fund. However, they agreed to such a deduction with their next salary increase.

Conditional Cooperation: An approach to cooperation in which one party only agrees to cooperate with another if certain conditions are met.

Confirmation Bias: Is the tendency we have to look for data or information, which supports the belief or opinion we already have, and to ignore data which does not.

Conforming: An alternative term for the 'following the herd' heuristic, and separately a general tendency for people to prefer to adhere to norms rather than stand alone. Conforming is a survival instinct because it aligns oneself with a group, avoiding confrontation and risk. Conforming also produces mutual feelings of affirmation, and a feeling of safety through strength in numbers. Conformity also protects us from feeling regret in case our decision turns out to be wrong, because we can justify it by saying 'I just did what everyone else did.' It's an enormously significant aspect of human/group behaviour/behaviour, without which there could be no wars, no religion, fashion industry, football fans, etc.

Crowd Wisdom: Much literature has been written about the foolishness of crowds, including Charles Mackay's 1841 book *Extraordinary Popular Delusions and the Madness of the Crowds,* and more recently Irving Janis' *Group Think* in 1982 which showed that a group might make faulty decisions that an individual would not make on his own, due to group dynamics. See *Group Think.* However, in 2004 James Suroweicki published his now classic book *The Wisdom of Crowds,* in which he suggests that some groups can be smarter than other groups, and even smarter than the smartest group member provided four conditions are met in the group: diversity (group members are different with respect to background, gender, age, education, cultural background, etc.), independence (each group member gives her opinion without influence from other group members), decentralization (group members have local knowledge related to their specialization), and aggregation (having a mechanism to turn the individual inputs into a collective decision).

Decision Architecture: The way in which decisions or choices can be affected by the structure or sequence of the decision process. For example, in a self-service cafeteria, people eat more sweets than salads because they see sweets first, when they are hungry. A traditional method to encourage people to eat more salad would be providing information (e.g. messages about healthy eating and the importance of vegetables), or rewards and punishments (e.g. make sweets more expensive and salad less expensive). The nudge approach would simply involve changing the decision architecture and putting salads first and sweets last. Design of course does not have to be physical. It can be done on a paper template, or a digital website.

Default: This refers to the effective option/outcome where no action or decision is taken. The concept of 'default' is a crucial aspect of Nudge theory, specifically equating to opting for the status quo or inaction, or no decision at all. Any of these things can, according to 'choice design,' be helpful or unhelpful options. Default is what happens when the box is not checked. Since people very commonly 'default' to inaction, or make no decision or change, the option that the leadership/authority or corporation assigns to 'no decision' or 'default' is seriously crucial. This is why 'opt in' and 'opt out' are such important aspects of policy and law in matters of audience response.

Default Options: An automatically generated response desired to encourage an individual to agree—as in the default to 'agree.' Default options facilitate decision-making since the easiest thing to do is to do nothing. Even when no default option is explicitly provided, we use our past experience as the default option.

Delayed Gratification: It is a crucial aspect of temptation, or more precisely the resistance of temptation. The inability to delay gratification produces the human weakness succumbing to many types of temptation. Even laziness or inertia is a sort of inability to delay gratification, where gratification equates to rest and relaxation.

Design of Choice: See 'choice design,' it means the same. 'Design' here refers to writing communications, creating other types of signals and interventions based on the heuristics explained, and the formulation of bigger strategic engagements between a 'choice architect' organisation and its audience, all of which equate to using Nudge theory to offer helpful options to people that are easy for people to understand and adopt.

Diminishing Sensitivity: According to Kahneman diminishing sensitivity applies to both sensory signals (e.g. turning a bit of light in a dark room will have a stronger effect than increasing the light by the same amount in an already lit room), and money (e.g. the subjective difference between \$100 and \$200 is larger than the difference between \$900 and \$1000).

Fundraisers should keep this numeric relativity in mind when presenting numbers or asking for certain amounts of money.

Diversification Heuristic: The tendency when in doubt, to diversify or choose alternative options.

Don't Think of An Elephant: This is the title of George Lakoff's book and refers to the fact that we cannot not think of something, illustrated by the example of not being able not to think of an elephant when asked to do so. People notice what you say more than what you omit to say. According to Dobelli, absence is much harder to detect than presence. As an exercise Dobelli asks readers to detect what the following numbers have in common: 724, 947, 421, 843, 394, 411, 054, 646.

Then he asks the same question for another series: 349, 851, 274, 905, 772, 032, 854, 113.

People detect that the all numbers in the first series include a 4, but have a harder time detecting that the numbers in the second series do not include a 6. We are better at noticing events than non-events.

One important implication for communication is that we are more likely to follow positive advice than negative advice, or positive framing vs. negative framing.

Drop in The Ocean Effect (or Drop in the Bucket Effect): This effect occurs when we feel that the little good we can do, or money we can give, is too small to have an impact on the big problem we are trying to solve.

This may be addressed by stressing that 'every little bit helps,' showing what the requested contribution will do or buy, and by referring to the identifiable victim.

Dunning-Kruger Effect: The tendency of individuals to over-or underestimate their own ability at a given activity. People with low abilities tend to suffer from an illusion of superiority, and over estimate their capabilities. This is attributed to the ignorance of low-ability people, 'They don't know what they don't know.' See Lake Wobegon Effect.

Econs: Thaler and Sunstein's term for the 'imaginary' people whom most leaders and politicians believe typify society; i.e., people whom leaders and governments imagine think like economists, whereas most people in society think like 'humans'—with very natural heuristic weaknesses. (Largely non-existent.) 'Econs' think logically, rationally, unemotionally, always correctly and rationally, whereas (in reality the highly prevalent) 'humans' think emotionally, instinctively, irrationally, and often wrongly.

Empathy: The ability to recognise the emotional state of another person and identify with it. Empathy is a big subject within communications, relationships and leadership which features strongly in Nudge theory and certain heuristics where the mood, personality and needs of the audience are significant. Empathy is significant in the supplementary heuristic 'sympathy'. Neurologically, empathy is related to Mirror Neurons. See Mirror Neurons.

False Consensus Effect: This refers to people's tendency to think that their beliefs, opinions, and actions enjoy greater public consensus than they actually do, according to Gilovich and Ross in *The Wisest One in the Room*.

For fundraisers, and people working in the development and humanitarian world in general, it is important to have an accurate assessment of the public's understanding of and support for their cause. No matter how important a cause is, most of the time most people are more concerned about their daily lives, than about global issues.

Facilitation: It's a supplementary 'nudge' or heuristic which extends the Thaler-Sunstein notions of feedback and priming. It's a sophisticated and deep concept, by which people are helped to think and decide, based on personalised feedback at suitable stages before and during a process of engagement.

Fear: It's a supplementary heuristic/nudge that is frequently referenced by Thaler and Sunstein, but never actually defined or categorized as a heuristic or 'nudge,' aside from being a factor within other named heuristics, notably loss aversion. Obviously fear can be a substantial influence on thinking and decision-making, and it is often exploited cynically and unethically by people and organisations seeking to control others. Fear is however a helpful heuristic in many situations, for example in guiding people's thinking and decisions in relation to fast-moving traffic, stormy seas, bad-smelling food, guns, knives, etc. So fear is also used in shifting group behaviours for example persuading people that tobacco smoke and obesity can be dangerous to health, etc. If not abused, the fear heuristic/nudge can certainly be potentially very helpful.

Feedback: It refers to the responses or reactions given by the 'choice architect' organisation or system to the audience during and after thinking/decisions, enabling adjustment and useful experience. Feedback is shown in this article as a 'nudge' and individual heuristic, although Thaler and Sunstein categorize 'feedback' more vaguely, as part of 'choice architecture'. In fact 'feedback' overlays potentially many other heuristics and 'nudges'. A more sophisticated type of 'feedback' is the additional (non-Thaler-Sunstein) nudge in this article called 'Facilitation.'

Fluency: It refers to the ease by which we process information. Fluency can be driven through familiarity and repetition. In the context of commercial products and not-for-profit organisations, fluency is developed through building strong brands, with consistent brand personalities and iconic assets.

Following The Herd: It's a Thaler and Sunstein 'nudge' which basically means conforming to a group view or behaviour. This may be due to the need to be af-

firmed or validated; to feel powerful (strength in numbers), or the attraction of being part of mob rule. There are other causes, and this is a very significant heuristic in group and societal behaviour. See Spotlight Effect.

Framing: Is a Thaler-Sunstein 'nudge' which refers to the way that a communication or intervention is styled and orientated, particularly in relation to the respondent or audience needs and interests, etc. This entails styling aspects such as accentuation of positive/negative, presentation of advantage/disadvantage, recommendation/dissuasion, endorsement, aspiration, etc. Traditionally, sales people who were said to have 'the gift of gab' or a 'silky tongue' would have been good at 'framing' an option, so as to increase its attractiveness to the potential client.

Framing is also the context in which something happens to the information surrounding inaction that impacts subconsciously on the decision we make. Reframing can be done by changing the unit of measurement (e.g. from annual donation to daily amount), by changing the layout of a template, or the order of money amounts presented, or even by how close or far the numbers are from each other. A common form of framing involves changing negative to positive framing. In one interesting experiment cited by Dobelli people preferred 98% fat free meat to 1% fat meat, despite its higher fat content.

Free-Rider: Is someone who benefits from collective action, without paying the price paid by other group members. On a social level, for example, someone who evades taxes, would still benefit from the roads or parks constructed using tax-payers money.

Fundamental Attribution Error: This refers to our tendency to put emphasis on other people's personality when evaluating their behaviour, while giving little or no weight to external factors, and doing the opposite for our own behaviour. For example, when the truth is not told, we accuse others of being liars and that lying is part of their personality. For ourselves, however, we justify not telling the truth by saying that we were under pressure to not tell the truth.

According to Dobelli in his excellent book The art of thinking clearly, we spend about 90% of our time thinking about other people, and only 10% assessing other factors and contexts.

In fundraising, it is easy for the audience to blame the victims for their own situation; they are at war because they are stupid, evil, or violent.

Games: Framework developed by Eric Berne as apart of Transactional Analysis to describe the routines or patterns of behaviour that develop between people.

Group Think: The tendency of groups to share a wrong, ill formed or inappropriate point of view or attitude. Groups might make faulty decisions that an individual would not make, due to group dynamics. The term was coined by Irving Janis in 1972, who identified eight symptoms of group think: illusion of invulnerability, collective rationalization, belief in inherent morality, stereotyped views of out-groups, direct pressure on dissenters, self-censorship, illusion of unanimity, and self-appointed mindguards.

Halo Effect: It occurs when one salient characteristic of a person (handsomeness), positively influences people's perception of other characteristics (e.g. kindness, or intelligence). In the world of commercial products, a laundry detergent with a pleasant perfume might be perceived to clean better than a detergent without such a perfume.

In the humanitarian world, having a popular celebrity as a goodwill ambassador might have a positive halo effect on the organisation. Partnering with a passionate tennis player might have a positive passion halo effect on the organisation.

Heuristics/Heuristic: In the context of Nudge theory, heuristics broadly refers to the various internal references and responses which people use in assessing things, developing views, and making decisions. Thaler and Sunstein equate a 'heuristic' to a 'nudge.' The word heuristics basically means self-discovery (from Greek heuriskein, 'find'). By its internal nature, heuristic thinking tends to be personal, emotional, subjective, and instinctive. Thaler and Sunstein's approach to heuristic thinking is that it is generally responsible for faulty judgment and unhelpful decision-making. Grammatically, the word heuristic may refer to a single thinking-tendency, or may act as an adjective. The word heuristics may be plural in referring to more than one heuristic thinking-tendency, or may be singular in referring to the study/theory/science of heuristics. Heuristics/heuristic outside of 'Nudge' theory refer to a more general sense of learning through self-discovery.

Hindsight Error: It occurs when past events seem predictable after the fact. We convince ourselves that we could see it coming 'Of course, it was bound to happen,' even if we had predicted the opposite outcome. The hindsight error also happens in organisations when they run assessments of past strategies or campaigns. The hindsight error is a serious impediment to learning. If you never made mistakes to begin with, then there is nothing to learn.

Homo-Economicus: This is the perfectly rational being portrayed in books of classical economics. He is the person who makes a decision after reviewing all the facts, comparing the benefits and costs, and calculating an overall utility.

Humans: Thaler and Sunstein's term for the 'real' people who largely represent societies, and who think heuristically (irrationally, emotionally, often wrongly), about whom most leaders and politicians are basically ignorant or oblivious, believing instead that societies are populated by logical rational 'Econs,' who supposedly think rationally and logically.

ID: *Battling the Inner Dummy: The Craziness of Apparently Normal People* is the name of a book by David L. Weiner in which he suggests that we have five basic drives: power, sexuality, survival, territoriality, and nurturance.

Identification Effect: Or victim identification takes place in the humanitarian context when we refer to a person by name and recognize her as an individual.

IKEA Effect: The tendency to value anything which we have been involved in making or shaping. As is the case with assembling IKEA furniture, we feel proud about having put together the desk for our study room or the kids' cupboard, even if the quality of work does not come close to that of ready-made furniture.

In the world of fundraising, making donors feel they are contributing to the organisation's work, not only by demonstrating how their money will be used, but also by engaging them as volunteers or advocates, co-creating, and more, will increase their commitment to the organisation and its cause.

Immediacy Bias: It refers to the perception that immediate emotions are more intense than previous emotions, possibly due to the salience effect. See Present Bias.

In-group Bias (In-Group/Out-Group): Due to our long history of living in small communities where the world was divided into two groups: our family and friends (In-Group) and strangers and enemies (Out-Group), we have internalized a tendency to classify individuals as either in-group or out-group. We have less empathy towards those in the out-group and tend to perceive them as more similar than they actually are (out-group homogeneity bias). Neurological tests, summarized in Eagleman's book The Brain: The Story of You, show that our brains feel the pain of those in our group more than the pain of those outside it. This obviously has clear implications on our likelihood of donating to others. If we see refugees as an out-group, we'd want to keep them out of our country and not help them. However, if we believe we are all refugees, one way or another, then we all belong to the same group.

Independence Axiom: This rationality rule says that the choice between two alternatives, should not be affected by the introduction of a third alternative. For example, if you are asked to choose between A and B, and you choose A, and then you are given a choice between A, B, and C, you shouldn't choose B. The preference between A and B should be independent of C. But it is not, and in many cases people violate this simple rule of rationality, possibly due to reframing.

Inertia: It means 'unchanging.' This is a very significant aspect of human decision-making, and of group behaviour/behaviour. Inertia relates to defaults and status quo. Inertia specifically refers to the tendency for people and groups do do nothing when faced with choices that are difficult to understand or which seem to offer threat or disadvantage.

Influence: Is the ability to cause a change in others' behaviours or attitudes, in indirect ways. In his classic book *Influence*, Cialdini outlined 6 influence tools: *Reciprocation:* People feel obliged to give back to anyone who gives them something, be it a gift or a favor, or a free sample.

In fundraising, it is easy to imagine offering a gift, so that the donor feels obliged to reciprocate by donating. However, this risks turning, or reframing, an altruistic act into a commercial transactional one, as well as making the organisation look wasteful, spending its money on gifts to donors instead of spending it on its ultimate beneficiaries. Some creative thinking is needed to define reciprocity in a humanitarian context. Perhaps, promising a matching gift from a major donor or a corporate partner can do the job.
Social Proof: When people don't know what to do, they imitate others. Those others may be people like us, people we aspire to be like, experts, etc.

In fundraising, reference to other people's positive behaviour can influence potential donors to do the same, be it donating money or changing behaviour.
Commitment and Consistency: People are more likely to do something after they've committed to doing it, verbally or in writing, and if it fits with their pre-existing values.

In fundraising, being aware of, and affirming, people's values may drive potential donors to act in line with their values, that is, to support the values they believe in by donating.
Liking: People are more likely to respond positively to requests coming from those they like, either because they are attractive, or because they've been kind to them.

In fundraising, using likeable personalities from within the organisation, popular goodwill ambassadors, or corporate partners with a positive brand image, may all be ways to encourage donations to the organisation.
Authority: People respect and follow those with authority, or the appearance of it. Authority may come from power, technical knowledge, or experience. Brands get people to support them through testimonials and expert opinions.

In fundraising, referring to experts, objective academics, or scientific research findings are all ways to influence potential donors behaviour.
Scarcity: The less something is available, the more valuable it is, or it seems to be. Belonging to, or owning, something scarce adds to our self-worth.

In fundraising, making potential donors feel that they belong to a small group of special donors can be helpful. Paradoxically, sometimes making something look difficult to obtain, makes it more desirable.

Intrinsic Reciprocity: This occurs when people reward or punish other people's behaviour even at their own expense.

Instrumental Reciprocity: When people respond to kindness with kindness in order to maintain a profitable relationship over the long run.

Input: An alternative word for an intervention. Not a specific Nudge theory term, but a useful word in describing any sort of intervention.

Intention-Action Divide: The gap between what we declare or decide we would like to do and what we actually do. This gap might be due to decision making processes whereby rationally we are convinced of the need for a certain course of action, but emotionally we cannot get ourselves to take action due to one of many psychological factors; habituation, procrastination, fear, etc. The gap may also be simply due to practical reasons. For example, we may want to donate to a cause but we don't know which organisation to trust, how to donate, or how much.

Intervention: A very useful term, referring to any sort of input or communication or alteration of a situation by a choice architect. Intervention is not specifically a Nudge theory word; it's used in most fields concerning relationships, education, management, training, communications, counselling, etc.

Lake Wobegon Effect: Originally, Lake Wobegon referred to a fictional town and community created by Garisson Keilor, where '... all children are above average.' The term has been used by psychologists and others to refer to our natural tendency to think that we, and our children, countries, companies, etc, are above average. Several tests have demonstrated that most people think they are above average on intelligence, leadership, getting along with others, driving, love-making, just to mention a few. In his book *How We Know What Isn't So*, Thomas Gilovich cites a survey of one million high school students which found that 70% of them thought they were above average on leadership ability, and only 2% thought they were below average. In terms of the ability to get along with others all the students thought they were above average, and 60% thought they were in the top 10%. A survey of university professors found that 94% thought they were above average at their jobs compared to their colleagues. In our workshops, we sometimes ask participants to give themselves a score on intelligence, compared to everyone else in the room, on a scale of 0-100 with 0 being the least intelligent, and 100 the most intelligent. We then ask for a show of hands: how many gave themselves a score of exactly 50 (i.e. average). Usually one or two hands are raised. What about a score of less than 50 (i.e. below average). Again, we see one or two hands. Then everyone starts laughing, realizing that more than 90% think they are above average.

The Lake Wobegon Effect can be detrimental to an objective assessment of one's capabilities, competitive reaction, and to planning for the future.

Least Effort Law: The tendency for an individual to look for the quickest and easiest solution to any decision or challenge.

In fundraising, every effort should be made to make it easy for the potential donor to donate. A clear call for donating is a simple pre-requisite that is often forgotten or buried in details, making the potential donor wonder 'What do you want me to do?'

Using default options is one way of making life easy for donors.

Tell the donor that all they need to do is to 'Click a banner.'

Likeability: It's a supplementary heuristic/nudge which refers to the reputation and credibility of the 'choice architect' (or the choice architect organisation, or figureheads and leaders which are associated with the intervention or 'nudge'). This heuristic acts on the simple principle that an audience is less likely to engage with and respond to an intervention if they do not respect or like the source of the intervention. This obviously applies to interventions where the audience is aware of the source of the intervention or 'choice architect' (sometimes interventions are perceived to be quite anonymous). Within this heuristic, *likeability is subjective* (i.e., different audiences like different leaders and organisations), and *reputation is relative*, i.e., the source must be seen as relevantly credible for the type of intervention; (e.g., we might be more influenced by a book about ethics written by the Dalai Lama than Tony Blair, but conversely we might be more influenced by a book about becoming a Roman Catholic or accumulating a multi-million dollar fortune by Tony Blair than the Dalai Lama). This heuristic relates to several others, notably framing, priming, and sympathy.

Limbic Brain: When exposed to a strong emotional stimuli such as a life threatening menace, an anger inducing situation, or a sexually attractive subject, the limbic brain can react quickly and instinctively, and bypass the rational neocortex. This is what happens when we say about someone else 'How could someone so smart do such a stupid thing?' or even we say about ourselves 'I just wasn't myself.' See Triune Brain.

Limbic Drives: According to David L. Weiner we have five basic limbic drives: power, sexuality, survival, territoriality and nurturance.

Limiting: It's a supplementary heuristic/nudge referring to human tendencies to desire something more if it is perceived to be in short supply, or its availability is subject to a time limit or expiry. It is related to Cialdini's concept of scarcity. See Influence.

Loss Aversion: Is a Thaler-Sunstein 'nudge', originally identified by Kahneman and Tversky. 'Loss aversion' refers to the heuristic tendency that people value something more when they possess it than when they do not. This produces a resistance to change (inertia/status quo bias) if a change is proposed or faced that threatens to deprive the person of a possession, or a current position. The driving force in this heuristic is a heightened sensitivity to, or exaggeration of risk. The Loss aversion 'nudge' is an opposite effect to optimism/over-confidence.

According to Kahneman 'When directly compared or weighted against each other, losses loom larger than gains.' Kahneman explains that this bias has evolutionary basis 'Organisms that treat threats as more urgent than opportunities have a better chance to survive and reproduce.'

Mammalian Brain: The part of the brain we share with mammals, and involved in basic emotions. See Limbic Brain.

Maslow, Abraham: The work of motivational theorist Abraham Maslow (1908-70), helped to lay the foundations of Nudge theory in the mid 1900s; its mechanisms/heuristics and ethos/philosophy. Maslow's famous Hierarchy of Needs model is effectively a presentation of the most fundamental human heuristics, which provide many of the ultimate driving forces behind the heuristics identified by Thaler and Sunstein, and Kahneman and Tversky. Maslow was also a strong 'libertarian' who argued that corporate and managerial power was a damaging feature of society in suppressing people's free choice and natural potential.

Mental Models: Any way—conscious or unconscious—in which we shape and organise data or information. Sometimes these models are referred to as schema. We have a schema for school that includes concepts and items related to school (e.g. education, teachers, classes, books, exams, students, etc.).

Fundraisers should understand what the donating model or schema includes, so that they can respond to donors' expectations.

Mental Short-Cuts: See Heuristics.

Mindlessness: Is a Thaler-Sunstein nudge which equates to negligence, avoidance, not concentrating, etc. When people make mistakes called 'human weakness' this is often 'mindlessness.' The effect may be prompted or increased when the brain is 'tricked' by some sort of illusion or technique of semiotics. Where communications/interventions are poorly designed, mindlessness can be a major factor in large group-wide poor 'thinking' (not actually thinking properly) and poor decision-making (especially deciding to do nothing, or not realising that a decision should be made).

Mirror Neurons: These are neurons that fire when we perform a task (e.g. eat an ice-cream) and when we see someone else perform the same task, provided we have been through a similar experience. That is why we cry when we watch a sad movie even though we know very well it's just a movie.

In the humanitarian world, people will be moved to support victims when they feel they have been through a similar situation, or emotion.

Mood/mood-changers: Is a significant aspect of heuristics, because it governs how people feel, and this influences how people respond to interventions. People's moods are subject to change, and so it's useful for choice architects to appreciate this and to allow for people's moods and emotions as far as possible. Transactional Analysis and Neuro-linguistic programming (NLP) are helpful supporting methodologies.

Negativity Bias: When stimuli are of equal intensity (news, stories, images) the negative ones will have a stronger psychological effect on us than the positive or neutral ones. See also loss and risk aversion.

Neuro-linguistic Programming (NLP): It's a commonly used abbreviation for Neuro-linguistic programming. NLP is a controversial psychological concept. Like Transactional Analysis, NLP explains and offers ways to interpret and manage the (often hidden and counter-intuitive) effects of communications/signals to and between people. NLP is not specific Nudge theory terminology or methodology, but the NLP concept relates to Nudge theory and supports it very well.

Neuroscience: The study of how the brain responds chemically and physically to various activities.

Nudging: A psychologically subtle change in a situation or process that leads to a change in behaviour.

Nudge: Thaler and Sunstein's 'brand' name for a heuristic effect which influences a person or group's thinking/decision-making. Thaler and Sunstein actually equate the notion of a 'nudge' to a 'heuristic' tendency, so that the words mean virtually the same. Technically such a direct equivalence is a little tenuous given that conceptually 'heuristics' are rather a passive and a constant tendency, compared to a 'nudge,' which is may be an intentional intervention, but the basic understanding of nudge theory is probably made easier by seeing these two words as essentially meaning the same thing.

Obliquity: Explored in the book by John Kay, obliquity refers to the paradoxical idea that many of our complex and long-term goals from wealth to happiness are best achieved in indirect ways.

Optimism/Over-Confidence: Is a Thaler-Sunstein 'nudge' and refers to people's heuristic tendency to under (or over) estimate the ease or difficulty of situations leading to **complacency**, which inevitably influences thinking and decisions. This heuristic was originally identified by Kahneman and Tversky. Optimism/over-confidence has an opposing effect to the 'Loss aversion' heuristic, which tends to restrict thinking and decision-making.

Opt In/Opt Out: Opt in means check the box to agree to sign-up or join, etc. Opt out means the 'default' is you are in unless you check the box to say you are not.

Oxytocin: A hormone involved in social bonding and involved in empathy and trust.

Peak-End Effect: This refers to the strange phenomenon that what matters most in how we feel about an experience, pleasure or pain, depends not on how long the pleasure or pain lasts, but on the peak and end moments of the experience. For example, in a medical operation in which pain is felt, operation A would be perceived as less painful than operation B if operation A ends less painfully than operation B, even if the total duration of pain is longer in operation A than in operation B.

Peer Pressure: The desire to conform that individuals have when confronted with behaviour from an individual or group.

Pilot: The individual in charge or the person who believes they are in charge.

Positioning: Is a supplementary heuristic or 'nudge' which refers to the location or relocation of anything which influences people's thinking or behaviour, for example the site of a notice-board, or a litter-bin, or the layout of headings on a poster or document or webpage.

Pre-Frontal Cortex: The part of the brain that covers the front part of the frontal lobe, and is responsible for planning and decision making.

Present Bias: The preference that individuals have for a payoff that is delivered sooner rather than later. For example, we'd rather receive $100 today than $110 next week. However, this bias is not linear. We'd probably prefer to get $110 in 53 weeks than $100 in 52 weeks.

In fundraising, it is important to consider the time factor when asking for donations. For example, a potential donor might be willing to start regular donations in a month or three, but not today. The method of payment also has an impact on the time dimension. When we pay in cash the money goes out of our pocket immediately and we feel the pain right away. But when we pay by credit card or through a bank transfer, the actual payment is delayed. In general, delaying the pain is a good idea.

Pre-Suasion: A term and book by Robert Cialdini referring to how the impact of our message can be magnified by what we do prior to delivering our message. In one interesting example, a company that sells comfortable sofas increased its sales by showing bubbly clouds on its landing page, prompting shoppers to think about comfort, the company's competitive advantage.

Primacy Effect: We are disproportionately influenced by the information or facts that come first, than by what comes last. First impressions are a form of the primacy effect.

Strong communication should balance the primacy and recency effects. Think of James Bond movies. They always start with an exciting scene and end in a climax. In fundraising, ensure that the start of the message or DRTV is powerful.

Priming: Is a Thaler-Sunstein 'nudge' referring to ways in which people can be made ready or prepared before thinking and deciding, for example, visualization, role-modelling, building belief, educating, giving information before options, and offering methods rather than directions. Like 'feedback' it extends to the more sophisticated notion of Facilitation.

Prisoner's Dilemma: This is a game theory ethical and decision-making dilemma based on a hypothetical situation in which two suspects, call them A and B, are arrested for a given crime. They are questioned, each one in a separate room, so that they cannot talk to each other. They are offered the following options:

If both confess on each other, each will serve two years in jail.

If A confesses on B, but B doesn't, A will be set free and B will serve three years, and vice versa.

If both remain silent, each will serve one year in jail.

The prisoner's dilemma is used to illustrate some of the real life situations dealing with issues involving cooperation vs. competition.

In the world of organisations, collaboration and competition often take place at the same time; collaboration on addressing world issues, and competition on raising funds from donors. The prisoner's dilemma offers a conceptual model to analyze some of the issues involved. It requires analyzing how the other party is likely to react to one's actions, in the short and long run.

Reach: This is a marketing term that's useful in understanding certain aspects of Nudge theory. Reach refers to the extent of a 'target' audience which sees/experiences a communication or intervention (which may be used to apply a nudge). Reach is significant in all communications designed to impact on a group, because if the reach is only 50% (i.e., only half the audience sees the message), then generally this is the actual maximum response rate. It's very difficult to achieve 100% reach of course, but it's not difficult to achieve a 75% reach compared to say a 25% reach, in which case the potential success rate is multiplied by three times. Such an example illustrates that reach is hugely significant in determining success of group interventions. In other words, the intervention may be fabulous, but if the reach is only 10% then the results will be relatively poor.

Recency Effect: When it comes to recalling information, we tend to recall what comes at the end. See also Primacy Effect.

In fundraising, make sure that the key message, or whatever you'd like your audience to recall, comes at the end.

Recipient: A general term, not specific to Nudge theory, which refers to a single member of an audience or target group or society, that is subject to a communication or intervention. When we talk to another person, the other person is the recipient. An alternative term is respondent.

Recognition: This refers to the ability of the audience to identify items connected with an organisation, be it its logo, tagline, colours, goodwill ambassadors, etc. The more items, and iconic assets, a brand is associated with, the more fluency it will enjoy with the audience.

Reference Point: Kahneman points out that any evaluation we perform is relative to a neutral reference point. This point may be the room temperature, our school average-grade, or our current salary.

Fundraisers must know what their donors' reference points are, with respect to donations. For example, what is their usual regular donation amount.

Reflective System: Thaler and Sunstein's term for rational logical thinking, equating to Kahneman and Tversky's System 2 thinking, as opposed to Automatic (Thaler-Sunstein) and System 1 (Kahneman/Tversky):
System One (Automatic) Thinking = 'Human', instinctive, emotional, subjective, irrational, heuristic.
System Two (Reflective) Thinking = 'Econ', logical, rational, objective, unemotional.

Relevance: Is a supplementary heuristic/nudge which refers to how well the intervention fits the needs of the audience. This is different to sympathy which mainly concerns fitting the mood and personality of the audience. Relevance requires that the option for the audience is seen as meaningful by the audience.

Representativeness: Is a Thaler-Sunstein 'nudge' originated by Kahneman and Tversky. It refers to **similarity** and relies largely on **stereotyping**, so that when people seek to assess or characterize an unknown thing or option they tend to refer to perceived stereotypical examples, on which they base assumptions about the unknown thing/option, and which may be very inaccurate. This heuristic is greatly influenced by mass media, which is responsible in the modern age for proliferating millions of stereotype references, on which people form faulty assumptions and decisions.

Respondent: An alternative term for recipient. Basically a respondent is the person who receives a communication or intervention. The term is a general one and not specific to Nudge theory.

Risk Aversion: See Loss Aversion.

Rule of Thumb/Rules of Thumb: This term is used by Kahneman and Tversky, and also by Thaler and Sunstein, in referring to a heuristic or several heuristics. The term is used quite vaguely. Thaler and Sunstein initially use the term in referring to the Kahneman-Tversky heuristics ('first identified') Anchoring, Availability and Representativeness, but imply it has a wider meaning. Kahneman and Tversky use the term to refer to heuristics more broadly. It's probably more accurate to suggest that 'rule/rules of thumb' is a general substitute term for the heuristics which entail some sort of instinctive comparison, calculation, or assumption based on a preconception.

Examples of rules of thumb from everyday life include: add three spoons of oil to one spoon of vinegar when preparing a salad dressing, leave the equivalent of one car for every 10 miles of speed when driving (e.g. leave the equivalent of six cars between your car and the car in front of you when driving at 60 miles per hour).

Corporations and organisations can develop simple and practical rules of thumb with experience (e.g. you need to intercept 100 pedestrians in order to recruit 2 regular donors).

Salience: This refers to the presence of a brand (organisation, commercial brand, celebrity, etc.) in people's mind and the ease by which it is recalled. It is more than just awareness. We might be aware of 20 brands in a category, but only two or three would come to mind in a given context. For example, I might know Coca-Cola, Pepsi-Cola, 7 Up, Sprite, Fanta, Schweppes, Mountain Dew, Dr. Pepper, etc., but only Coca-Cola and Pepsi-Cola come to mind when I am thirsty. Similarly, I might know The Red Cross, Doctors Without Borders, Greenpeace, Amnesty International, Save the Children, War Child, UNHCR, UNICEF, Operation Smile, WWF, etc., but only The Red Cross and Doctors Without Borders come to my mind when a natural disaster strikes.

Mind presence, driven by salience, is a key driver of any brand's success.

Samuelson Bet: Named after economist Paul Samuelson, this bet suggests that if you offer people a one-time bet of a 50-50 chance of either winning $150 or losing $100, they usually decline it. However, if you offer to repeat the same bet 100 times, most people would accept. This bet is also related to Risk Aversion and Loss Aversion.

This bet is a reminder that what might be true of a single transaction, may not be true in the long-run.

Schemata: The mental principles by which we organise ideas or information—from alphabetic to by impact.

Self-control Strategies: Is a Thaler-Sunstein 'nudge' which refers to the many routines and habits that people develop to counter their known or perceived weaknesses. Common examples are seen in the ways that people manage money, and devise quirky methods to save, budget, and transfer money (from various accounts, jars and pots, savings funds, etc). A different example is the tendency for many people to put alarm clocks out of reach (because they know they have a temptation to switch them off and go back to sleep). These unnatural routines become part of the reality that influence thinking and decisions in response to communications and interventions.

Self-image: Is a general term in psychology and relationships, empathy, etc., not specific to Nudge theory, but is especially significant in heuristics concerning relevance and framing. It's a crucial aspect of communications and interventions which is often overlooked, as follows: Authorities or leaders design interventions and communications based on the personalities and moods that they believe people have; whereas usually people's personalities and moods are quite different. Therefore interventions or communications are inappropriate or irrelevant, quite aside from the content or purpose of the intervention. People don't recognise the intervention to be relevant or meaningful in terms of their self-image. Principles of empathy offer ways to understand self-image.

Self-Serving Bias: In order to preserve their self esteem, humans tend to ascribe their successes to their own skill and effort, while blaming circumstances and others for their own failure. See Fundamental Attribution Error.

Semiotics/Semiology: It refers to making and analysing meaning through signs, language, symbols, stories, and anything else that conveys a meaning that can be understood by people. This is not specific Nudge terminology; it's an entirely separate and major area of communications. Semiotics is however hugely significant in Nudge theory, and especially the heuristic called Stimulus Response Compatibility. Semiotics relates to linguistics, which refers to language structure and meaning. Semiotics more broadly encompasses language and all other signage, metaphor and symbolism. The processing aspect of semiotics is called semiosis. Semiotics comprise **logical** elements, and **anthropological** [humankind] elements, which is to say that the effects are partly based on unchanging logic (for example big is generally more impactful than small), and partly based on human factors such as genetics, evolution, culture, and conditioning.

Sensory: Sensory nudges are supplementary heuristics in terms of Thaler-Sunstein's listing, which basically ignores these effects. Sensory influences besides traditional semiotics (language, symbols, signs, etc.) can be immensely influential on people's thinking and decision-making. Consider for example: the effect of music in films and other media, and on people's moods and decision-making when partying; the effect of smells such as freshly baked bread and coffee; or antiseptic, or bleach, or petrol, or tobacco smoke; or the effects of heat and cold on people's bodies and moods, or of dampness, humidity, etc. There are hundreds of other sensory stimulants which can be regarded and potentially used as sensory nudges.

Signage: A general non-Nudge term which is useful in Nudge theory in referring to visual signals which convey a meaning of some sort to an audience, for example colours, symbols, graphic design, headings, visual media, layouts, signposts, notices, etc.

Signal: It means a communication or other sort of non-verbal sign or conveyance of meaning or mood to a person or group. Signal is not specific Nudge theory terminology, but it is very useful in explaining Nudge theory, because 'signal' has such a wide meaning of different types of messages or influences that humans are receptive to. Changing the colour or size or typestyle of text is a signal. So is direct eye contact, or repositioning a litter-bin. Signal broadly equates to the word 'intervention'.

Social Identification: This refers to a person's perceived belonging to a social group, based on natural characteristics (nationality, ethnic group), common beliefs (political party, religious group), or some other factor (sports-club fans). Since humans are social beings, identifying with a specific group increases our self worth.

Organisations can try to create a sense of identity by being members of a social movement working together towards a common goal.

Spotlight Effect: Is a Thaler and Sunstein 'nudge' which refers to people's anxiety when they feel isolated, as if being watched and judged by others. This produces pressure and a heightened fear of making errors, typically producing inertia or conforming (following the herd). Thaler and Sunstein assert that people have a false sense of self-significance when making these judgments, so that they can greatly exaggerate the significance and visibility of their actions and decisions.

Status Quo/Bias: Is a Thaler-Sunstein 'nudge' which equates to inertia, and the default option (i.e., what happens when the respondent takes no action, like not checking the box). Status quo bias is a hugely powerful effect, and much exploited by corporations and much under-regulated by protective authorities. It's basically why we receive so much junk mail, email, text spam, and unwanted marketing phone calls—because authorities/governments traditionally permitted corporations to assign an 'opt-in' agreement, which committed consumers to receive follow-up mailings, and have their details sold to other corporations, when people divulged personal contact details on forms when buying things. Status quo refers to the 'existing situation'. A Latin term, *status quo* means literally 'situation in which.' Almost always 'status quo' means preserving the existing situation, and this is its meaning in Nudge theory. This is similar to inertia, and is related to defaults.

Stimulus Response Compatibility: Refers to the design of signage and language, so that it looks and seems appropriate for the message it conveys. For example, a red X symbol generally conveys a meaning of 'no' or 'stop' or 'negative,' and a green check or tick generally conveys a meaning of yes or positive, so to use a red X with the word 'yes' or 'go' would be heuristically misleading and unhelpful (i.e., the stimulus of the red X does not match, [is not compatible], with the audience response, which would tend to be negative rather than positive).

Story Bias: In his book *The Art of Thinking Clearly,* Dobelli illustrates that we have a story bias that makes us recall stories better than news, even when a story is longer than a piece of news. He cites an example from E.M. Forster, the English novelist: a) The king died, and the queen died and b) The king died, and the queen died of grief. Most people retain the story version better (b) because it has meaning and involves emotions.

For fundraising, many studies have illustrated that a story about an individual child generates more support than a reference to millions of deaths. See Identification effect.

Substitution: Substitution happens when people do not know the answer to a question or are too lazy to think about it, so they answer another question. One common form of substitution is a decision based on what we feel, rather than what we think. For example, if asked 'Who do you think would make a better president for the country?' someone might answer 'I really like X. I think he is cool.' This can happen in our choice of which organisation to support, company to partner with, or celebrity to engage as a Goodwill ambassador.

Sunk-Cost Fallacy: This occurs when we persist in pursuing a wrong path just because we've already invested in it. In everyday life we stay in a movie theatre watching a long boring movie just because we have spent $20 on the movie ticket. The error is due to the fact that the past is irrelevant. The money is already spent and we have two hours ahead of us that we can spend either continuing to torture ourselves in front of the screen, or to go out and do something more interesting. In business, companies and organisations continue to invest in failed projects just because they've already invested so much money in it, and think it'd be a waste to abandon it. This is faulty thinking, throwing good money after bad money. One reason we

fall victim to the sunk-cost error is that we don't like to admit we were wrong.

Supplementary/Additional Nudges and Heuristics: In this article a 'supplementary' or 'additional' nudge/heuristic is one which Thaler and Sunstein do not specifically categorize and name as such, although they may refer to its effects and existence to a degree. Some are not mentioned or alluded to by Thaler and Sunstein, but have been discussed, proposed, implied by other theorists with interests in what might be termed Nudge theory heuristics.

Supposedly Irrelevant Factors (SIF): In his book *Misbehaving: The Making of Behavioural Economics*, Thaler stresses that economic theory is based on flawed premises of rationality, optimization, unbiased choices, etc. Thaler suggests that a model of human behaviour should take into account the many systematic biases and errors that humans commit, and not be based on assumptions. As a professor, Thaler noticed a strange reaction from students to their grades; they were disappointed with an average grade of 72%, but when Thaler changed the grading score to total 137, students were satisfied with an average score of 96/137, which is actually only 70%, less than the 72% they were disappointed about. Thaler then started noticing and collecting such biases which he labelled Supposedly Irrelevant Factors, or SIF for short.

Sympathy: Is a supplementary heuristic/nudge which refers to the ease of engagement that an audience feels for an intervention—in other words is the intervention 'sympathetic' to the mood and personality of the audience? Is the communication 'in-tune' and resonant with the audience. Self-image is often a factor. So is empathy.

Syntactics/Syntax: The study/science of the arrangement of words within language (i.e., syntax) and especially within sentences which seek to convey clear meaning.

System 1 and System 2 (Thinking): The two basic decision-making frameworks identified by Kahneman—one automatic and fast, and one slow. These terms were originated by Kahneman in referring respectively to the two main types of human thinking in heuristics, which Thaler and Sunstein call Automatic (System One) and Reactive (System Two).
System 1 (Automatic) Thinking = 'Human', instinctive, emotional, subjective, irrational, heuristic.
System 2 (Reflective) Thinking = 'Econ', logical, rational, objective, unemotional.

Temptation: Is a Thaler-Sunstein 'nudge', referring to human tendencies to seek maximum reward for minimum effort. Other drivers of temptation include greed, ego, insecurity, desperation, etc. Thaler and Sunstein argue reasonably that this heuristic is a natural urge in humans, which has evolved due to it being mostly a successful tendency, although it is a vulnerability in the modern age, or at any time where it can be used as a trap. Temptation—and the tendency for people to succumb to temptation—relates to delayed gratification, and the dilemma that this offers to many people.
Theory of The Mind: This refers to our ability to infer the intentions and anticipate the reactions of other people. As we mature and become more socially and emotionally intelligent, our ability to understand other people's perspective increases. This also involves the realization that others do not necessarily know what we know or share our perspective. In a famous experiment with children, with different variations, the researcher shows kids in a class a box of crayons. He then removes the crayons and puts candles in the box instead. He then asks the kids, if someone comes from outside, what will they think is in the box? Very young kids, whose sense of others is not yet well developed, say candles. They cannot realize that others do not know what they know. Older kids, usually around four years old will say crayons because they realize that the person coming from outside does not know that the crayons were replaced by candles.

Neurologically, The Theory of the Mind is related to Mirror Neurons which allow us to experience milder forms of what others think and feel. It is easy to see that many adults lack the ability to see things from other people's perspectives.

In fundraising, it is important to acknowledge that not everyone thinks our cause, values, or opinions are the correct one. This will have implications on who to communicate with, and what to tell them. See Walter Mischel's *The Marshmallow Test*.

Transitivity: It states that if you prefer A to B, and you prefer B to C, then you should prefer A to C. However, this rule of rationality is often violated.
Triune Brain: This model was developed by the American physician and neuroscientist Paul D. MacLean. In a simplified format it says that from an evolutionary

biology perspective, our brain consists of three parts, from oldest to youngest:

The Reptilian Brain: Shared with reptiles it is responsible for automatic functions such as blood circulation and maintaining body temperature.

The Mammalian Brand or Limbic Brain: Shared with mammals it is in charge of basic emotions such as anger, fear, nurturing behaviour, etc.

The Neocortex: Shared with higher primates, but most developed in human beings, is responsible for higher cognitive functions such as control, planning, and simulation.

Ultimatum Game: In this game the first player (proposer) is given $100 and asked to share it with the second player (receiver) the way he likes; 50/50, 90/10, 70/30, etc. The receiver can either accept the split, in which case the money is split accordingly, or reject the offer in which case no one gets anything. According to traditional economics, the Homo economicus proposer should propose the maximum for himself (e.g. 99/1) and the Homo economicus receiver should accept whatever he is offered because anything is better than nothing. However, this is not what usually happens in reality. Many proposers offer a 50/50 split, some 60/40 and 70/30, and when the receiver is offered something less than 30/70, he usually rejects it. This experiment suggests that we have a sense of fairness. This is what we have observed in our workshops, and when we probed why the recipient didn't accept the small amount they were offered since it is better than nothing, they said 'It's not fair.'

In development and humanitarian work the notion of fairness and equity is a powerful case to make.

Vividness Effect: Information presented in a vivid way, with stories, images, colours, metaphors, music, etc. is more noticeable and memorable than dry information. It becomes more available to the mind than mere facts or statistics.

What Fires Together Wires Together: The process of synaptic connections being made in the brain between different stimuli.

What You See Is All There Is (WYSIATI): A phrase developed by Kahneman to describe the tendency for people to decide on the basis of available information even if it's not really enough, and assume that that's all the information they need. This tendency can distort our decision-making by not basing our decision on the key relevant information, but only on what's available.

Zeigarnik Effect: Named after the Russian psychology student Bluma Zeigarnik, this refers to our bias to remembering uncompleted tasks, and forgetting them once the task is completed. It was prompted by an incident with a restaurant waiter who delivered a complicated large order from memory but forgot who the guests were minutes after they left. When questioned, he said 'I keep every order in my head—until it is served.' This phenomenon is complementary to the need for completion effect. When something is not completed, it stays active in our mind, so we remember it, and only forget about it once it is completed. This dynamic can be used smartly to maintain the attention of the audience. Teaser campaigns are just one example.

Zero-Sum Game (and Non-Zero-Sum Game): In game theory refers to situations in which gains by one player come at the expense of losses by another player, or players, because the sum total is fixed. This is the nature of competitive activities such as sports. In non-zero sum games, both parties can lose, and ideally gain.

In practical terms, a zero sum mentality focuses on gaining a large share of the pie from other players. A non-zero sum mentality thinks about ways of making the pie bigger so that everyone wins.